In Search of
HISTORY

TEACHER'S RESOURCE PACK

Martyn Whittock

ACKNOWLEDGEMENTS

The publishers would like to thank the following for permission to reproduce illustrations in this volume: **The changing lives of women in the Middle Ages**, 'Problems with the evidence', source B, British Library (ms. no. Harl 4425, folio 9, order no 1605); 'How did the rights of women change during the Middle Ages', source A, The Bridgeman Art Library, London; **Sources of evidence from the Middle Ages**, 'Kinds of evidence from the Middle Ages', source B, Andrew Ward (Life File, London); source C, Cambridge University Collection of Air Photographs; **The world turned upside-down!**, 'Why did so many revolutionary groups spring up after the English Civil War?' source A, Fotomas Index (UK); **Making a United Kingdom, 1500-1750** 'What were the results of these changes?', source A, Smithsonian Institution, courtesy of the Freer Gallery of Art, Washington DC; **The beggars are coming...**, sources A and B, Hulton-Deutsch Collection; **The image of the Queen**, source A, Her Majesty Queen Elizabeth II; source B, The Bridgeman Art Library, London; source C, the Marquess of Salisbury; **What kind of king was Henry VIII?**, Walker Art Gallery, William Brown Street, Liverpool; **Their house and my house**, top photo, The National Trust; bottom photo, Martyn Whittock; **The British Empire**, 'What was the influence of the Empire on the British?, source A, The Bridgeman Art Library, London; 'What image did British people have of the Empire by the end of the 19th century?' sources A and B, Robert Opie Collection, London; **Growing towns - Liverpool**, sources A to C, Fotomas Index (UK); **The Slave Trade**, source A, Mary Evans Picture Library, London; **Interpretations of the past**, sources B and D, *Punch*; The dangers of railways! source A, Iron Gorge Museum Trust; source B, *Punch*; source C, Mary Evans Picture Library, London; **The Western Front**, source A, The Imperial War Museum; source B, Private Collection; source C, Robert Opie Collection, London; **The Nazi treatment of the Jews**, source A, Private Collection.

The publishers would like to thank the following for permission to reproduce material in this volume: Addison Wesley Longman for extracts from *King John* by RU Turner (1994) and *Sir Robert Peel* by N Gash (1976); BBC Worldwide Limited for permission to reproduce an extract from *1914-1918 The Great War and the Shaping of the Twentieth Century* by J Winter and B Baggett © Community Television of Southern California 1996; BT Batsford Ltd for extracts from *The Somme* by AH Farrar-Hockley (BCA, 1961); Cambridge University Press for extracts from *Domination and Conquest* by RR Davies (1990) and *Workshop to Warfare* by C Adams, P Bartley, H Bourdillon and C Loxton (1990); Duckworth for an extract from *Peel* by G Kitson-Clark (1936); George Sasson for an extract from 'The General' by Siegfried Sasson; Heinemann Educational Publishers, a division of Reed Educational and Professional Ltd, for an extract from *The French Revolution* by P Mantin (1992); Ian V Hogg for an extract from *The Weapons that Changed the World* (Ebury Press, 1986); Macmillan Press Ltd for extracts from *The Making of Britain: The Middle Ages* by J Gillingham (1985) and *The Age of Expansion* by L Smith (1986); Methuen and Co for an extract from *Victorian England* by LCB Seaman (1973); an extract from *World History* by W McNeill (1967) by permission of Oxford University Press; an extract from *In Pursuit of the Millennium* by Norman Cohn (1970), reprinted with permission of the Peters Fraser and Dunlop Group Ltd; University of Exeter Press for extracts from *Nazism 1919-1945, Volume 3: Foreign Policy, War and Racial Extermination* edited by J Noakes and G Pridham; Weidenfeld and Nicolson for extracts from *The Battle of the Somme* by MM Evans (1996); Routledge for an extract from *Victorian England* by LCB Seaman (1973); Allen Lane, The Penguin Press, for an extract from *Total War: Causes and Courses of the Second World War* by Peter Calvocoressi and Guy Wint (1972).

Every effort has been made to trace and acknowledge ownership of copyright. The publishers will be glad to make suitable arrangements with any copyright holders whom it has not been possible to contact.

To my good friend, Fiona Jane Holland, fellow labourer at the chalkface!

Orders: please contact Bookpoint Ltd, 39 Milton Park, Abingdon, Oxon OX14 4TD. Telephone: (44) 01235 400414, Fax: (44) 01235 400454. Lines are open from 9.00 - 6.00, Monday to Saturday, with a 24 hour message answering service. Email address: orders@bookpoint.co.uk

British Library Cataloguing in Publication Data
A catalogue record for this title is available from The British Library

ISBN 0 340 704 896

First published 1998
Impression number 10 9 8 7 6 5 4 3 2
Year   2004 2003 2002 2001 2000 1999

Design and layouts by Fiona Webb
Illustrations on the front cover and inside the book by Phil Page
Printed in Great Britain for Hodder & Stoughton Educational, a division of Hodder Headline Plc, 338 Euston Road, London NW1 3BH by Hobbs the Printers, Totton, Hants

Contents

PART I GENERAL GUIDANCE

- **i** Following commands!
- **i** Using posters in history
- **i** Note-taking to answer a question
- **i** Carrying out a research project

PART II MEDIEVAL REALMS

- **TN** 1066–1485: Medieval Realms
- **DS** The English conquest of Wales, 1272–84
- **DS** The power of talking – the growth of Parliament
- **DS** The changing lives of women in the Middle Ages
- **EX** Sources of evidence from the Middle Ages
- **EX** Changing castles
- **F** Newspaper report: 14 October 1066
- **F** The Christian Church in the Middle Ages
- **F** The Black Death
- **F** Living in towns in the Middle Ages
- **F** Changing weapons and equipment of knights

PART III THE MAKING OF THE UNITED KINGDOM

- **TN** 1485–1714: The Making of the United Kingdom
- **DS** The end of merrie England?
- **DS** The world turned upside-down!
- **DS** Making a United Kingdom, 1500–1750
- **EX** The beggars are coming …
- **EX** The image of the Queen
- **EX** Kings from Hanover
- **EX** Changing kingdoms
- **EX** Timeline search…
- **F** What kind of king was Henry VIII?
- **F** Why was the Catholic Church less popular in the 16th century?
- **F** The poor in Tudor England
- **F** Their house and my house

- **F** 'Remember, remember … '
- **F** Quarrels with Parliament!
- **F** The 'Glorious Revolution'

PART IV BRITAIN 1750–1900

- **TN** 1750–1900: Britain
- **DS** The Napoleonic Wars
- **DS** The British Empire
- **EX** Growing towns – Liverpool
- **EX** The slave trade
- **EX** Changing 19th-century Britain
- **EX** Interpretations of the past
- **F** How did ideas about farming change in the 18th century?
- **F** Changing industry
- **F** Writing about the changes in making cloth
- **F** The dangers of railways!
- **F** Factory reform
- **F** A changing world

PART V THE TWENTIETH CENTURY WORLD

- **TN** The Twentieth Century World
- **DS** The Western Front
- **DS** The Nazi treatment of the Jews
- **EX** Redrawing the map of Europe, 1919
- **EX** A new kind of war: Blitzkrieg
- **EX** The war on the Eastern Front
- **EX** The war in the Far East
- **EX** The dropping of the first atom bomb
- **EX** Why did Germany lose the Second World War?
- **F** Letter from the trenches
- **F** The first day of the Battle of the Somme
- **F** Why did Hitler come to power in Germany in 1933?
- **F** The road to war, 1935–39
- **F** What events caused a 'Cold War' to start after the Second World War?

SHEET IDENTIFIERS

Throughout the text, the following symbols are used to identify the different sheets:

(i) Information section which can be found in **Part I General Guidance;**

(TN) Teacher's Notes;

(DS) Depth Study;

(EX) Extension Sheet;

(F) Foundation Sheet.

Part I
General Guidance

i Following commands!

History students are often asked to do different things with the evidence they are looking at. The words which tell you what to do are called 'command words'. You need to understand them or you will do the wrong things. Command words are as follows:

- *Describe* means say in your own words what is going on in the source you are reading. But only write about the bit you are asked to look at.

- *Explain* means say what something means, what evidence there is for it and why something is said.

- *Compare* means show how sources are similar or different.

- *Evaluate* means make a judgement about evidence. Can you trust it? Is it useful? Do you think it is right?

On this sheet are different sources of evidence. They are opinions about King John. After the sources are questions. These questions contain command words. To help you, the questions have been answered for you. This shows you what the command words want you to do.

SOURCE A

❝While John's reign was a failure, he had some successes and even came close to regaining Normandy and then defeating the rebel barons. John's efforts in the British Isles, 1209–12, strengthened the English monarch's position. The Barnwell Chronicler wrote at the peak of John's power, 'There is no one in Ireland, Scotland and Wales who does not obey the commands of the king of England.'❞

Historian Ralph V. Turner in the book King John *(1994).*

SOURCE B

❝He managed to lose Normandy, Anjou and much of Poitou. His murder of his nephew had led him to be regarded with distrust and dislike. In contrast to his brother Richard he could not keep the support of the most powerful princes in France.❞

Historian John Gillingham in the book The Making of Britain, The Middle Ages *(1985).*

SOURCE C

❝Rumours that the king himself was responsible for the murder of his nephew created an atmosphere of fear, a feeling that the land was ruled by a tyrant. But he was also a generous, able and lavish king.❞

Historian Doris Mary Stenton in the book English Society in the Early Middle Ages *(1965).*

USING THE EVIDENCE

1 Look at Source B. *Describe* the reasons why King John might be thought of as a failure.

> In Source B there are three main reasons why John was a failure. First, he lost control of lots of land. Second, he murdered his nephew, and people did not trust him after this. Third, he was not as good as his brother had been at getting on with the people who ruled France.

2 Look at Source A. *Explain* why this historian thought John was quite successful in ruling England between the years 1209 and 1212.

> This historian thinks John was successful because he was able to make people obey him. He quotes a person who lived at the time of John who wrote that all the countries near England did what John told them to do. This means he was a strong king.

3 Look at Sources B and C. *Compare* their views about King John.

> These two historians are the same in some ways but different in others. They both say that people did not like him because he killed his nephew. But the person who wrote Source B also says that it was his fault he lost so much land and did not get on with the rulers of France. The writer of Source C does not mention this at all. Instead she mentions some good things about John. The person who wrote Source B did not mention any good things about John.

4 All of the sources are secondary sources. They were written hundreds of years after John lived. *Evaluate* how useful they are if you want to find out what John was like as a king.

> Some people think that because they were written so long after John died they cannot be useful. But this is wrong. They are written by historians who will have looked at lots of evidence before they come to their opinions. This is very useful as they have thought a lot about the evidence. This does not mean they all think the same. It does not mean that they are right. But it does mean they are useful when trying to get an idea about what John was like by looking at lots of different evidence.

i Using posters in history

The kinds of questions history students answer do not always involve a lot of writing. Sometimes, a question might ask you to design a poster. These are fun ways to show what you understand about something in history. You can illustrate your ideas with pictures and cartoons. You can think of serious or funny things to write on a poster! The problem is, sometimes they end up as just a piece of artwork. This does not show your history knowledge. Always remember:

◆ the drawing is important but the history information is more important;

◆ think about what history information you are trying to show in your poster;

◆ try to include as much relevant information, or evidence, as you can;

◆ whose point of view are you trying to show?

Here are two examples of posters. They are trying to show 'Why Harold was the true king of England in 1066'. To do this, you would need to imagine that you were one of his supporters. You would need to think of all the things in favour of him being king.

An example of a good poster: one which makes historical points.

An example of a bad poster.

USING THE EVIDENCE

1 Look carefully at the two posters.
a Explain why the first poster is a good one.
b Explain why the second poster is worse.

2 Look at pages 20-21 of *In Search of History 1066–1485*. Imagine you are a villein. Design a protest poster complaining about your life. Remember to show as much historical information in your poster as you can.

 # Note-taking to answer a question

BEING A HISTORY DETECTIVE

History students are like detectives:

◆ They have questions and problems to investigate.

◆ They decide how they should examine the evidence.

◆ They sort out the relevant clues from the things they do not need to know.

◆ They look at all the evidence they have sorted. They use it to solve the problem. They write up their report using the relevant clues.

These are skills that are not just important in history. They are useful in other subjects too. They can be used out of school. They can be used in lots of different jobs.

Often, though, it is tempting to just copy chunks out of a book, or off a CD-ROM. This is not investigating at all! In this unit we will be looking at how to carry out an investigation without doing that!

ANSWERING A QUESTION – KEYWORDS

Answering a question is easier if you follow these simple rules:

◆ Rule 1. Think about the question. What does it ask you to do?

◆ Rule 2. Read the words in a textbook carefully. Make a note of the keywords. These are the words which help you answer the question.

Before you do this on your own, you will see an example of how it can be done. After this you can try it out for yourself!

ANSWERING A QUESTION – TAKING NOTES

> **How well prepared was King Harold for the Battle of Hastings?**

◆ Rule 1. The question is about two things:
a The Battle of Hastings.
b How well prepared was King Harold?

◆ Rule 2. Look at page 7 of *In Search of History 1066–1485*. You only need to look for clues which help answer the question. Ignore the rest!

Look at the next sheet. The work has been done for you. The writing from page 7 is printed. Arrows take you to all the keywords. These are the clues which tell you about how prepared Harold was. The other pieces of information you can ignore. They do not help you answer the question.

His army fought the Norwegians at Stamford Bridge, where Harold won a great victory. Both Tostig and the King of Norway were killed. Their army was crushed. The survivors only needed 24 of their ships to get home.

Meanwhile, Duke William had been busy. He had got together men and supplies, put them in 100 ships and set sail for England. Just three days after Harold won his battle in the north, William landed in the south.

This was more bad news for Harold! His men were resting when they heard about it. The army was (tired) out after the long march and the battle. Many men had been (killed.) Others were badly (wounded.)

Harold was advised to wait until his army had recovered and he had found fresh troops. But he thought a (delay) would be dangerous. While William was building a wooden castle at Hastings, Harold set off to march the (400 kilometres) south to meet him.

Harold had lost a lot of his soldiers.

Harold thought he did not have time to waste!

Harold's army was tired out!

Quite a few of Harold's soldiers were wounded.

A long way to march South!

KEYWORDS AND SPIDER DIAGRAMS

You should not draw arrows on your textbooks! Instead you can write down the keywords to help you remember them. One way to do this is to use a spider diagram. This is a simple way to remember the important pieces of information. Here is one done for you. It records the keywords that are found in the writing above.

Harold's army was tired. It had marched a long way and had already fought a big battle.

Harold had a long march south to get to William. It was 400 kilometres.

Many of Harold's soldiers had been killed at the Battle of Stamford Bridge.

How well prepared was King Harold for the Battle of Hastings?

Harold was worried about delaying marching to fight William. So he could not wait for his army to recover. He could not wait to get fresh soldiers.

Many of Harold's soldiers had been wounded in the battle.

Using keywords to write a report which answers a question

After you have made a note of the keywords, you can use them to answer the question. Here it is done for you.

> Remember: you need to organise the information that you have got. You need to explain what you are doing: write about the evidence (the most important first) and draw it together in a conclusion which links back to what you were supposed to be doing.

'How well prepared was King Harold for the Battle of Hastings?

To find out how well prepared King Harold was for the Battle of Hastings, we need to see what happened to him and his army before the battle.

Shortly before the battle, he had had to fight another battle. This was at Stamford Bridge, 400 kilometres north of Hastings. Although he won this battle, his soldiers were tired from marching and from fighting. Many of Harold's men had been killed, and others had been wounded. This meant that Harold could not use these men to help him fight William. When Harold heard that William had arrived, he thought it would be too dangerous to wait and collect more soldiers. So he marched 400 kilometres south again with the soldiers he had left.

This meant that when he fought William, he had fewer men than at the Battle of Stamford Bridge, and the men he had were worn out. So he was not well prepared for the battle at all.'

INVESTIGATION

1 Read page 38 of *In Search of History 1066–1485*. The question you are investigating is:

> **'What problems did King John face in trying to rule England?'**

a Remember the rules:

◆ Rule 1. Think carefully about the question. What does it ask you to do?

◆ Rule 2. Look carefully at the page. Find the keywords (the information to help you answer the question). Make a spider diagram with them. Write the question in the middle of the spider diagram. This will remind you of what your keywords are all about.

b Next, use the keywords and your own words. Explain what problems King John faced. Use your own words to link up and explain the keywords.

By doing this you will be able to answer the question. You will not be just copying words out of the textbook. Instead you will be thinking about the question. You will be selecting only that information you need to answer the question. You will be answering the question using the keywords and your own understanding of what they are telling you. Follow this way of writing up your answer:

◆ Introduction. Say whom you are writing about. Say what you are trying to discover.

◆ Then write the main part of your essay. Write about each one of the problems John faced. Say why it was a problem. Say what he did about the problem, if you know this. Say how successful he was.

◆ Conclusion. Remind the person reading your essay of what you were looking at and what you have discovered. You can suggest which problem you think was the most important. Remember to say why you think this.

 # Carrying out a research project

When you are studying history, you sometimes need to carry out a research project. This is longer than just answering a question using one source of information like your textbook.

A research project gives you a chance to:

◆ study an area of history in depth, or over a long period of time (in outline);

◆ get information from a range of different sources (textbooks, videos, CD-ROMs, etc.);

◆ look at more than one question. If you are trying to answer a large question it may help to split it up into smaller questions. You can decide on what questions to ask yourself. This is one of the interesting things in carrying out your own research. You need to decide what you need to know in order to answer your main research question. For example, if your research project was:

> **How and why did castle defence change during the Middle Ages?**

you would need to write an introduction saying what area of history you are looking at, what you are trying to discover and how you intend to find out about the area you are investigating.

Then you would need to split it up into a number of smaller questions. These make a 'route of enquiry'. These are questions which will help you answer your overall question. You will need to write at least one paragraph on each question. These smaller questions should include:

> **How were the first castles defended?**
>
> **How did ways of attacking castles change?**
>
> **How did this lead to changes in how castles were defended?**
>
> **How were castles defended at the end of the Middle Ages?**
>
> **In what ways were they different from the earlier castles?**
>
> **In what ways were they similar?**

◆ After you have answered the smaller questions you will need to write a conclusion summing up what you have discovered. You might say what the biggest change was, what caused it and why you think it was important.

◆ At the end of the project, you can list all the sources of evidence that you used. This is called a 'bibliography'. You can also say how useful they were and how they helped you.

◆ You can say how you went about your project and any way you would do it differently (and better) if you were doing the project again.

Your own research project

Now carry out a research project on some part of the history of the Middle Ages. You will need to decide on a question, or a problem, that you want to explore. Try to choose something that you can investigate in order to find an answer.

RESEARCH PROJECT ON THE MIDDLE AGES

Name: _____

The big question I am going to investigate is: _____

_____

Why I chose to investigate this question: _____

_____

_____

The smaller questions I will need to explore to find out the answer to my big question are:

Question 1_____

Question 2_____

Question 3_____

Question 4_____

Question 5_____

(You do not need to use as many questions as this. It is up to you.)

I got my information from (list the places and say how useful they were): _____

_____

Problems I faced doing my research project: _____

_____

What I did to overcome these problems:_____

_____

If I was doing my research project again, I could do it better if I … _____

_____

New words I discovered and what they mean:_____

_____

Part II
Medieval Realms

CAERPHILLY CASTLE WITH OUTER WALLS AND A SECOND SET OF INNER WALLS.

THE SQUARE STONE KEEP OF ROCHESTER CASTLE.

THE ENTRANCE GATE TO CARISBROOKE CASTLE.

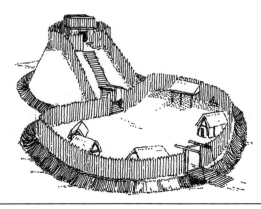

A DRAWING WHICH SHOWS A RECONSTRUCTION OF A MOTTE AND BAILEY CASTLE.

BODIAM CASTLE AND ITS MOAT.

The sheets for this and the other three study units aim:

a to provide an introduction to key study skills used throughout Key Stage 3 and beyond;

b to provide greater rigour in study through a series of Depth Studies which are clearly identified in the Orders, but have only a very limited coverage in the *In Search of History* series;

c to extend other areas of study which, while not being covered in the detail of the Depth Studies, nevertheless repay examination in greater detail. These have been selected due to their importance within the overall study unit, the requirements of the Orders and the extent to which these core areas were covered within the existing textbook;

d to provide a mixture of resource sheets, some of which arise directly from the existing textbook, others free-standing, which can be used in class, or as home-work exercises. A number of those which arise directly from the existing book offer structured assistance to less-able students, to enable them to extract and use key information and concepts.

In addition, the tasks suggested within the pack aim to encourage a more rigorous approach to evidence and enquiry with: critical comprehension of sources; comparison of sources for usefulness and reliability; reference to provenance of sources as part of critical enquiry; opportunities for extended writing, accompanied by structures which encourage students to adopt a logical and ordered progression of ideas; and, opportunities to pose their own questions.

SPECIFIC POINTS

The study skills sheets in the previous section are of two main kinds: those which are probably best slotted in when the skill is called for and those which could be used as an introduction to study at the start of the study unit. **Following commands,** and

Note-taking to answer a question may be used as an introduction to the study unit and to these skills. **Using posters in history** and **Carrying out a research project** are probably best introduced when these skills are called for within this (or other) study units at Key Stage 3.

Depth Study: Wales gives an opportunity to examine relationships between two of the 'realms' of the study unit title. It can be used as a substitute for Chapter 12 in *In Search of History 1066–1485*, or this can be used as an introduction, followed by the Depth Study. The final task could be attempted as group work followed by class discussion. **Depth Study: Parliament** would work well after a study of John and Magna Carta (book Chapter11) as both examine limits to kingship. **Depth Study: Women** gives an opportunity to redress something of the gender imbalance in medieval history, though it should not be taken as sufficient in itself. As a Depth Study that ranges across the period, it could be placed within the study unit where a social/economic focus is given to the work, or at the end, drawing a number of threads together. Again, the final question could be addressed via group work, then extended writing.

The sheets which extend knowledge cover a number of essential areas. **Sources of evidence** would work well as an introduction to the study unit. The first task works well as introductory homework. **Changing castles** would work very well as the culminating assessment of an extended study on castle development.

Of the Foundation Sheets, **Newspaper report** and **The Christian Church** assist students to access and record information from the book and make decisions on the basis of their explorations. **Black Death** and **Living in towns** can be used as summing-up exercises after class work. **Knights** makes the point that the Middle Ages were not a static period of time, and this would probably work best towards the end of the study unit but linked to previous work on knights and/or castles.

The English conquest of Wales, 1272–84

KEY QUESTIONS

Why was England able to control Wales even before it was conquered?

How did the English manage to finally conquer Wales?

What were relationships like between the English and the Welsh after the English conquest of Wales?

 WORD BOX

chronicle a record of events, in the order in which they happened.

markets places where goods were bought and sold.

medieval (also called the Middle Ages) the period of time between the Norman Conquest in 1066 and the start of the rule of the Tudor monarchs in 1485. Some historians start it in the Anglo-Saxon period after the fall of the Roman Empire and call

this early medieval. But in this book it is taken as lasting between 1066 and 1485.

monarch a ruler who is a king, or a queen.

reliable something that you can trust. Something that is true.

rivalry competition between people to be best, or most powerful.

underdeveloped poorer, with fewer towns, roads and large buildings.

At the start of the Middle Ages, or the **medieval** period of history, what is now Britain was made up of a number of independent countries. These countries were England, Wales, Ireland and Scotland. England, Scotland and Ireland had their own **monarchs** – there were several in Ireland – and in Wales different princes ruled. There was often war between these different countries. Many of these wars happened because the rulers of England wanted to rule these other countries too. Most Welsh, Irish and Scottish people did not want to be ruled by the English.

During the 13th century, King Edward I of England conquered Wales. This Depth Study looks at how and why this happened. There are three key questions to be answered in order to understand this. You will find them at the top of this sheet.

WHY WAS ENGLAND ABLE TO CONTROL WALES EVEN BEFORE IT WAS CONQUERED?

The English King Edward I conquered Wales after 1272. However, long before this, the rulers of England had thought they had the right to interfere with how Wales was ruled. They were able to do this for a number of reasons. First, Wales was not a united country. It was split up and ruled by different princes. There was often **rivalry** between these different princes and their families. This made it easy for English rulers to help one Welsh prince against another. Often, the different Welsh princes would not work together against the English. These Welsh princes did deals with different English rulers. This encouraged the English to get more involved in Wales. Before the Norman Conquest, Anglo-Saxon rulers had treated Wales as a country under their control. The Anglo-Saxon King Ethelred II, for example, had the title: 'King of the

English and governor of the nearby lands'. This included Wales! The Norman kings treated Wales in the same way.

Second, Wales was an **underdeveloped** country compared with England. It had fewer towns and **markets**, there was less trade and fewer coins were used. England was richer, and, because it was close to Wales, it was able to control much of the trade with Wales. Many things sold by the Welsh went to England. Many of the things bought by the Welsh came from England, or were brought in by English merchants. After the Norman Conquest, southern Wales fell under the control of Norman lords. Around 1100, many English people moved into southern Wales. These newcomers brought in a new language and new laws.

The geography of Wales made it easy for it to be dominated by England. It was not far from the south and midlands of England which were wealthy and heavily populated areas of England. This made it easier for English merchants to trade with Wales and for English rulers to move large armies into Wales. On top of this the richest parts of Wales were in the low-lying lands found in the south and north-east of Wales. These were areas close to England and were easily invaded and controlled by people from England.

Third, even though the Welsh and the English were both Christian people, it was the English Church which was the most powerful. This was important because the English Church tended to support the rulers of England against the Welsh rulers.

In all these ways, the rulers of England were able to control things happening in Wales long before they defeated the Welsh and took over their country.

The evidence on the next two pages shows what people living at the time thought about this.

SOURCE A

❝Prince of the Normans and king of the Saxons and Britons and the Scots.❞

*An 11th-century Welsh **chronicle** describing William the Conqueror. The word 'Britons' means the Welsh.*

SOURCE B

❝Wales is unable to supply all its people with food, without buying things from England. Since it cannot control this trade, without the generosity and permission of the king of England, it is of course under his control.❞

Written in England, by William of Newburgh in the late 12th century. Although he lived in Yorkshire – a long way from Wales – he tried to find out about what he was writing about. He was a fair man, who did not just look at things from an English point of view.

SOURCE C

❝It is part of the kingdom of England, not a kingdom in itself.❞

Written by Gerald of Wales, a Welsh church leader in the 11th century. Gerald had strong opinions about people. Not everyone agreed with his ideas. He was partly Welsh, but most of his family were Normans. Gerald lived for some years in France and England. He worked for the English kings Henry II and Richard I. He wrote advice to the kings of England, telling them about the best ways to conquer Wales. He failed to become Bishop of St David's Cathedral in Wales, though he tried to get help from the English king. Eventually Gerald retired to Lincoln in England.

USING THE EVIDENCE

Reason:	Source:	What it says:
Ideas amongst church leaders.		
Old beliefs that England was stronger than Wales.		
Trade.		

1 Look at Sources A–C. Then complete the table above. The sources suggest different reasons why the English were able to control some of the life in Wales, even before they conquered it. Find which source fits each reason. Then write what each source tells you about how England was able to control Wales.

2 Using your completed table and any other relevant information, explain how rulers of England were able to control life in Wales even before they conquered it. Write a paragraph about each of the following reasons:

◆ the closeness of England to Wales and what the land was like in Wales;
◆ old ideas about the relationship between Wales and England;
◆ trade;
◆ relations between the Church in Wales and in England.

Say which one of these reasons you think gave rulers of England greatest power over the Welsh, and explain why you think this.

3 Look at Source C. Gerald of Wales was descended from the Norman conquerors of England, as well as from the princes of Wales. Look at the information written about him under the source. From what you have learned about Gerald, how much do you think you can rely on him to find out about what the Welsh felt about the English?

4 Look at the information about the writer of Source B. Do you think he would be a **reliable** person to write about life in Wales? Give the reasons for your answer.

5 Imagine you are a Welsh person living in 1200. Design a protest poster complaining about the ways English rulers interfere in Wales. Use some of the ideas you have read about which tell you how the English treated the Welsh.

DEPTH STUDY: The English conquest of Wales, 1272–84   Page ☐

HOW DID THE ENGLISH FINALLY MANAGE TO CONQUER WALES?

Rulers of England invaded Wales in 1114, 1121, 1157-58, 1165, and 1211–12. But it was King Edward I of England who finally conquered Wales and brought it completely under English rule. The timeline shows the main events of his conquest of Wales.

1272: Edward I became King of England.

1277: Edward I invaded Wales after the Welsh leader, Llewellyn, refused to obey him. Edward I forced the Welsh to recognise him as ruler.

1282–3: Llewellyn's final rebellion. Edward I finally conquered Llewellyn's strongholds in north Wales, and Llewellyn was killed.

1284: Welsh crown jewels taken by the English. Welsh laws changed to fit in with English laws.

1301: Edward I gave his own English son the title 'Prince of Wales'.

How Edward I succeeded in completely conquering Wales

THE ENGLISH FOUGHT THE WELSH REBELS.

ENGLISH CASTLES DOMINATED WALES AND THE COUNTRY WAS SPLIT INTO COUNTIES CONTROLLED BY THE ENGLISH.

CAERNARFON
FLINT
MERIONETH
CARDIGAN
CARMARTHEN
ENGLISH MARCHER LORDSHIPS

THE ENGLISH GOVERNMENT WAS WELL ORGANISED AND POWERFUL.

SOURCE

“Wales, which always rightfully belonged to us, has now been completely and entirely brought under our direct rule and has been taken over and united under the Crown of England.”

Edward I, in 1284, in the law called the Statute of Wales. The words 'united under the Crown' mean controlled by the English king.

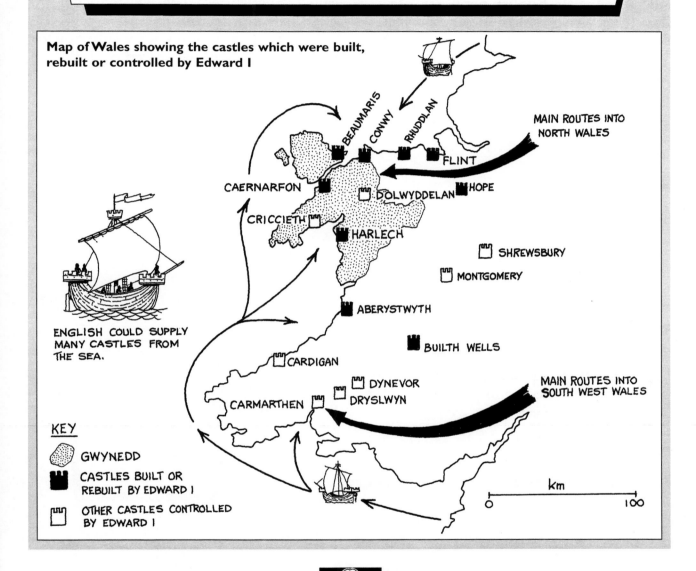

Map of Wales showing the castles which were built, rebuilt or controlled by Edward I

USING THE EVIDENCE

1. Look at the cartoons. Imagine you are one of Edward I's advisers looking back on how the English conquered Wales. Explain how you managed to do it. You will find ideas in the cartoons.

2. Look carefully at the map. Explain how the location of Edward's castles made it very difficult for the Welsh to rebel again.

3. Look at Source A. In what way did Edward try to show he was right to conquer Wales? Look carefully at the words, and identify what he said in order to give this impression.

WHAT WERE RELATIONSHIPS LIKE BETWEEN THE ENGLISH AND THE WELSH AFTER THE ENGLISH CONQUEST OF WALES?

After Edward I conquered Wales, relationships between the English and the Welsh grew worse. The English were determined to keep the Welsh under strict control. It became unfashionable for an English person to marry anyone who was Welsh. English people wrote about the Welsh as if they were savages. Welsh people were ruled strictly by new laws, which applied only to Welsh people (see the illustrations on the next sheet).

Areas of Wales were split up according to whether they were lived in by English people with English laws, or by Welsh people covered by the laws that the English rulers said should apply to Welsh people. The English areas were called 'Englishries'. The Welsh areas were called 'Welshries'.

The English felt they were superior to the Welsh but still felt scared of them. They did all they could to try to make it difficult for Welsh people to carry on with their customs and ways of life.

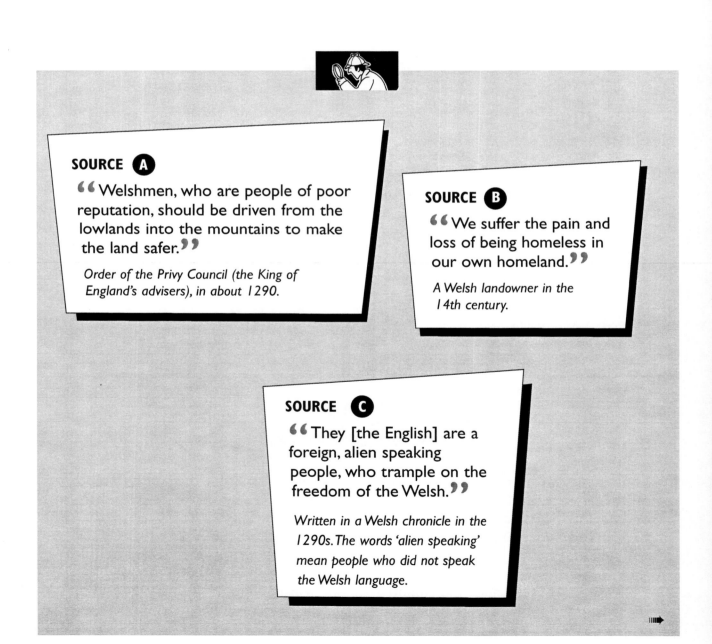

SOURCE A

❝Welshmen, who are people of poor reputation, should be driven from the lowlands into the mountains to make the land safer.❞

Order of the Privy Council (the King of England's advisers), in about 1290.

SOURCE B

❝We suffer the pain and loss of being homeless in our own homeland.❞

A Welsh landowner in the 14th century.

SOURCE C

❝They [the English] are a foreign, alien speaking people, who trample on the freedom of the Welsh.❞

Written in a Welsh chronicle in the 1290s. The words 'alien speaking' mean people who did not speak the Welsh language.

THE WELSH COULD NOT RUN GOVERNMENT OR BE POWERFUL OFFICIALS AND COULD NOT OWN LAND IN AN ENGLISH TOWN.

THE WELSH COULD NOT TRADE FREELY.

THE WELSH COULD NOT USE ENGLISH LAW COURTS.

USING THE EVIDENCE

1 Read Source B and look at the other information in this section. The Welsh person who wrote Source B was not really homeless. He was actually quite a well-off person. What did he mean by what he wrote, and why did he write it?

2 A *cause* is why something happens. A *consequence* is what an action makes happen, or leads to. Look at Sources A and C. Which one of these is a *cause* of Welsh people's loss of land? Which one is a *consequence* of what the English did? Explain how you decided.

3 Imagine you are a Welsh person living in the 14th century. Explain what you feel about the English conquest of Wales and why you feel the way that you do. Try to follow these three steps:

◆ Write an introduction. Describe how the English conquered Wales and that many Welsh people were unhappy about this.

◆ Write the main part of your essay. Describe how the English treated the Welsh. Explain why these things might have made Welsh people happy, or unhappy.

◆ Write a conclusion. Say what would have had the biggest impact on the way the Welsh felt about the conquest of Wales.

The power of talking – the growth of Parliament

KEY QUESTIONS

What were Parliaments?
Why did rulers set them up?

 WORD BOX

barons the most powerful landowners in the country. They were given land directly by the ruler. Also called the **nobility (nobles)**.

commoners ordinary people, who were not royal, or great landowners.

government the group of people, under a ruler, who run a country and carry out the wishes of a ruler.

knights landowners who were given land in return for fighting for their lord. Knights were important people in their local communities. Some were very powerful.

state a nation – a large group of people – which comes under one government. It can also mean the government and its servants who run the country.

WHAT IS PARLIAMENT?

Today, the laws in Britain are made by Parliament. Parliament makes many laws that affect the lives of ordinary people. The word 'Parliament' comes from a French word meaning 'to talk'. This was because the first Parliaments were groups of people called to give advice to the ruler, to bring complaints and to agree to new taxes. They became part of the **government** – the way by which the kings and queens ran and controlled the country. People who share the same ruler and government are said to be part of the same **state**.

When did the first Parliaments meet?

Rulers of England had always discussed important matters with the powerful people in the country. The Anglo-Saxon rulers had had a group of advisers called the 'Witan'. These people were powerful landowners, the **nobility**. After 1066, William the Conqueror and his sons met with their advisers three times a year: at Christmas, Easter and Whitsun. These are great Christian celebrations. Later, these meetings happened more regularly. These meetings came to be called the

'Great Council'. They helped the ruler govern the country.

In 1258 the English nobles or **barons** decided that the king at that time, Henry III, was not ruling properly. They made him discuss the running of the country three times a year with a group of people whom they called a 'Parliament'. This was another name for the old Great Council.

How and why did Parliament change in the 13th century?

In 1264 another baron, Simon de Montfort, led a revolt against Henry III. Simon wanted more people to support him. To do this, he changed the kind of people who came to a Parliament. As well as the most powerful landowners, Simon also called **commoners** too. His Parliament was made up of two **knights** from every county and two people from the most important towns.

In 1265, Simon was killed. However, the new king (and Simon's enemy) King Edward I carried on with Simon's ideas about Parliament. This was because they were useful. Parliament agreed what taxes should be paid and brought complaints to the ruler.

SOURCE A

❝Look at the state of the country and deal with its common business and that of the king. It should have the power to advise the king in good faith concerning the government of the kingdom, in order to change and improve everything that they shall consider in need of being changed, or improved.❞

The job of Parliament, decided by Henry III's barons in 1258.

SOURCE B

❝In the king's Great Council, in Parliament, doubts about laws are decided. New solutions suggested for new problems. Justice is done to people as they deserve.❞

From the Law Book of King Edward I.

SOURCE C

❝They are to give clear answers to the Council on the matter of a tax.❞

The orders given to knights called to the Royal Council, in 1254.

Responsibilities of Parliament

- TO HELP AND SUPPORT THE RULER.
- TO GIVE ADVICE.
- TO AGREE TO RAISE TAXES.
- TO DISCUSS LAWS.
- TO BRING COMPLAINTS TO THE KING.

USING THE EVIDENCE

Source	Job(s) of Parliament
Source A	
Source B	
Source C	

1 Read Sources A, B and C. For each one of them, fill in the table above.

2 From what you have read, explain why Parliament was useful to a ruler in the Middle Ages. How did it help a ruler to rule?

◆ Mention how Parliament started and how it changed over time.

◆ Describe the jobs it did (like making laws, advising the king, making complaints) and say why each was important and useful to a ruler.

THE GROWING POWER OF PARLIAMENT

KEY QUESTIONS
Why did Parliament become more powerful?
Did everyone think this was a good thing?

During the 14th century, Parliament became more powerful. Rulers needed Parliament to agree to more taxes to fight wars with France.

The evidence shows that different people had different opinions about whether this was a good, or a bad thing.

SOURCE A

❝Our lord the king has asked from the church and the commons…taxes on wool and other goods. In my opinion it is too much to give him, for the commons are so weakened by the many taxes which have been paid up to now that they cannot afford such a charge. All the money that we have given for the war has been lost because it has been badly spent.❞

Speech by Peter de la Mare to Parliament in 1376. Peter was a knight, not a great landowner or member of the royal family. He led a group of members of Parliament who thought that the King, Edward III, should give Parliament greater power.

SOURCE B

❝What are these worthless knights trying to do? Do they think they are the kings and princes of this land? Or where have they got their pride and arrogance from?❞

The words of John of Gaunt, brother of King Edward III, in 1376. He is talking about Parliament who would not agree to new taxes. This report of what he said was written by Thomas Walsingham, who thought it was right for Parliament to limit the power of the King if he was behaving badly. He also disliked John of Gaunt.

USING THE EVIDENCE

❶ What was happening in the 14th century which made rulers rely more on Parliament? How did this increase Parliament's power?

❷ Look at Sources A and B.
  ◆ What different opinions do they give about the power Parliament should have?

◆ Think about who said these things. What kinds of people were they? How might this have caused them to have such different views?

❸ Look at the information about the writer of Source B. How reliable do you think his account may be? Give the reasons for your answer.

 **DS** # The changing lives of women in the Middle Ages

 **KEY QUESTIONS** **Why were women given little power after the Norman Conquest? How did the rights of women change during the Middle Ages?**

 WORD BOX

nunnery places where nuns lived, away from the world, worshipping God.

will a document which says whom a person wants their possessions to go to after they are dead.

WHY WERE WOMEN GIVEN LITTLE POWER AFTER THE NORMAN CONQUEST?

Women had less power after 1066 than before. Anglo-Saxon women had been important landowners. They had been able to give away, or sell, the land that they owned. Women in charge of important **nunneries** possessed a lot of power. These women could read and write and were involved in the complicated business of organising both the lives of their religious communities and links with the people outside the community.

After the Norman Conquest, women lost many of their rights. This did not happen straight away, but soon they had less power and freedom. This happened for a number of different reasons.

Landowners were supposed to serve the king as soldiers, in return for their land. Women were not allowed to fight and so it was thought they should not own large amounts of land.

From 1100 onwards, laws controlling women became stricter. This was because the royal laws began to follow Church law more than they had before. Church law (called Canon Law) treated women as inferior to men. Many leaders of the Church thought that women were more sinful than men, less intelligent and should not hold positions of power. Even nuns running nunneries found they were more strictly controlled and more cut off from the outside world.

Rulers found they could increase their power by controlling women. If a man died, then his widow could be made to marry again. Her land would then belong to her new husband. The ruler could use this as a way to reward a man he trusted without it costing the ruler anything! Girls as young as five years old were married so that their husband could have their land. Less powerful lords found they could do similar things to women too. They could make peasant widows marry or move out of their homes.

All this reduced the power and rights of women. By the 12th century they could not be witnesses in a court case. They could not take complaints to court to get justice. They could not make a **will**.

Problems with the evidence

We do not know what women felt about the way they were treated. Most of the laws and other written documents were written by men – often by monks who had promised never to marry and have sex and who often distrusted and feared women. We have few letters and books written by women before the 15th century. Even after this, there are very few. Often, we can only guess what women felt about their lives.

SOURCE A

" There is a fault in the way women are made, since she was formed from a bent rib. Through this defect she is an imperfect animal. She always tempts others to do wrong. "

This is what some men in the medieval Church thought about women. It was written in the 15th century. The words 'bent rib' refer to Eve being made from Adam's body in the Bible. The Bible does not say that this made women wrong in any way, but this medieval writer is making it seem as if the Bible does say that!

SOURCE B   A picture from a 15th-century French manuscript showing 'greed' as a woman.

SOURCE C

" When her husband comes home she dares not say a word. He rants and raves like a madman. She can do nothing, say nothing that pleases him. Often when she has done nothing wrong she gets his fist in her teeth. "

A writer's view of the problems faced by some wives. It was probably written by a man in the 12th century.

USING THE EVIDENCE

1 How might ideas like those in Source A affect how women were treated?

2 Does Source B seem to agree, or disagree with the ideas found in Source A?

3 Both Sources A and B were probably written and drawn by monks. How might this explain their view of women?

4 Make a spider diagram to show different reasons why women were given less power and freedom than men. Which reason do you think was most important, and why?

5 Why would it have been difficult for the woman in Source C to get her violent husband punished?

HOW DID THE RIGHTS OF WOMEN CHANGE DURING THE MIDDLE AGES?

Not all women behaved in the way some men thought that they should.

Many wives of rich landowners looked after their husband's lands and castles while they were away. Many were skilled and clever and did this as well as any man. In 1075 Norwich Castle was commanded by the wife of the Earl of Norwich when he was in a revolt against William the Conqueror. In the 12th century the Empress Matilda led her forces in a civil war against King Stephen, whom she believed had stolen the crown from her. Nicola de la Haye held Lincoln Castle in a revolt against King John in the early 13th century. In the 15th century the wives of the wealthy Paston family in East Anglia often ran the family homes and lands while their husbands were away.

In 1215 King John agreed to the Magna Carta. This listed what people's rights should be. One of these was that widows would not have to pay a fine to the ruler for the right to stay unmarried.

In the towns less wealthy women gained more freedom. Many jobs were done by women who were in charge of the business. The London bakeries were run by women, and so was the making of silk and beer. In 1363 women were given the right to change their trade if they wanted to. Men did not have this freedom!

The wives of rich craftsmen could often carry on the trade of their husband when he died. This was so even if it was a trade that only men should do. The law treated these widows as men! But they lost this power if they remarried.

In the countryside there were changes too. During the 13th century lords began to pay workers to do jobs for them, instead of making them work for no pay. Many unmarried women were allowed to leave their villages to get work for money. In many areas all the dairies had women workers, who worked for pay. This gave them more money and power.

SOURCE A A picture of the famous 15th-century French writer, Christine de Pisa. But she was unusual. Most women did not write about their lives or what they thought about the world. This made it hard for them to change ideas men had about women.

SOURCE B

" No widow shall be forced to marry again. She can live without a husband if she wishes to. But she must not remarry without the king's permission if she is the widow of a wealthy landowner. **"**

Words from the Magna Carta.

SOURCE C

" This agreement is that John Nougle of London, maker of ribbons, has sent Katherine Nougle, his sister, to be an apprentice trained by Avice Wodeford, silkthread maker of London, to learn her trade. **"**

An agreement made in 1392. It shows how women were in charge of silk making, and could train others too.

Women were still much less powerful than men

These changes made great differences to the lives of many women. This was especially true for women in towns and also for poorer women in the country-side. But women still had far fewer rights than men.

◆ If a widow remarried, her new husband took control of her land and property. In the 15th century, fewer than 10 in every 100 landowners were women.

◆ Married women could not leave property to other people.

◆ Women could not go to university.

◆ Women could not be members of a jury in a court.

◆ No woman could be an official of a guild, which made rules for the different trades in towns.

◆ Nuns were strictly controlled.

◆ Between 1066 and 1485, only one woman was given a noble title! Margaret de Brotherton became Duchess of Norfolk in 1397.

We must always remember that many men were strictly controlled too. Many men could not read either.

• • • • • • • • • • • • • • • • • • • **USING THE EVIDENCE** • • • • • • • • • • • • • • • • •

❶ Draw two columns. In one, put all the things which changed to give women more freedom and power. In the other, put the things which still reduced their freedom and power.

❷ Look carefully at your columns. In your opinion how much did the position of women really change in the Middle Ages? 'A lot'? 'A little'? 'In some ways but not in others'? Say what you think. Back up your opinion with evidence.

• •

 # Sources of evidence from the Middle Ages

Historians use evidence from the past to find out what life was like in the past. Evidence from the period in the past that you are studying is called primary evidence. Primary evidence about life in the Middle Ages comes from that period of time and tells you about life in that time. Different periods of history leave different kinds of primary evidence for historians to study. People in the future studying your life will have different kinds of evidence to look at, compared with the kinds of evidence which survive from medieval times.

> **Beware!** Just because something is primary evidence does not mean you can always trust it, or that it will tell you all you need to know. Some people who wrote things in the past made mistakes, told lies and got things wrong. Just like these things happen today. Also, a piece of evidence will not tell you everything you would like to know.

INVESTIGATION

1 Make a list of things which a historian in the future might look at to find out about your life. This list might include:

- things which you have written or recorded;
- things you have made;
- things you have bought, or own;
- official records about you (like a school register).

2 Look at all the things on your list. For each one of these things, say what it might tell a historian in the future about your life.

3 Which do you think would give the historian the most important information about you? Explain the reason for your choice.

EVIDENCE FROM THE MIDDLE AGES

Historians looking at the Middle Ages do not have as much evidence about ordinary people as historians in the future will have about you. Why?

- Most people in the Middle Ages could not read or write. They did not write diaries or letters.

- The few people who did write were almost all of them men. We do not know much about what women thought or felt.

- Most people owned fewer things than people do today. They have left little evidence for us to study because they did not own very much to start with.

- People did not own machines (like CD players, videos) because these had not been invented.

INVESTIGATION

1 **a** How many of the clues from your life would ordinary people *not* have had in the Middle Ages? Explain why.

b What difference does this make to what we can find out about their lives?

Kinds of evidence from the Middle Ages

Different kinds of evidence survive from the Middle Ages. Here are some:

- manor court records, telling about life in the villages. These often record the names of people punished for breaking the rules made by the lord of the village;

- laws made by the ruler;

- prayer books and Bibles written by monks and nuns. These sometimes have pictures drawn in them showing scenes from ordinary life;

- fine buildings such as churches, castles and houses of rich people;

- jewellery and other expensive things made for the rich;

- coins used for buying and selling;

- pieces of pot and the remains of houses. These are found by archaeologists. These are people who dig for clues in the ground. The houses of poor people just leave pits and holes in the ground, which show where the posts stood which held up the house.

On this sheet are examples of the kinds of evidence which survive from the Middle Ages. We need to think carefully about what these kinds of evidence can tell us about life in the past. Different kinds of evidence can tell us different things.

SOURCE A

“ He must plough two and a half acres of the lord's land each winter, or pay six pence an acre each time. He has to do a day's harrowing, providing his horse if he has one and to bring his own plough to do extra ploughing at sowing time, providing his own meals. At Christmas he has to give one cock, one hen and a loaf [to his lord] and at Easter thirty eggs. He must do one day of hay carrying at hay-making time, the lord providing food and he must mow until the lord's meadow is finished. He must help the lord at harvest as the lord commands. He must carry corn for the lord and clean out the water channel for the mill and spend half a day doing it. ”

An extract from the rules of the village of Codicote, in Hertfordshire, in 1332. These rules said what a villein had to do for the lord of the manor. A 'villein' was a farmer who had only a little land. He was not free and had to do work for nothing at certain times of the year for the lord of the manor. Another word for a farmer with only a little land is a 'peasant'.

SOURCE B
A photograph of Salisbury Cathedral. It was built in the 13th century.

SOURCE C

A photograph of the deserted village of Upper Ditchford, Gloucestershire. All that remains of the houses are ditches and bumps in the field.

SOURCE D

" All the labourers, skilled and unskilled, were so determined to do whatever they wanted that they would not obey the king, or the law. "

A monk from Rochester describing how poorer people were behaving in 1349.
A lot of writing was done by monks. Many ordinary people did not write about their own lives.

INVESTIGATION

1. **a** Look carefully at Source A. What could you find out about life in a village in the Middle Ages from this source?
   b What questions might you want to ask about this source? Do you think it would be easy to answer your questions? Explain your answer.
   c How useful would this source be if you wanted to find out what peasants thought about life in the village? Explain your answer.

2. Look at Source B. What questions might a historian ask about a building like this when trying to find out about the importance of religion in the lives of medieval people?

3. Look at Source C. How useful would this be in trying to find out about the houses of ordinary people in the Middle Ages? Think about what it

could tell you. Think about what it could not tell you.

4. Why might a historian have to be careful about using Source D to find out how ordinary people behaved in the Middle Ages?

5. Look at Sources A and C. Which would be most useful to a historian trying to find out what life was like in villages in the Middle Ages? Give the reasons for your answer.

6. Compare all of the sources. Which do you think is most useful and which least useful to a historian trying to find out about the lives of ordinary people living in the Middle Ages? Give the reasons for your choices, saying why your chosen source is more, or less, useful than the other sources.

Things do not stay the same. Over time new ideas bring changes. Many castles were built between 1066 and 1485. But they were not all the same. Over time, ideas about how best to build castles changed.

Look carefully at the information about changing castles on pages 12–13 of *In Search of History 1066–1485*. Then look at the information on this sheet.

CHANGING IDEAS ABOUT HOW TO BUILD CASTLES

◆ The first castles in the 11th century were motte and bailey castles. These were built quickly using earth and wood.

◆ Square keep castles were made with a great square stone tower. This was harder to break into. The doorway was often on the first floor. Stairs led up to it. These were being built by 1100.

◆ Round keep castles had a tower built of stone. Because it was round it was stronger. Attackers could not dig under a corner to make the wall fall down. Most were built later than the square keep castles.

◆ Curtain walls of stone were built around castles during the 12th century to help keep out attackers. Later they had towers which stuck out from the walls. Sometimes these castles were surrounded by a water moat.

◆ Entrance gates were places where attackers could break into a castle. These became protected by strong gateway towers called barbicans.

◆ Later in the 13th century, concentric castles were built. These had walls one behind the other. This meant that if attackers broke through one wall, they then had to break through another.

◆ During the 15th century, new cannons were used to break down castle walls. Castles began to be built with lower walls so that they were a harder target to shoot at. Earth banks were used again to absorb the force of a cannon ball. Walls were made thicker. Sometimes they were hollow with earth in them to absorb the force of a cannon ball.

INVESTIGATION

1 Look at the castles shown in the diagram on the following page. List them in the order in which they were probably built. Explain how you decided this.

2 Look at the pictures of the castles, then look at *In Search of History 1066–1485*, pages 12–13.

Explain how and why the building of castles changed during the Middle Ages.

3 If you have a local castle, research what type of castle it is. How is it defended? Were its defences changed at all during the time it was used as a castle? If so, how and why did they change?

CASTLE IMPROVEMENTS

CAERPHILLY CASTLE WITH OUTER WALLS AND A SECOND SET OF INNER WALLS.

THE SQUARE STONE KEEP OF ROCHESTER CASTLE.

THE ENTRANCE GATE TO CARISBROOKE CASTLE.

A DRAWING WHICH SHOWS A RECONSTRUCTION OF A MOTTE AND BAILEY CASTLE.

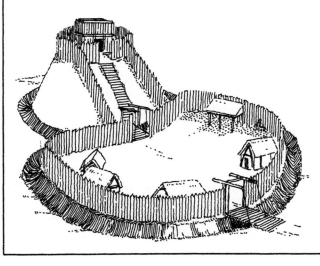

BODIAM CASTLE AND ITS MOAT.

F Newspaper report: 14 October 1066

Look at pages 8 and 9 of *In Search of History 1066–1485*. These tell you about the Battle of Hastings.

Look at the cartoons on this sheet. They show you what happened in the battle.

What happened in the Battle of Hastings

HAROLD'S ARMY WAS ON FOOT. WILLIAM'S KNIGHTS WERE ON HORSES.

HAROLD CAMPED ON SENLAC HILL.

THE NORMANS CHARGED UP THE HILL. THE SAXONS CHASED THEM DOWN.

THE NORMANS FIRED ARROWS. HAROLD WAS HIT IN THE EYE AND KILLED.

WRITING A NEWSPAPER REPORT OF THE BATTLE OF HASTINGS!

In 1066 there were no newspapers. Imagine that there *was* one! Imagine you were a journalist watching the battle. Write an account of the battle. Be either a Saxon, or a Norman. Tell the battle from their point of view. Remember they will have different thoughts about the battle!

◆ Explain how each side was armed.

◆ Describe how the battle was fought. Use the cartoons to help you get it in the right order. Source B on page 9 of your textbook might help you too.

◆ Tell how the battle ended. Again, source A on page 9 might help you. Say who won. Explain why they won.

◆ Imagine you can talk to soldiers on each side. What might they tell you about the battle? Write what they might tell you. They are imaginary eyewitnesses.

◆ Say what you think about the battle. Say who you think deserved to win.

F The Christian Church in the Middle Ages

Look carefully at the information on page 24 of *In Search of History 1066–1485*. In the Middle Ages the Christian Church played an important part in the lives of people. It still does so today. But more people went to church in the Middle Ages than today.

Things the Church did that people would have liked:	Things the Church did that people might not have liked:

1 A person living in the Middle Ages might have liked some things the Church did. They might not have liked some other things that it did. Using the information on page 24 of your textbook, fill in the table above. Try to find things the Church did that people would have liked. Then try to find things the Church did that people might not have liked.

What you have just done is an important thing to learn. You have shown that people in the past might have had mixed feelings about something as important as the Church. It would be a mistake to say people liked everything the Church did. It would also be a mistake to say people did not like the Church.

2 Look at each of the columns in your table. Using what you have discovered, explain:
a *why* people liked some things about the Church;
b *why* people might not have liked some things about the Church. Remember: do not just copy out your list again. Instead, explain how these things would have made people's lives happy or sad.

3 Design a poster to show all the things the Church did in the Middle Ages. Divide your poster in half. On one side show things that people might have liked. On the other side show things that people might not have liked.

F The Black Death

The Black Death was a terrible disease. It killed many thousands of people in the Middle Ages.

Imagine that you were living in Britain in 1348. This was the year that the Black Death first came to this country. You are going to write a letter to a friend in another part of the country.

Imagine that the disease has not reached there yet. In your letter, tell your friend about how terrible the disease is. The cartoons below tell you important things about the Black Death.

In your letter, tell your friend all about the disease. Use the cartoons to remind you about things to say. Write your ideas in proper sentences.

1. WHAT WERE THE SIGNS OF THE BLACK DEATH IN A PERSON?

LUMPS ON THEIR BODY.

SPOTS.

SMELLY BREATH.

2. WHAT DID PEOPLE THINK CAUSED THE BLACK DEATH?

GOD WAS PUNISHING PEOPLE FOR DOING WRONG THINGS.

ENEMIES.

DIRTY STREETS.

BAD AIR.

3. WHAT DID PEOPLE DO TO TRY TO AVOID CATCHING THE BLACK DEATH?

VISIT CHURCHES AND PRAY.

SMELL SWEET-SMELLING THINGS.

WHIP THEMSELVES.

LETTER TO A FRIEND ABOUT THE BLACK DEATH

Look carefully at the sheet with the cartoons telling you about the Black Death. On this sheet, there are some ideas to help you write your letter.

Written in the Year of Our Lord, 1348.

Dear.......................................

I am writing to you about a terrible disease called the.......................
.... It is killing hundreds of people where I live in
....

You know a person has the Black Death when you see these things:
....
....
....
....
....
Most people never get better. They die horribly.

People cannot agree what is causing the Black Death. Some people say it is caused by...
Other people say it is caused by...
Some think it is..which causes it.
Other people say... makes the disease happen.

Here are some ideas about how to keep the Black Death away:
....
....
....
....

I hope you do not get the disease.
Signed, your good friend,

 # Living in towns in the Middle Ages

During the Middle Ages, towns grew in size. Many people found that it was better living in towns than in the country. They felt they had more freedom. They felt they could make more money. But living in a town was not all easy. Play the game on this sheet. It shows you the good things and bad things about living in a town.

All you need is:

◆ this sheet;

◆ a dice or numbered pieces of paper (1–6);

◆ a cup to shake the dice in.

 # Changing weapons and equipment of knights

Life did not stay the same through the Middle Ages. Many things changed. Knights changed. Their armour changed. Their weapons changed.

Here are pictures of two knights. One comes from 1066. The other comes from 1450. There were about 400 years between them. Ideas about weapons and armour changed in this time. But some things stayed the same. In history it often happens that things change. But some things sometimes stay the same.

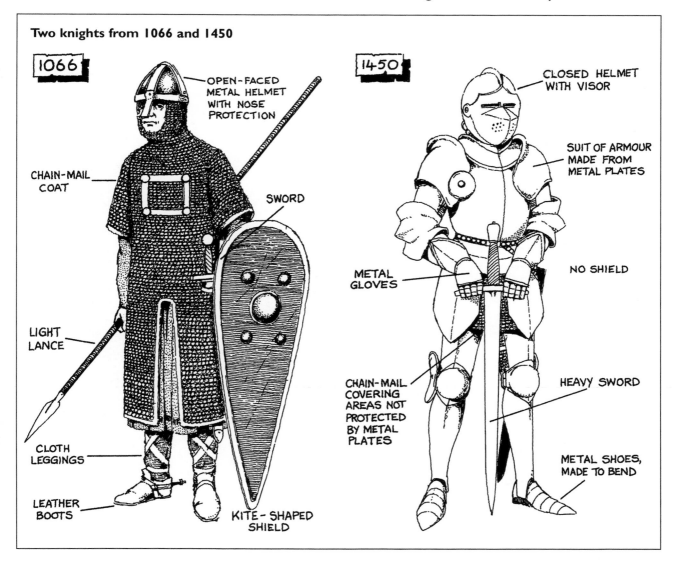

Two knights from 1066 and 1450

1066
- OPEN-FACED METAL HELMET WITH NOSE PROTECTION
- CHAIN-MAIL COAT
- SWORD
- LIGHT LANCE
- CLOTH LEGGINGS
- LEATHER BOOTS
- KITE-SHAPED SHIELD

1450
- CLOSED HELMET WITH VISOR
- SUIT OF ARMOUR MADE FROM METAL PLATES
- NO SHIELD
- METAL GLOVES
- CHAIN-MAIL COVERING AREAS NOT PROTECTED BY METAL PLATES
- HEAVY SWORD
- METAL SHOES, MADE TO BEND

❶ Look carefully at the two knights. Make a spider diagram. In the middle, write: 'Ways in which knights changed'.

❷ Now make another spider diagram. In the middle, write: 'Ways in which knights stayed the same'.

❸ Look at this statement: 'Knights were the same through the Middle Ages'.

Say whether you agree, or disagree with this statement. Use your spider diagrams to help you decide what you think. Think about:

◆ the chain-mail they wore;

◆ the shields they used;

◆ the weapons they carried;

◆ the armour they wore.

Part III
The Making of the United Kingdom

NON SINE SOLE
IRIS.

TN 1485–1714: The Making of the United Kingdom

The subsequent sheets for this study unit follow the same format as that of **Part II Medieval Realms**. However, a number of the concepts covered and activities test higher levels of response in order to build progression into the overall work of students across the study units.

One particular feature of this part of the pack is to extend the coverage from 1714 to the middle of the 18th century. This is because the study unit covers a longer time-span than the original book, which was written long before the National Curriculum.

Depth Study: The end of merrie England? is based on Chapter 8 of *In Search of History 1485–1714* but takes the study well beyond the changes brought about within church services. This reflects what has been a developing research area amongst academics, and that is the impact of the Reformation on popular culture and particularly on seasonal celebrations, both religious and secular. When introducing the 'Ritual Year', it might help to first identify those events which are seasonally celebrated by students within the class. This is an opportunity to identify the wide range of such activities which now exist within a multi-cultural society. Then look at the list of pre-Reformation celebrations. How many of these are still celebrated today, and in what form? The extended writing which arises from an examination of the Ronald Hutton quote might repay small group work and whole-class discussion before it is attempted individually. **Depth Study: The world turned upside-down!** looks at some of the radical groups that flourished in the aftermath of the breakdown of order in the 1640s. The spider diagram and the first activity are crucial as they help explain why there was such an upsurge in the late 1640s and 1650s. Before the Fifth Monarchy Men poster is attempted, students may benefit from referring back to the sheet on posters in **Part I General Guidance**. The radical groups covered here could be taken as research areas by different groups in the class who could first identify what they intend to find out about each radical group and then carry out research, concluding with a report to the whole class. Such research could include information from other sources provided by the teacher. **Depth Study: Making a United Kingdom** focuses on one of the central themes of this study unit and extends the focus beyond 1714. While this is a very challenging area of study, it draws together otherwise disparate threads and provides background to the next study unit.

The Extension Sheet on **The beggars are coming...** works well as an assessment, focused on hierarchies of causation and provenance of sources related to their utility. **The image of the Queen** would be enhanced if, prior to attempting it, textbooks and library books are trawled for contemporary images of Elizabeth I. These could then be subjected to the same scrutiny as those given in the pack. **Kings from Hanover** and **Changing kingdoms** fill gaps in the existing textbook while relating back to work covered in the **Depth Study: Making a United Kingdom**. The **Timeline search...** could be carried out as a concluding exercise (homework?) to revisit key events and explore the nature of 'turning points'. This would repay being discussed in class first.

In the Foundation Sheets, **What kind of king was Henry VIII?** can be used to draw together work on Henry. **Why was the Catholic Church less popular?**, **The poor in Tudor England**, **Quarrels with Parliament** and **The 'Glorious Revolution'** encourage more critical awareness of causation. **'Remember, remember...'** looks at two sides to the controversy and offers a structure for extended writing. **Their house and my house** could be attempted as homework linked to a critical examination of students' own homes. It is probably best placed at a midway point in the study unit prior to looking at the 17th century.

 **The end of merrie England?**

 WORD BOX

Reformation changes to the Christian Church in England which started while Henry VIII was king. England changed from being a Catholic country to being a Protestant country.

rituals things which are done which are thought to be special, or holy. They are ways of doing things which show what people believe and think is important.

parish the area served by a church.

fasted ate less or went without food for a time.

relics bones or possessions of a holy person.

saint a person who was thought to be very holy. Many medieval people prayed to saints to help them.

Look at pages 20–21 in the book *In Search of History 1485–1714*. These tell you about the great changes which happened in the Christian Church in England in the 16th century. There were changes in:

◆ who was head of the Church in England;

◆ the language used in Church services;

◆ the Bible (from the Latin to the English language);

◆ how people worshipped God;

◆ how they decorated churches.

These new ways replaced old ways of doing things. The people who believed in the new ways thought that the 'old' religious ideas and ways of doing things were wrong. But how much did these changes alter people's lives? This is a big and a very important question you will be investigating in this Depth Study.

HOW DID RELIGION AFFECT THE LIVES OF PEOPLE BEFORE THE REFORMATION?

Before the **Reformation,** the Christian Church in England was part of the Catholic Church. By the end of the Middle Ages, there were Christian festivals, holidays and special events throughout the year. The Church had a big impact on people's lives. Most of the big events in people's lives were connected with the Church. This happened in many ways.

Some of these celebrations had a lot to do with religious beliefs. Others were less connected to the Church – these were times to play sports, meet people, feast and sometimes to make fun of the rich and powerful people in the country. Altogether, the year was filled with special events.

Some of these events across the year are shown on the next sheet. Together they make up what is sometimes called a **Ritual** Year. This means a year full of events which help people live their lives, show what they believe and bring their communities together.

Celebrations across the year

- Churches and homes were decorated with greenery at Christmas.

- People **fasted** for four weeks before Christmas.

- Special dramatic services took place at Christmas. Churches were lit up with many candles.

- There were 12 days of feasting, plays and games after Christmas. In the feasts people were elected as 'Lords of Misrule'. These were people who were not rich and powerful. They led the parties and sometimes made fun of the rich and powerful! On New Year's Day, people exchanged presents.

- On the Twelfth Day, services remembered the Wise Men visiting baby Jesus. Great golden stars were hung up in some churches.

- In January, services and processions asked God to bless the crops. Candles were lit in front of ploughs.

- In February, churches were lit up with candles on Candlemas. This was in honour of Jesus and Mary, his mother.

- On 14 February, people sent gifts to friends they loved.

- People fasted for 40 days before Easter. At the start, on Shrove Tuesday, they feasted. The next day,

Ash Wednesday, the priests put ashes on people's foreheads, and the fast started.

- On Palm Sunday, branches were blessed and used to decorate the churches.

- At Easter, people made models of Christ's tomb in their churches. On Easter Sunday, the model was opened and there were processions and celebrations.

- On 23 April there were St George's Day processions and feasting.

- May started a time of summer celebrations. Many raised money for the Church.

- People paraded around their **parishes** asking God's blessing on their area.

- On Pentecost Sunday there were more great services, and parades the next day. These celebrated God filling the first Christians with the Holy Spirit.

- On Midsummer Day, there were bonfires and houses were decorated.

- In August and September, harvest suppers were held at the end of the harvest.

- In November, bells were rung and candles lit to remember the dead.

USING THE EVIDENCE

1 Draw a large circle on a piece of paper. Imagine that this represents the year. Christmas is at the top. Midsummer is at the bottom. Draw arrows to the various parts of your circle (the year) where big events happened in the Ritual Year before the Reformation. Say briefly what these events were.

2 Which parts of the year had the most celebrations? Can you think of any reasons why this might have been so?

3 Take two colours. Colour in all the religious celebrations in one colour. Colour in the celebrations which you do not think were connected with religious beliefs with the other colour. How important was religion in the year's celebrations?

DID THE REFORMATION PUT AN END TO THIS WAY OF LIFE?

Not everyone liked the celebrations. This was because:

◆ they said that because some of these celebrations were not mentioned in the Bible, they were wrong;

◆ they thought it was wrong to honour, or pray to **saints**;

◆ they did not like ordinary people holding feasts and celebrations. They were worried they might get drunk and cause trouble.

Many of the people who did not like the old celebrations were Protestants. Under Henry VIII, the law began to be used to stop the old celebrations. Henry died in 1547. When his son, Edward VI, was king, there were great attacks on the old celebrations. Many of these were led by Protector Somerset, the man who helped the young king to rule the country.

Attacks on the 'old' celebrations

1538: churches could not be filled with candles. Any statues people had prayed to were removed. **Relics** were removed. There were no more St George's processions.

1539: the London Midsummer Marching was banned.

1547: only two candles could be lit in a church. Palm Sunday processions were banned.

1548: the government banned the blessing of candles at Candlemas, ashes on Ash Wednesday and branches on Palm Sunday. Pentecost processions were banned. Models of Easter tombs were attacked. The November ringing of bells for the dead was banned. Religious marching around the parish was banned.

1552: the feast of St George was completely banned.

• • • • • • • • • • • • • • USING THE EVIDENCE • • • • • • • • • • • • • • •

1 Look back at your circle of the year. Put a date after each celebration, to show when it was banned.

2 Make a list of the celebrations which were left. Do these have anything in common?

3 Look at the following comment by a historian: 'Within 18 months of its start the government of Protector Somerset had virtually demolished the yearly rituals of the English Church.' (Ronald Hutton,*The Rise and Fall of Merrie England*,1994). Use the evidence to explain why he might have thought this. Your answer should contain the following parts:

◆ An introduction to explain that many things changed in the way that people celebrated yearly events in the 16th century. Many Protestant people wanted to get rid of celebrations they thought were wrong.

◆ The main part of your essay showing what celebrations were banned in 1547 and 1548.

◆ A conclusion saying how different church life would have been in 1549 compared to 1547. But you should also say that this did not all start in 1547. Changes had started before this. You could mention some of the changes that had happened before 1547. Remember to say that these celebrations were not all connected with church.

• •

<table>
<tr><td>

Why were the old celebrations destroyed?

</td><td>

Some of the people who disliked the old religious celebrations wrote about why they wanted to get rid of them. By looking at these primary sources of evidence we can see some of the reasons why they wanted to ban these old ways of celebrating through the year.

</td></tr>
</table>

SOURCE A

❝It is wrong to try to do magic with the ploughs.❞

Written in about 1550 by a Protestant preacher named John Bale. He was against praying for the ploughs and lighting candles by them so that God would make crops grow.

SOURCE B

❝Shrove Tuesday was a time when people ate too much and got drunk.❞

Written by William Kethe, a Protestant preacher at Blandford in Dorset, in 1570.

SOURCE C

❝Ringing bells for the dead should be stopped because it is part of the belief in purgatory.❞

Attacks by Archbishop Cranmer on a November ritual, about 1547. The belief in purgatory was a Catholic idea that if people prayed for the dead, their sins could be removed and it would become easier for them to get to heaven.

SOURCE D

❝Football is to be banned on Shrove Tuesday because of great trouble caused by evil people.❞

A rule from the city of Chester, 1540.

SOURCE E

❝Church feasts and celebrations encourage people to be lazy and less holy.❞

The House of Commons, 1532.

USING THE EVIDENCE

1 Using the sources on this page, explain how people who opposed the old celebrations did so partly because they thought they were not really Christian beliefs and partly because they thought some caused trouble and made people behave badly.

2 Why does this make it difficult for a historian trying to find a simple reason why these changes happened?

 # The world turned upside-down!

KEY QUESTIONS
Why did so many revolutionary groups spring up after the English Civil War?
What did these groups believe in?

 WORD BOX

blasphemy words attacking God.

heresies bad religious beliefs, which are not true Christian ideas.

holy living a good life that pleases God.

orgy having sex with many people. A bad thing to do.

republic a country which does not have a king, or queen, to rule it.

revolutionary wanting big changes.

After the English Civil War, some very **revolutionary** groups were started. These groups wanted big changes in the way England was run. You will look at some of these revolutionary groups in this Depth Study. These different groups did not all want the same things:

◆ Some wanted to change what people believed about religion and how to live a good life. They wanted freedom to believe anything they wanted to.

◆ Some wanted poor people to have more rights and more land to farm.

◆ Some believed that Jesus would soon return to the earth. They believed he had given them the job of preparing the country for his return. They thought only they should rule the country because they thought only they were good and **holy**.

These revolutionary groups were all very different. Most did not work together. Often they disliked each other. But they had one thing in common. They all wanted to change England in a big way. They all wanted to turn their world upside-down.

WHY DID SO MANY REVOLUTIONARY GROUPS SPRING UP AFTER THE ENGLISH CIVIL WAR?

The old church courts stopped punishing people for breaking rules about religious beliefs.

Many people had fought in the Civil War and ordinary people had become used to thinking their ideas and beliefs were important.

Why were there so many revolutionary groups?

King Charles I was killed in 1649. England became a **republic.** To some people, it seemed as if the old ways of life were over.

There were many people whose lives had been disrupted by the Civil War. They wanted better living standards and treatment for ordinary people.

SOURCE A

The front cover of a small book published in 1647. It was called 'The World Turned Upside Down'. It looked at the way great changes were sweeping the country.

SOURCE B

❝ It is no new work of the devil to start **heresies** but they never came up so thick as in these present times. They used to peep up one at a time but now they sprout up in huddles and clusters. They now come thronging on us in swarms like the caterpillers of Egypt. **❞**

Written in 1651 by John Taylor. Taylor wrote books criticising the more revolutionary groups after the Civil War. He felt they were using their greater freedom to live badly.

USING THE EVIDENCE

1 Look carefully at the spider diagram. Explain why each one of the causes may have led to some people forming revolutionary groups. How might they have made some people think that the old ways of life were over?

2 Look at Source B. Look at the words in the source. Look at the way the author describes the people he is writing about. Was this person in favour of the changes he was writing about, or was he against them? Explain how you decided. Look at what the writer believed.

3 Look at Source A.
a What message was this picture trying to give to people who saw it?
b Do you think the person who drew this would have agreed with the writer of Source B? Explain how you decided.

THE FIFTH MONARCHY MEN: WHAT DID THEY BELIEVE IN?

One of the most revolutionary groups was called the Fifth Monarchy Men. They believed Jesus would soon return to rule the world. They thought that only people they believed to be good should have power, and that the Old Testament laws in the Bible should become the laws of England. Some evidence about the beliefs of this group are set out below.

SOURCE A

"God's people must be a bloody people!"

From a book published by the Fifth Monarchy Men in 1656.

SOURCE B

"Of all kings I am for Christ alone. For he is king to us though Charles be gone."

Written by the Fifth Monarchy Man, Vavasor Powell, in 1654.

SOURCE C

"If Moses did not dare set up any other law, how dare you?"

Question asked by the Fifth Monarchy Man, Rogers, to Parliament in 1654.

SOURCE D

"How can the kingdom be ruled by saints, if the ungodly are allowed to vote and rule?"

Fifth Monarchy Men petition to Parliament in 1649.

SOURCE E

"No poor man shall have too little, nor the rich too much."

Written by the Fifth Monarchy Man, Morgan Llwyd.

SOURCE F

"I long to murder and destroy the rich!"

Written by a Fifth Monarchy Man named Mary Cary. A number were women.

USING THE EVIDENCE

❶ Look carefully at all the evidence on this sheet. What kinds of people do you think might have supported the Fifth Monarchy Men? What kinds of people might have opposed them? Explain why these people would not have liked them.

❷ Imagine you were a Fifth Monarchy Man living in the 1650s. Design a poster to show people what you believe in and how, in your opinion, England should be ruled.

Areas you might cover in your poster:

◆ your willingness to use violence;
◆ wanting to get rid of human kings;
◆ having only the Bible as the law of the country;
◆ only people you think are good should run the country;
◆ taking money from the rich and giving it to the poor.

THE DIGGERS: WHAT DID THEY BELIEVE IN?

What the Diggers believed in

EVERY FAMILY SHOULD ONLY HAVE ENOUGH LAND FOR ITSELF. THE LAND SHOULD BE TAKEN FROM RICH LANDOWNERS.

NO ONE SHOULD WORK FOR WAGES.

What the Diggers did

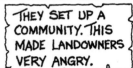

IN 1649 THE DIGGERS MOVED TO COMMON LAND AT ST. GEORGE'S HILL, SURREY. THEIR LEADER WAS GERRARD WINSTANLEY.

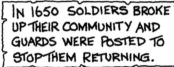

THEY SET UP A COMMUNITY. THIS MADE LANDOWNERS VERY ANGRY.

IN 1650 SOLDIERS BROKE UP THEIR COMMUNITY AND GUARDS WERE POSTED TO STOP THEM RETURNING.

SOURCE A

66 We plough and dig so that the poor may get a living. We joined Parliament relying on promises of freedom of land. They said: 'Give us your taxes and risk your lives with us. Cast out the oppressor Charles, and we will make you free people.' So we claim the freedom to enjoy the Common Lands, bought by our money and blood. 99

A letter sent to Parliament by the Diggers in about 1649.

USING THE EVIDENCE

1. Imagine a conversation between one of the Diggers at St George's Hill and a rich landowner living nearby. In the conversation, let the Digger explain what she believes in. Let the rich landowner say why he does not agree. Start the conversation with the Digger saying: 'We fought the Civil War to make life better for poor people. What we want is…'

2. Parliament in 1650 was mostly made up of landowners. Why did this make it difficult for the Diggers to get what they wanted?

THE RANTERS: WHAT DID THEY BELIEVE IN?

The Ranters were a group which got a lot of attention in the 1650s. It was said that they were very bad people. It was said that they did not believe in right or wrong but instead thought they could do anything they wanted to. It was said they carried out sex orgies and used bad language. Look at some of the evidence and decide for yourself.

SOURCE A

66 They taught that God does not care about people's actions. They spoke most hideous words of **blasphemy** and many of them had sex with many people. **99**

Written by the Puritan minister Richard Baxter in 1696. He was looking back to the 1650s. We do not know if he actually saw any Ranter meetings.

SOURCE C

66 They swore a lot but there was no **orgy**... When they were arrested one of them took a candle and hunted around the room saying he was looking for his sins but there were none. **99**

The report of a police agent about a group of London Ranters who met in 1650.

SOURCE B

The title page from a 1650 book, *The Ranters Declaration*, written by a man who claimed to have once been a Ranter. It shows people having sex and saying they don't do wrong things.

USING THE EVIDENCE

1 **a** In what ways does Source C agree, or disagree, with Source A?
b In what ways does Source B agree, or disagree, with Source A?
c In what ways does Source B agree, or disagree, with Source C?

2 Source B was designed to make as many people as possible buy it. How might this affect how useful it is for finding out about the beliefs and actions of the Ranters?

3 Which of the sources do you think appears the most reliable for finding out what Ranters did? Decide by looking at:

◆ who wrote, or made, each source;
◆ why they may have written the source you are looking at;
◆ how this might affect the way they wrote about the Ranters.

Making a United Kingdom, 1500–1750

KEY QUESTIONS

How did the government of Britain change between 1500 and 1750?
Why did these changes happen?
What were the results of these changes?

 WORD BOX

empire land (colonies) which a country captures and rules.

Parliament a group of elected people (MPs) who discuss and make laws for the country. In this period of history, these people were usually wealthy and elected by other wealthy people. Ordinary people did not share in this power and were not involved in the making of the laws of the country.

HOW DID THE GOVERNMENT OF BRITAIN CHANGE BETWEEN 1500 AND 1750?

In 1500 there was no united country called the United Kingdom. Instead England and Scotland were two independent countries, each with its own ruler. In addition, England dominated Ireland and Wales.

By 1750 this had changed! England, Scotland, Wales and Ireland were all united under one ruler. They had become part of one kingdom. Because this kingdom was made up of more than one country, it became known as the United Kingdom.

Maps showing Britain in 1500 and 1750

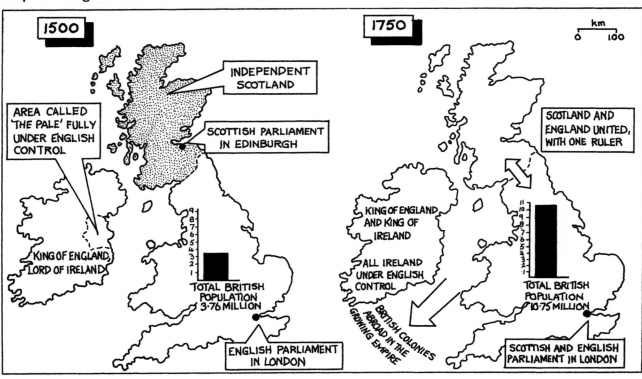

Timeline of events

1541: Henry VIII declared himself King of Ireland. Before this, English rulers had been Lords of Ireland. This new title gave him more control.

1603: King James VI of Scotland became ruler of England as well. In England he was called King James I.

1650s: Cromwell united England, Scotland and Ireland under one government. One **Parliament** made laws for all the three countries. This one Parliament was in London.

1660: This ended when Charles II became king. He ruled England, Scotland and Ireland but each country had its own Parliament once more.

1707: England and Scotland united. One Parliament made laws for both countries. But Ireland kept its own separate Parliament until 1800.

• **USING THE EVIDENCE** • • • • • • • • • • • • • • • • •

1 Look carefully at the maps on the previous sheet. Make a list of the ways in which Britain was different in 1750 compared to 1500.

2 In pairs, or small groups, look at the timeline of events. Do you think these changes would have made Britain:
a weaker, or **b** stronger?
Give the reason for your answer.

• •

WHY DID THESE CHANGES HAPPEN?

Between 1500 and 1750, the way Britain was ruled changed a lot. Historians have many ideas about why these changes happened when they did. When they look at reasons why events happen, historians use the word *causes* to describe these reasons. There can be many different kinds of causes. Some of these causes are:

◆ *political*, which is to do with how a country is ruled. Political causes are to do with things like who ruled the country, how they ruled the country and whether the power was held by one person or shared.

◆ *economic*, which is to do with buying and selling. Economic causes are to do with things like what industries there were, who controlled them and who was in charge of the wealth of the country.

◆ *social*, which is to do with how people behave. Social causes are to do with things like people's religious beliefs, what they think is right and wrong, how they organise things like marriage and families and how they get on together.

Often, causes are mixed up. They do not always fit neatly into one of these ways of describing things.

Reasons why Britain changed

BRITISH TRADE WAS CONTROLLED FROM LONDON.

LONDON

THERE WAS ONE PARLIAMENT FOR ENGLAND AND SCOTLAND. THIS MADE IT EASIER FOR RULERS TO CONTROL THE COUNTRY.

THE POPULATION WAS GROWING.

SCOTTISH AND IRISH PEOPLE HAD MORE JOB OPPORTUNITIES IN A BRITAIN WHICH WAS BECOMING MORE UNITED. MANY JOINED THE ARMY.

IRISH PROTESTANTS LIKED CLOSER LINKS WITH ENGLAND BECAUSE IT HELPED THEM TO CONTROL IRISH CATHOLICS.

THE EDUCATED PEOPLE ACROSS BRITAIN SPOKE ENGLISH.

USING THE EVIDENCE

1 Look carefully at the cartoons above. Write out three headings: 'Political', 'Economic' and 'Social'. Decide which reasons should go under each heading and write them under the heading which best describes them. You will see from this that there were many reasons why Britain changed.

2 Look carefully at this quote, written in the 18th century: 'The best view facing a Scotsman is the road to London' (Samuel Johnson).
a Explain what this means in your own words.
b Why do you think he wrote this? (The cartoons may help.)

3 Look at what an Irish writer, Baron Willes, wrote in 1760: 'Imagining that London is a kind of paradise, and that England is like it, is the reason why so many from my country swarm in London in all jobs.'
a Explain what this means in your own words.
b How does it help explain why some Irish people accepted being part of Britain?
c Did this writer have an opinion similar to, or different from, that of Samuel Johnson? Give reasons for your decision.

WHAT WERE THE RESULTS OF THESE CHANGES?

The great changes between 1500 and 1750 in how Britain was ruled had big effects on Britain. Historians call these effects *consequences*. These consequences were important in Britain, but they did not stop there. Because Britain became more powerful and united, it became more powerful across the world. British merchants began to trade across the world in the 17th and 18th centuries more than ever before. Britain won wars with its rivals, especially with France. Britain began to build an **empire**.

Effects (consequences) of the changes for Britain

BRITAIN WAS VERY RICH AND CONTROLLED A LOT OF THE TRADE IN EUROPE AND ACROSS THE WORLD.

BRITISH RULERS BECAME MORE POWERFUL.

RICH LANDOWNERS AND BUSINESS PEOPLE WORKED WELL TOGETHER IN LONDON.

BRITAIN WAS ABLE TO WIN WARS (ESPECIALLY AGAINST FRANCE) AND BUILD AN EMPIRE IN INDIA AND CANADA.

BRITAIN WAS MORE UNITED THAN ANY OTHER EUROPEAN COUNTRY.

SOURCE A

An Indian picture dating from about 1615. The man in the centre is Emperor Jahangir, ruler of the Mughal Empire in India. On the right are other rulers offering him gifts. The third one down is King James VI of Scotland and I of England. It shows how British trade grew after he united Scotland and England in 1603.

SOURCE B

66 It must be stressed that if the British empire has a parent it is that clever Scot, James VI [James I of England], who united the British Isles under his sceptre in 1603. Not all his subjects agreed with his characteristically modest theory that this union was part of God's plan for mankind's salvation, nor were they very cooperative in pushing forward with schemes for political integration [union]. James nevertheless assumed the title of King of Great Britain to symbolise the birth of a new European great power. 99

B. Lenman, in The Age of Expansion, *1986. When this historian says that James was modest, he is being sarcastic, because he thinks that James was not really a modest man. James thought that his plans for Britain were very important and were part of God's plan to save the world from wrongdoing.*

USING THE EVIDENCE

1 Look at Source B. From what you have done so far in this Depth Study, explain why James may have thought that the uniting of England and Scotland under one ruler would make Britain more powerful in the world.

2 Look at Source A. Does this seem to agree or disagree with what James

thought? Give the reasons for your answer.

3 *Research*. Find out when and how British power in the world grew during the 17th and 18th century. Try to find out reasons why this happened. Do these reasons link with the reasons suggested in this Depth Study?

The beggars are coming...

Historians are interested in the causes of events in the past. When they look at the evidence, they often find that there are different causes. They are also interested in which causes are the most important. This involves them making a decision. Not all historians agree – there are sometimes disagreements. This is often because the sources they use do not agree. One question historians ask is:

> **Why was there an increase in the number of poor people in Tudor England?**

Look at the different sources of evidence and see what you think the answer is. Remember, some of the sources give different reasons. These show the ideas of different people. These different people had different experiences of life. They had different beliefs. Because of these things they had different opinions about why things were happening.

SOURCE A A picture of a harvest in 1510.

SOURCE B A country scene in 1540.

SOURCE C

66 If you look in any part of the country that grows the finest and dearest wool, there you find noblemen and even certain abbots have greatly abused the public interest. They leave no ground for ploughing. They enclose all for grazing. They tear down houses and leave nothing standing but the church to be made into a sheep-house. 99

Written in 1516 by Thomas More. He was a very educated man and a member of the government. He wanted things to stay the same in the countryside. He thought this would give people happier and better-run lives.

SOURCE D

"My father was a yeoman [well-off farmer] and had no lands of his own. He only had a farm costing three or four pounds rent a year. Yet he could afford to keep me at school and gave each of my sisters five pounds on their marriage. He [the farmer] who now has the farm pays sixteen pounds a year and is not able to do anything for himself, his children or the poor."

Bishop Hugh Latimer, in 1549. He came from a farming family. This meant he understood the way farmers lived and the problems that they faced.

SOURCE E

"How many cities are decayed, how many towns that have shrunken to hamlets would improve if a third of England did not live idly [lazily]?"

Written in 1536 by Richard Moryson. He was trying to explain why there were more poor people. He was worried about the cost of helping the poor.

SOURCE F

"1) Weak and ill. 2) Injured, or unlucky. 3) Lazy."

The three causes why people were poor, according to William Harrison in about 1560. He was quite wealthy and worried about the cost of helping poor people.

INVESTIGATION

1 **a** Look carefully at Sources A and B. In what ways had some parts of the countryside changed between 1510 and 1540? Use Source C to help explain what had happened and why.
b How might this have caused there to be more poor people?

2 Look at all the sources. Make a spider diagram to show all the possible reasons given in these sources for there being more poor people. Remember that the same reason may appear in more than one source.

3 Of all of these reasons, which do you think was probably the most important one? To help you decide, you might consider: which seems most likely to have affected a large number of people, and which is supported by other evidence. You might decide to reject causes which seem to be simply rich people blaming the poor for being poor!

4 Which of Sources C, D, E and F in this unit do you think is the most reliable one for trying to find out why there were more poor people in Tudor England? Explain the reason for your choice. To do this, first of all look at *each* source and say who wrote it, what things worried them, and how these things might have affected what they thought. Then say which one you think is *most* reliable and why.

EX The image of the Queen

Read pages 46–47 of *In Search of History 1485–1714*. These pages show you what Queen Elizabeth looked like. However, Queen Elizabeth was very careful to only let people see the pictures of herself that she approved of. She used pictures to tell people what kind of queen she was and about the things that she did. She encouraged painters to paint her as beautiful, wise and powerful.

We call this propaganda. This is saying or doing things that give people your version of events. The aim is to make people think that what you say is true. On this sheet and the next you will see some examples of Elizabeth's propaganda. She wanted people to have only her view of what she was like. The pictures are full of messages. Messages that Elizabeth wanted people to believe.

Look carefully at the pictures and at the messages that they are giving people. Think about how Elizabeth and her supporters were trying to make sure people thought she was a good queen.

SOURCE Ⓐ Elizabeth I confounds the goddesses. Painted in about 1569.

Elizabeth looks young and beautiful. She carries an orb and wears a crown to show she is queen.

Roman goddesses of majesty, wisdom and beauty make way for Elizabeth.

INVESTIGATION

❶ Look carefully at Source A. What messages about Elizabeth was the person who painted this trying to get across to people?

❷ Using the evidence of the painting, explain *how* the painter tried to get these messages across.

SOURCE B

Elizabeth and the Armada. Painted in about 1590.

The Armada threatens England.

The Armada is destroyed by a storm sent by God.

The crown shows she has the right to rule.

The hand on the world shows how powerful she is.

SOURCE C

The Rainbow Portrait of Elizabeth I. Painted in about 1600. Elizabeth looks young and pretty. She was 67 when this was painted! The eyes and ears on the dress show she knows everything that is going on in England. The rainbow is a sign of peace. The snake on the sleeve symbolises wisdom. The English flowers on the bodice symbolises Elizabeth uniting all English people.

INVESTIGATION

1. Look carefully at Sources B and C. For each one of them, explain what messages about Elizabeth each contains and what the painter did to try to get these messages across.

2. Do the messages in these pictures give an impression of the Queen similar to, or different from, the messages given in Source A? What is similar and what is different?

 **Kings from Hanover**

WHY DID THE RULER OF HANOVER BECOME RULER OF BRITAIN?

In 1714 Queen Anne died. She was the last ruler of Britain who came from the royal family of the Stuarts. She had no children. Who would rule Britain after her? The choice had already been made. In 1707 Parliament had passed a law deciding who would rule after Anne. The law decided that this should be Princess Sophia, Electress and Duchess of Hanover in Germany. She was the cousin of King James II, who was Anne's father.

Sophia had married the ruler of Hanover. She was a Protestant, and so Parliament thought she would be acceptable as ruler. This was because members of Parliament were Protestants. King James II had had a son, but Parliament did not want him to be king. This was because he was a Catholic. He was called James the Old Pretender. He had a son who was called Charles Edward Stuart – some people later called him 'Bonnie Prince Charlie'. He was a Catholic too. Because of this Parliament did not want him to be king either. In 1714 Sophia died, and so it was her son, George I, who came to rule Britain. The members of this family, from George I to Victoria (1714–1901), are called 'Hanoverians'.

SOURCE **A**

❝ The succession to the Monarch of the United Kingdom of Great Britain should remain and continue to be the most excellent Princess Sophia, Electress and Duchess of Hanover and the heirs of her body, being Protestants. ❞

The law called the Act of Union made by Parliament in 1707.

INVESTIGATION

1 **a** Look carefully at Source A. What do the words "heirs of her body" mean?
b What evidence is there in this source about what members of Parliament thought a British ruler's religion should be?

2 Some people in the 18th century thought that James the Old Pretender and later Charles Edward Stuart had a better claim to the throne than Sophia and her son. Why would Parliament have not agreed with this view?

HOW AND WHY DID THIS EVENT CHANGE THE WAY BRITAIN WAS RULED?

The new king, George I, did not speak English! He had to rely on people that he trusted to govern the country for him. Because he did not speak English he did not meet with the chief members of Parliament who ran the country for him. Instead of the King running these meetings, his most trusted adviser did it for him. This person became known as the prime minister. This means the most important minister. A minister was a person who ran the government for the ruler. People were often jealous of the power of the prime minister.

Different groups in Parliament – parties – competed to be more powerful. This was because the king was less involved in government, so ordinary people became more powerful. It was also because not everyone agreed with the way James II had been driven from Britain and with the later decision to let George I become king.

What happened when the rulers of Hanover became rulers of Britain?

THE KING WAS LESS INVOLVED IN GOVERNING THE COUNTRY. THE PRIME MINISTER BECAME POWERFUL. THE FIRST PRIME MINISTER WAS ROBERT WALPOLE (1721-42).

THERE WERE RIVAL PARTIES IN PARLIAMENT.

THE 'WHIGS' SUPPORTED KING GEORGE AND WANTED A STRONG PARLIAMENT.

THE 'JACOBITES' SUPPORTED CHILDREN OF JAMES II.

THE 'TORIES' WANTED A STRONG KING.

THERE WERE JACOBITE REVOLTS AGAINST GEORGE I AND GEORGE II. 1715: A REVOLT LED BY JAMES 'THE OLD PRETENDER' FAILED. 1745: A REVOLT LED BY CHARLES EDWARD STUART (BONNIE PRINCE CHARLIE) FAILED.

INVESTIGATION

❶ Look carefully at all of the ways that the government of Britain changed.
a In your own words, explain each of these changes.
b Think carefully. For each of these changes, explain *why* it happened.

❷ Look again at these changes. Which one do you think looks like it was the most important change? Explain why you think it was the most important.

❸ *Research.* Bonnie Prince Charlie's revolt in 1745 is very famous. Find out:
a where the revolt took place;
b who supported the revolt;
c how the revolt ended;
d different reasons historians give for why it failed;
e the evidence they use to help them reach these opinions.

EX Changing kingdoms

Between 1500 and 1750, Britain changed in many ways. One of the most important ways it changed was in the way different parts of Britain became united under one ruler. Other important changes came with the different families, or branches of families, who ruled the country. These changes can be seen in the ways the coats of arms of the rulers of Britain changed between 1500 and 1750. Look at the coats of arms shown in the diagram and use the clues to decide which changes they tell you about.

Royal coats of arms from 1500–1750

HENRY VII, HENRY VIII, EDWARD VI, MARY I, ELIZABETH I (1485-1603)

JAMES I, CHARLES I, CHARLES II, JAMES II (1603-1688)

WILLIAM AND MARY AND THEN WILLIAM III (1688-1702)

ANNE (1702-1714)

GEORGE I, GEORGE II (1714-1760)

CLUES:

 BADGE OF ENGLAND.

 BADGE OF SCOTLAND.

BADGE OF FRANCE (BECAUSE ENGLISH RULERS CLAIMED IT WAS THEIRS).

BADGES OF HANOVER, BRUNSWICK AND LUNEBURG (ALL IN GERMANY).

 BADGE OF HOLLAND.

INVESTIGATION

1. Look at each of the coats of arms in the diagram. Look at the clues. Explain what changes in the way this country was ruled you can find out about from each coat of arms. Explain how each of the coats of arms was altered to show the changes which had happened.
To help you, here are some of the changes which took place. They are not in the right order.

◆ England and Scotland united with one Parliament, 1707.

◆ England has a ruler from Holland, 1688.

◆ England and Scotland have the same ruler, 1603.

◆ Britain has a ruler from Germany, after Queen Anne dies, 1714.

EX Timeline search ...

Understanding the correct order, or sequence, of events is important in history. Without this, events are muddled and it is impossible to explore cause and consequence. On this sheet is a timeline running from 1485 to 1750. On it are marked some dates when important events occurred. On the right-hand side of the page are key events. Match up the right event with the date that it happened.

Clue: if you are unsure about the events, look them up in the book *In Search of History 1485–1714*. You can find many of them using the index.

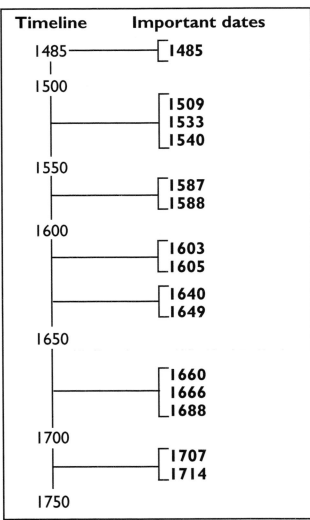

Timeline	Important dates
1485	1485
1500	
	1509
	1533
	1540
1550	
	1587
	1588
1600	
	1603
	1605
	1640
	1649
1650	
	1660
	1666
	1688
1700	
	1707
	1714
1750	

Key events

1   Spanish Armada

2   Glorious Revolution

3   Battle of Bosworth

4   Start of the Civil War

5   Divorce of Catherine of Aragon

6   Fire of London

7   Gunpowder Plot

8   Execution of Mary Queen of Scots

9   James I becomes king of England and Scotland

10 Pilgrimage of Grace

11 Restoration of Charles II

12 Death of Queen Anne

13 Henry VIII becomes king

14 Execution of Charles II

15 Union of England and Scotland

USING THE EVIDENCE

❶ Historians call some events 'turning points'. These are events which bring great changes. After them, things are not the same. Look at your timeline. Mark any events which you think were turning points. Then explain why you think this.

❷ Choose any two events which you think are related to each other. Explain why these events happened in the order that they did and what the link is between them.

F What kind of king was Henry VIII?

1 Look carefully at the information about Henry VIII that you find on pages 16-17 of *In Search of History 1485–1714*.

2 Next look at the diagram on this sheet. Around the picture of Henry VIII are pieces of information about him. Some are true. Some are false. Draw a circle around the boxes that are true.

Henry VIII had eight wives.

When he became king he was very poor.

While Henry was in France, a Scottish army beat an English army.

His children were called Mary, Elizabeth and Edward.

He wanted to divorce his first wife, Catherine of Aragon, but the Pope would not let him.

He beheaded all his wives.

He beheaded two wives, he divorced two wives, one wife died of illness and one wife was still living when he died.

He was the son of King Richard III.

His father, Henry VII, left him lots of money when he died.

In 1513 he defeated the French in a battle. This was called the Battle of the Spurs.

When Henry VIII died, the Pope was still head of the English Church.

He made himself head of the English Church so he could divorce his wife, Catherine of Aragon.

Henry did not mind whether a son or a daughter ruled England after he died.

He wanted a son to rule after him but his first wife had a daughter. Henry was worried England would be weak with a woman ruler.

3 Look at the true information on this sheet about King Henry VIII. Imagine that you are describing Henry VIII to someone who has never heard of him. Use these words and your own words to describe him.

4 From what you have seen on this page and in the book, why did King Henry VIII make himself head of the English Church?

Why was the Catholic Church less popular in the 16th century?

King Henry VIII changed the English Church. His son, King Edward VI, made even bigger changes. They were helped to do these things because many people were not happy with the way that the Church was run. On this sheet are some of the reasons why the Catholic Church had become less popular.

1 Look at the list of reasons carefully. Then put these complaints in the right boxes on the table below. If you think something should be in two boxes, then write it twice.

◆ Leaders of the Church were too rich.

◆ Some leaders of the Church lived bad lives.

◆ The Church owned lots of land.

◆ People were not allowed to read the Bible in English.

◆ The Pope tried to get involved in how countries were run.

◆ Some people did not like paying taxes to the Church.

◆ Priests paid no taxes to the king.

◆ The Church taught things that were not in the Bible.

◆ Priests claimed that only they could make sure a person's sins were forgiven.

◆ Rulers wanted to get their hands on money and land owned by the Church.

Political reasons (government and running the country)	Economic reasons (money and wealth)	Religious reasons (beliefs about God and the Church)

2 Look at what you have written in the boxes above. Now use this to explain why the Catholic Church was less popular in the 16th century.

F The poor in Tudor England

Historians describe some events in history as 'causes'. Other kinds of events they call 'consequences'. A *cause* is a reason why something happens. A consequence is a thing that happens because of a cause.

1 In the box below there are different pieces of information. Some are causes.

Other ones are consequences. The trouble is they are mixed up. Try to put the right consequence with the cause which made that event happen. You will be helped if you look at pages 30–33 in the book *In Search of History 1485–1714*.

Causes	Consequences
◆ There was no unemployment pay.	◆ This meant fewer jobs.
◆ Henry VIII closed the monasteries.	◆ This worried the government.
◆ Landowners enclosed land.	◆ They were given help and a licence.
◆ Landowners kept more sheep.	◆ Local people were taxed more.
◆ Prices were going up more than pay.	◆ People worked, or starved.
◆ The numbers of beggars went up.	◆ They were punished for begging.
◆ The government decided the sick could not help being poor.	◆ Poorer people had nowhere to graze their animals.
◆ 'Sturdy beggars' were not given a licence to beg.	◆ This meant there were fewer people to look after the poor.
◆ The government did not have enough money.	◆ People found their pay did not buy as much as it used to.

2 Imagine you are one of Queen Elizabeth I's ministers. Write a report to her about the poor. In your report:

◆ explain why there are more poor people than before;

◆ say whether this worries you, or not;

◆ suggest ways to deal with this problem.

Use the information on this sheet and in the textbook to help you.

F Their house and my house

Little
Moreton Hall,
Cheshire.
Built between
1450 and
1580.

A modern
house,
Wiltshire.
Built in 1981.

Look at the two houses on this sheet.

❶ Make a list of anything the same, or similar, about both houses.

❷ Make a list of anything different about both houses.

❸ Which house would you prefer to live in? Explain the reasons for your choice.

❹ Why do you think that there are so few Tudor houses that have survived into modern times? Here are some ideas which might help you. Use them and your own words to explain your answer in a short essay.

◆ Wood rots.
◆ Old houses burn more easily as they are made from wood.
◆ People often like to live in a new house.
◆ Old houses are often cold and damp compared to new houses.
◆ As towns change, old houses may be knocked down.

F 'Remember, remember ... '

Historians are not sure about exactly what happened in the Gunpowder Plot. They know that there were plans to blow up Parliament. But there are things they are not sure about:

◆ Did the people who planned to blow up the King really come close to doing it?

◆ Did the government really know all about the plan to blow up the King?

◆ Did the government secretly help the plotters? Was this because the government wanted to get Catholics into trouble?

Look carefully at pages 48–51 of *In Search of History 1485–1714*. Then look at the two versions of what happened shown in the boxes on this page. Remember, no-one is absolutely sure which of the two versions is right. Fill in the gaps using words from the Missing Word Box. Then look at the questions at the bottom of this sheet.

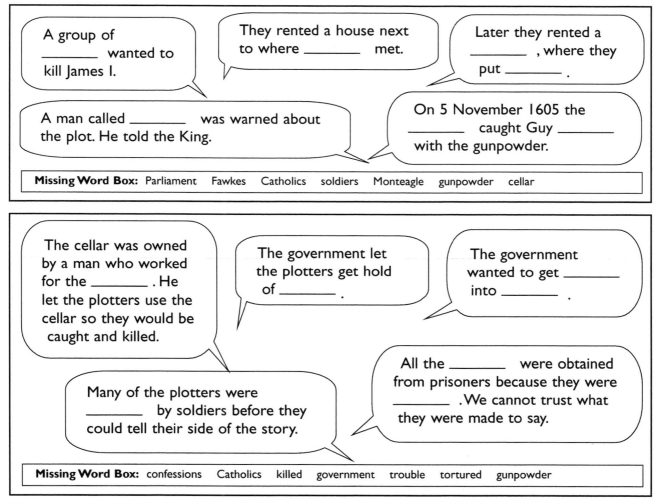

A group of _____ wanted to kill James I.

They rented a house next to where _____ met.

Later they rented a _____ , where they put _____ .

A man called _____ was warned about the plot. He told the King.

On 5 November 1605 the _____ caught Guy _____ with the gunpowder.

Missing Word Box: Parliament   Fawkes   Catholics   soldiers   Monteagle   gunpowder   cellar

The cellar was owned by a man who worked for the _____ . He let the plotters use the cellar so they would be caught and killed.

The government let the plotters get hold of _____ .

The government wanted to get _____ into _____ .

Many of the plotters were _____ by soldiers before they could tell their side of the story.

All the _____ were obtained from prisoners because they were _____ . We cannot trust what they were made to say.

Missing Word Box: confessions   Catholics   killed   government   trouble   tortured   gunpowder

❶ Look carefully at the two versions of what happened. Which one do you think is most likely to be true? Explain the reasons for your answer.

❷ Imagine you are one of the plotters in prison. Write a letter to the government telling them you have been 'set up'! Explain the two versions of what happened. Remember, you would *disagree* with the first set of statements on this sheet. You would *agree* with the second set of statements on this sheet.

'REMEMBER, REMEMBER ... ' LETTER

Use the ideas on this sheet to help you write your letter to the government. Remember, you want to tell them that people have deliberately encouraged you to get you into trouble.

---

10 November 1605.

Your Majesty,

I was arrested and charged with treason. But I have been 'set up'. People are saying that we Catholics thought up the Gunpowder Plot on our own [mention how people are saying that the plotters were not helped by anyone]...
They say we put together the plan to blow up Parliament [mention that the plotters rented a cellar under Parliament, bought gunpowder, put the gunpowder in the cellar] ....
....
....
I admit that we plotted, but people in the government encouraged us [mention that the cellar was owned by a government official, and that other important people let the plotters get hold of gunpowder]...
....
....
They just wanted to cause trouble [mention getting Catholics into trouble]...
....
If I am going to be punished, then they should be punished too.

Yours sincerely,
Guy Fawkes.

 **Quarrels with Parliament!**

Look carefully at pages 54–55 of *In Search of History 1485–1714*. They tell you about the quarrels that King James I and King Charles I had with Parliament. You are going to look especially at page 55. This shows reasons why Parliament did not like King Charles I. There were lots of reasons why the King and Parliament quarrelled. They are shown as cartoons on the spider diagram below. The cartoons show the problem. Next to them, write what the problem was in words. Use the textbook to help you decide.

King Charles had so many disagreements with people that a civil war broke out in 1642. Here are some of the steps which led to civil war. They are not in the correct order. Write them out in the correct order using your textbook to help you.

◆ 1639: Scottish army invaded England.

◆ 1642: Charles left London. Civil War started.

◆ 1641: Court of Star Chamber shut by Parliament.

◆ 1641: Parliament made complaints against the King.

◆ 1640: Charles called Parliament to give him money.

◆ 1642: Charles tried to arrest five MPs.

◆ 1641: Parliament had Charles's adviser killed.

F The 'Glorious Revolution'

In 1688 the king was overthrown. His name was King James II. The people who got rid of him were glad that he had gone. Because of this they called it the 'Glorious Revolution'. A revolution is a big change. The big change here was getting rid of James and finding someone else to rule the country. Glorious means something good and fine, something wonderful.

King James was replaced as ruler by two people. They were his daughter Mary and her husband William.

William was the ruler of Holland. After 1688 William and Mary ruled Britain together. They were invited by Parliament to come and rule this country. Looking back at this event we can ask:

Why did this revolution happen?

If we can answer this question, it will help us decide why some people at the time thought the revolution was so important.

Things wanted by most members of Parliament

BRITAIN SHOULD BE PROTESTANT AND THE CATHOLICS SHOULD NOT HAVE POWER. THE KING SHOULD SHARE POWER WITH PARLIAMENT. PARLIAMENT SHOULD CONTROL THE ARMY. THE COURTS SHOULD NOT BE CONTROLLED BY THE KING.

Things done by King James II

JAMES BECAME A CATHOLIC. MANY ARMY OFFICERS WERE CATHOLICS. JAMES ALLOWED CATHOLICS TO WORSHIP FREELY AND TO HAVE GOVERNMENT JOBS. BISHOPS WHO DISLIKED CATHOLICS HAVING MORE FREEDOM WERE ARRESTED. JAMES HAD A SON IN 1688 WHO WOULD BE BROUGHT UP A CATHOLIC.

1 Look at the list of what Parliament wanted. Look at the list of what King James II did. In your own words, explain why each of the things King James did would have annoyed many powerful members of Parliament.

2 In your own words, explain why King James II was overthrown. Use the cartoons and your answer to question 1 to help you.

Part IV
Britain 1750–1900

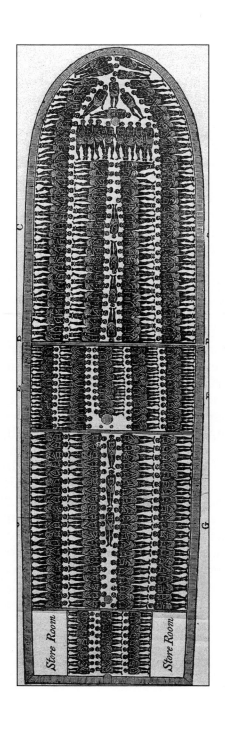

TN 1750–1900: Britain

The revised National Curriculum (1995) brought significant changes to the old study unit, Expansion, Trade and Industry. These changes produced less of a fit between *In Search of History 1714–1900* and the new Orders than there had been between the book and the original National Curriculum study unit (with the exception of the different date outlines). The main difference was with regard to studying 'in depth'. While this need has been recognised in the first two study units within this pack, it is particularly significant in the final two core study units.

Depth Study: The Napoleonic Wars focuses on a very large area, and does so by selective coverage. The main areas covered are: an outline of events of the Napoleonic Wars, the impact of the wars on Britain, and reasons why France lost the wars. The second area gives an opportunity to categorise causation, as well as to examine chains of causes/consequences. The final focus encourages students to critically compare sources of evidence. This critical comprehension uses sources in advance of those used in previous study units. The final extended writing would probably benefit from class discussion before it is individually attempted. Where to place this Depth Study is open to question. Chronologically, it fits well after examining 18th- and 19th-century industrialisation and before looking at the growth of the empire (though clearly there are overlaps here). **Depth Study: The British Empire** could follow on from the examination of the Napoleonic Wars, or replace it.

Extension work on **Growing towns – Liverpool** would fit in well after students have learned about industrialisation and the corresponding growth of cities. This little study makes the point about urban growth while also raising issues about utility of sources. **The slave trade** links with the overview provided by Chapter 11 of the textbook, but it provides greater depth concerning the processes involved in both the setting up and maintenance of the trade and its eventual decline. It could be linked to the extension work on Liverpool and shipping. Students could also carry out their own research project on William Wilberforce and the role of an individual in history. **Changing 19th-century Britain** gives an opportunity to use a long written source which encourages critical comprehension and awareness of the way in which a writer's social position can affect their concerns. This Extension Sheet would fit in as a homework exercise at the end of a period of study on the impact of industrialisation and urban growth in the 19th century. **Interpretations of the past** examines the role and importance of an individual (Sir Robert Peel) while also highlighting that different historical interpretations can arise depending on which factors and issues are studied. Thus Peel is judged sometimes as the party politician and sometimes as the national leader, and this can produce significantly different interpretations. This exercise could be used late in the study unit, when students are more familiar with some of the main issues confronting 19th-century Britain.

The Foundation Sheets **Ideas about farming**, **Changing industry** and **Factory reform** assist students in accessing and organising information in order to gain a greater understanding of the central issues involved. They arise out of the coverage provided by the existing textbook. **Changing Industry** is followed by a writing template – **Writing about the changes in making cloth** – which provides a structure to help students organise their knowledge coherently. **The dangers of railways!** could be used as a homework exercise after class work on the way in which pictures and cartoons can be used to convey messages about society.

DS The Napoleonic Wars

In 1789 there was a **revolution** in France. The king, Louis XVI, was overthrown. Later, in 1793, he was executed. One year earlier (in 1792), the new revolutionary government in France had declared war on Austria, whose ruler supported the French king. By 1793 the French were fighting Austria, Prussia, Spain, Sardinia, Britain and Holland. All these countries were frightened of the French Revolution and wanted to crush it. Wars between France and other countries in Europe continued until the French were finally defeated at the Battle of Waterloo in 1815.

From 1799 France was ruled by a man named Napoleon Bonaparte. In 1804 he made himself Emperor of France. He was a great military leader who conquered many of France's enemies. The wars he fought are called the 'Napoleonic Wars'. They lasted until he was defeated in 1815. The wars, fought between 1802 and 1815, are shown on this page.

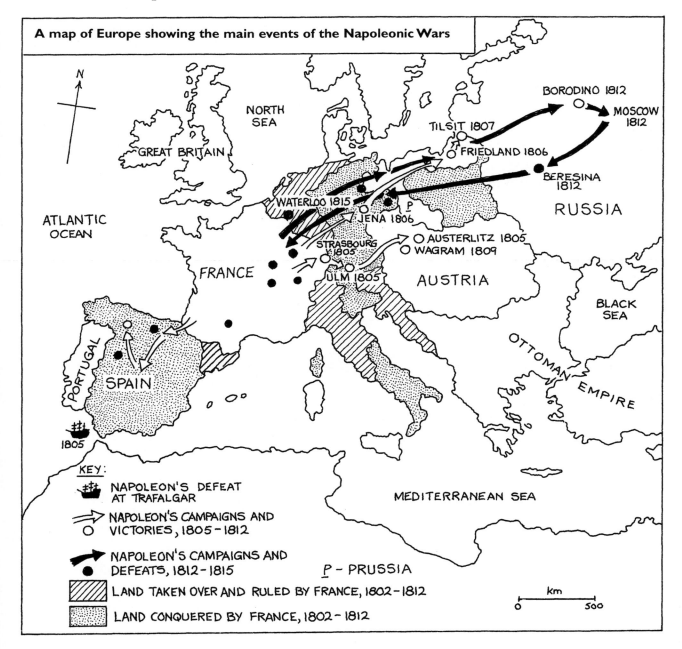

A map of Europe showing the main events of the Napoleonic Wars

KEY:
- NAPOLEON'S DEFEAT AT TRAFALGAR
- NAPOLEON'S CAMPAIGNS AND VICTORIES, 1805–1812
- NAPOLEON'S CAMPAIGNS AND DEFEATS, 1812–1815
- LAND TAKEN OVER AND RULED BY FRANCE, 1802–1812
- LAND CONQUERED BY FRANCE, 1802–1812

P – PRUSSIA

km
0 — 500

WHAT IMPACT DID THE NAPOLEONIC WARS HAVE ON BRITAIN?

Britain was one of the countries which fought Napoleon. These wars against the French had a big impact on Britain. Some of the effects are shown on this page. On the left side of the box are *causes*. On the right side of the page are *consequences* for Britain. Look at them carefully.

Causes

a Britain needed to pay for fighting the war. Britain also lent money to its allies to help them fight the French.

b War made it difficult to trade.

c Napoleon set up something called the Continental System in 1806 and 1807. This said that France and her allies would not buy goods made in Britain.

d Guns, ships and clothes were needed for the army and navy fighting the French.

e The French Revolution seemed to promise ordinary people the chance to change their government and get more freedom. These ideas quickly spread.

Consequences for Britain

◆ The government banned people in Britain from writing to people in France.

◆ In 1795 the government made it illegal to hold large meetings.

◆ The government borrowed money from the Bank of England.

◆ Britain struck back by using its navy to stop any ships taking goods to France and allies of France.

◆ Prices went up (especially of bread).

◆ People had to pay more taxes. Income Tax began in 1799.

◆ Farmers made a lot of money as cheap corn could not get into Britain and so they could put up their prices.

◆ Laws made it hard to publish papers ordinary people could afford.

◆ Some industries did well: ship-building, iron for guns, cloth for uniforms.

USING THE EVIDENCE

1 Draw a line from each cause to its consequence. You may find that some causes had more than one consequence.

2 Shade the consequences in different colours depending on whether they are: **social**, **political**, **economic**.

3 Which of the consequences of the war with France do you think was most important?

4 Some of the consequences became causes of other events. Here are some more events. Which of the events in the consequences column do you think made these happen?

◆ The USA did not like the British stopping its ships, and declared war on Britain in 1812.

◆ Farmers enclosed more land to grow corn. This changed agriculture.

◆ More steam engines were built for use in the iron and cloth industries.

WHY DID FRANCE LOSE THE NAPOLEONIC WARS?

France attacked Russia in 1812 but could not defeat the Russians. Napoleon's army was destroyed in the terrible Russian winter.

Britain was the first industrial country. It had lots of money to lend to other countries to help them pay for war with the French.

France was fighting too many countries at the same time. It could not beat them all.

Why did France lose?

Enemies of France began to copy things done successfully by the French – encouraging their people to be proud of their country to make them oppose the French.

Britain had a powerful navy. This stopped supplies getting to France and its allies, and made sure Napoleon could not fight a war outside of Europe.

SOURCE A

❝ The cost of the war was too great; France could not sustain it against the **coalition** of all the other European countries. When after his [Napoleon's] invasion of that country in 1812, Russia entered the field against him, and the greatest army he ever led crumbled into ruins in the snows of the winter, he was doomed to defeat unless his enemies should fall out with one another. This time they did not. Napoleon himself blamed the British, who had been at war with him (and before him, with the Revolution) with only one short break since 1792. British money financed the allies. A British army in Spain kept alive there from 1809 onwards a **front** which drained French resources and gave hope to other Europeans. ❞

J.M. Roberts, History of the World, *1980.*

SOURCE C

❝ Britain helped pay for this new war against Napoleon. Napoleon was short of money and soldiers. There was opposition to his government, both in the conquered lands and at home in France. There was little enthusiasm in France for a new war. Prices were high and there were shortages of food. ❞

P. Mantin, The French Revolution, *1992.*

SOURCE B

❝ It was only after the monarchs of Europe had learned how to stir **patriotic** enthusiasm by copying the French that their armies and peoples became capable of meeting and overthrowing Napoleon's forces. ❞

W. McNeill, A World History, *1967.*

1 **a** Look at Source A. What reasons might Napoleon have had for blaming the British for his defeat?
b Do you think that the writer of Source A would have agreed with Napoleon's view that this was the reason why he lost? Explain your answer.

2 What does Source B mean? Explain it using your own words.

3 Look at Sources A, B and C. Compare their interpretations of why Napoleon was defeated. In what ways are they similar to, or different from, each other?

4 Make a list of the reasons why Napoleon was defeated using Sources A, B and C. But only put in reasons that are *not* already covered in the spider diagram above them on the page.

5 **a** Look at your list and the diagram on the sheet. Now you have many possible reasons why Napoleon was defeated. Draw three interlocking circles (a Venn diagram). Label one 'Political', one 'Economic' and one 'Military'. Within each circle, write the different causes for Napoleon's defeat depending on their type. Where circles overlap, write again any causes which seem to be linked. In the middle, write any cause (if you can find one) which links all three categories.
b Select the most important three reasons. Explain why you think these are more important than the other reasons.

6 Essay question:

> ## Why did France lose the Napoleonic Wars?

To answer this question, you will need to look at the map and at what you have learned about possible reasons why France lost. When you have done this, use the following suggestions for how best to tackle answering this question:

◆ Write an introduction saying when the wars with France were fought, who Napoleon was, when he was defeated and what it is you are going to try to explain.
◆ Write different paragraphs looking at the possible reasons why Napoleon lost:
   a mistakes Napoleon made;
   b the part played by Britain;
   c the numbers of enemies he faced and how they encouraged their people to fight the French;
   d problems he faced in France.
◆ Explain which reasons were **political, economic** and **military**. You could **quote** some of the ideas of the historians you have looked at. Do not copy great chunks of their words. Only use the words which sum up their ideas.
◆ Write a conclusion in which you say which reasons you think were the most important and why you think this.

 WORD BOX

coalition when several countries join together to fight another country.

economic how money is earned, how industries are run.

front where armies are fighting.

military to do with armies and navies and how they fight.

patriotic loving your country.

political to do with governing a country.

quote to copy someone's words.

revolution a great change – in France, overthrowing the king.

social how people live and behave.

DS The British Empire

The word **empire** is used when one country captures a lot of other countries. These other countries, which form part of an empire, are often called **colonies**. The British Empire was the largest empire in the history of the world. It covered more square miles of the Earth and included more people in it than any other empire. On this page are five maps showing the British Empire at different times in its history. You will see how it grew bigger over time, and then how it finally came to an end.

When you are looking at these maps, make a list of the questions you would like to find answers to about the British Empire. At the end of this Depth Study, tick the ones you have found answers to. Where you have not found answers, you could carry out your own personal research to find the answers.

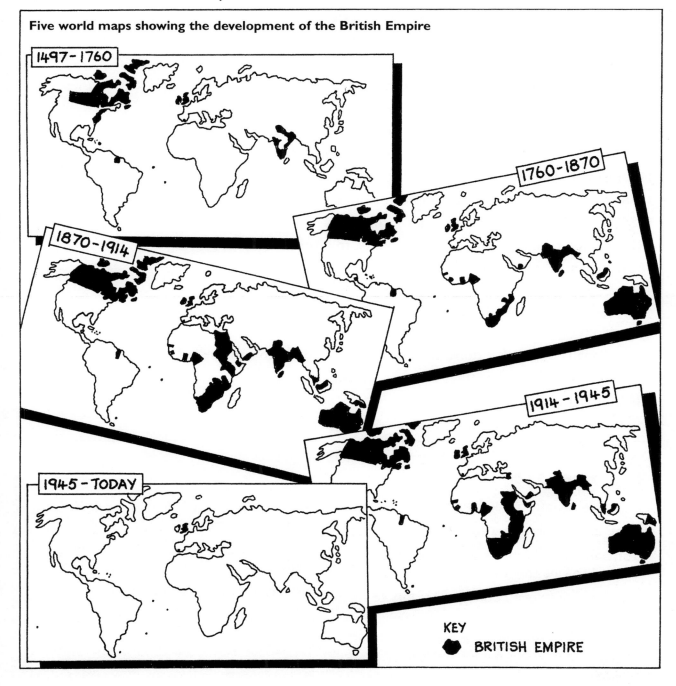

Five world maps showing the development of the British Empire

1497–1760

1760–1870

1870–1914

1914–1945

1945–TODAY

KEY

BRITISH EMPIRE

HOW AND WHY DID THE BRITISH GET AN EMPIRE?

This is a very important question. Below is a timeline of the main events in the growth of the British Empire. Some of the events are marked with a *. These are some of the 'growth points' of the Empire. These were times when the Empire changed in some important way.

On the next sheet is an explanation of why each 'growth point' was important and what it led to. These explanations are not printed in the right order. Match up the explanations to the correct growth-point dates and events as indicated by the asterisks.

Main events in the growth of the British Empire

1497: John Cabot sails from Bristol to North America.

1583: Sir Humphrey Gilbert claims Newfoundland for Britain. *

1585: first English settlement in America.

1600: beginning of East India Company. Britain **traded** with India and set up bases there.*

1617: tobacco plants grown in Virginia, America. *

1643: sugar grown in English colony of Barbados. *

1649: first Navigation Act gives Britain control over trade with colonies.

1655: after war with Spain, Jamaica added to British colonies in West Indies.

1667: Britain gives up colony of Surinam (in South America) to the Dutch.

1700: all British colonies in America founded (except Georgia).

1757: British East India Company defeats Indian and French army at Battle of Plassey. *

1759: British defeat French in Canada. *

1776: Britain loses control of American colonies but keeps Canada. *

1788: first settlements in Australia, by **convicts**.

1815: Britain takes control of Cape Colony, the southern tip of Africa. *

1821: Britain takes control of West Africa.

1842: China defeated. Hong Kong taken by British. *

1857: revolt against British rule in India. British government takes over running of India from the East India Company. *

1867: Canada becomes a **dominion**. It has more power to run itself. *

1877: Queen Victoria becomes Empress of India. *

1887: Zululand taken over by British.

1899–1902: British win Boer War and control all of South Africa.

 WORD BOX

colony a country ruled by another country.

convict a criminal serving a prison sentence.

dominions parts of the British Empire allowed to rule themselves.

empire where one country rules lots of other countries.

economic to do with how money is earned, and how businesses are run.

Hindu a follower of Hinduism, one of the religions of India.

raw materials things used in the making of other goods.

resources the wealth of a country.

textile cloth.

trade buying and selling.

USING THE EVIDENCE

The explanations in the box below of the growth points of the British Empire are not written in the correct order.

1 Decide which of the growth-point dates and events each explanation below refers to.

2 Then write out each date and event marked with a * from the box on the previous sheet. After each date and event you copy out, write out the explanation from this box.

- ◆ These plants needed lots of workers. Start of British slave trade to America.
- ◆ This began British control of large parts of Africa.
- ◆ Britain begins to give up power to different parts of its Empire.
- ◆ Start of British Empire. **Resources** in America brought wealth to Britain.
- ◆ This gave Britain a base from which to trade with China and other Asian countries.
- ◆ Start of British links with India, which would one day be a very important part of the Empire.
- ◆ This shows how important India and the Empire were to Britain.
- ◆ This made the British government become more involved in running the Empire.
- ◆ A terrible blow to Britain, but it kept control of Canada.
- ◆ This needed many workers. Most African slaves brought here. Britain gained wealth from selling sugar.
- ◆ This gave Britain control of North American resources.
- ◆ This made British East India Company the most powerful force in India.

WHAT WAS THE INFLUENCE OF THE EMPIRE ON THE BRITISH?

During the 19th century, the idea of having an empire became more popular in Britain. Looking back at the growth points, you will see that the British gained a lot from their empire.

- ◆ The British gained control over **raw materials** (like sugar, tobacco, cotton, rubber) which could be made into things and sold for a lot of money.

- ◆ The British gained control over the lives of huge numbers of people. British goods, made in Britain, could be sold to these people. For example, the British destroyed the Indian **textile** industry and then sold huge amounts of British cotton cloth to the Indians.

- ◆ Men from the colonies could be used in the army to fight the enemies of Britain. The Indian army was a very large army, and Indian soldiers fought for the British all over the world.

- ◆ British people felt proud of their empire. It made Britain look important.

However, the British Empire was not just about taking things from people. Many British people who went to the colonies learned a lot from the people they ruled. Many British habits, like drinking tea, came from the Empire. In India, some of the British rulers began to live like Indians.

SOURCE A

Sir David Ochterlony, a British official in India. This was painted in the early 19th century.

SOURCE B

"I am in love with the gopis [cowherd girls in Indian legends], charmed with Krishna [a **Hindu** god] and an enthusiastic admirer of Rama [a Hindu god]."

Written by Sir William Jones, a British judge in Calcutta. He arrived in India in 1784.

SOURCE C

"When I discovered that Fraser had given up eating pork and beef I felt it necessary to remind him of the religion he was brought up to. In truth he is as much Hindu as Christian."

Written by Lady Nugent in the 1820s. She was the wife of the British army commander. The person she was unhappy with was William Fraser. He was a member of the East India Company. He dressed and lived like a rich Indian prince.

USING THE EVIDENCE

1 'Britain gained economic power from ruling the Empire.' From what you have read so far, explain how and why this was true. What else did it gain?

2 Look at Source A. 'David Ochterlony lived like an Indian.' Make a list of all that you can see in this picture which supports this statement.

3 Look at Source C. Why was Lady Nugent so unhappy with William Fraser, according to this source? The clue is in the mention of pork and beef. You may have to do some research into Hindu beliefs to help you understand her complaint.

4 Do you think Lady Nugent (Source C) would have approved, or disapproved of the ideas of Sir William Jones (Source B) and the lifestyle of Sir David Ochterlony (Source A)? Look at each of these sources and explain what she might have felt and why she would have felt this way.

WHAT IMAGE DID BRITISH PEOPLE HAVE OF THE EMPIRE BY THE END OF THE 19TH CENTURY?

British people had many different ideas about the Empire. These ideas were shown in things they wrote, songs they sang and the way the Empire was pictured on posters and advertisements.

By looking at these things we can get an idea of the different kinds of images, or ideas, there were about the Empire by the end of the 19th century.

SOURCE A This is a late-19th-century advertisement for Queen's Honey Soap.

SOURCE B An advertisement for Rippingille Stoves.

SOURCE C

❝I no longer doubt about the benefits of English rule in India. The natives, gentle, simple and dreamy are dependent upon Englishmen for everything.❞

Herbert Maynard, 1887.

SOURCE D

❝Why should we not form a secret society with but one aim, the furtherance of the British Empire and the bringing of the whole uncivilised world under British rule?❞

Cecil Rhodes, 1876.

USING THE EVIDENCE

1. Look carefully at Sources A–D. Each one of them gives you a British impression of the British Empire. For each one of them, explain what ideas about the Empire it gives you. Here are some things you might think of while looking at each source:

   ◆ what native people get from being part of the Empire;

   ◆ what British people get from having the Empire;
   ◆ how people in the Empire get on;
   ◆ British attitudes towards non-British people.

2. Do you think that people ruled by Britain would have agreed with all these images of the Empire? Explain why.

 # Growing towns – Liverpool

During the 18th and 19th centuries, many towns grew enormously. One of these growing towns was the port of Liverpool. The three pictures on this sheet show Liverpool in three different years. You can use these pictures as evidence for how the town grew in size.

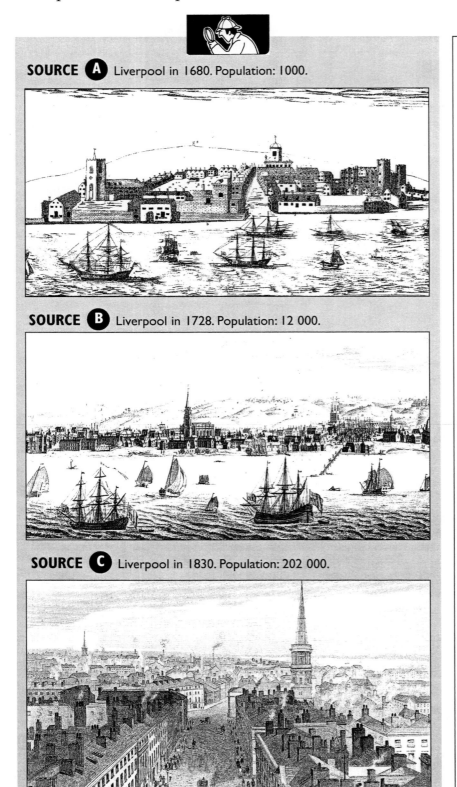

SOURCE **A** Liverpool in 1680. Population: 1000.

SOURCE **B** Liverpool in 1728. Population: 12 000.

SOURCE **C** Liverpool in 1830. Population: 202 000.

INVESTIGATION

1 Look at each of the pictures of Liverpool. Describe in as much detail as possible how the town changed between 1680 and 1830, according to these pictures.

2 Looking again carefully at these pictures, can you see any problems in using them for comparing the city at three different dates?

3 When towns grew as quickly as Liverpool did, the people living in them faced many problems.
a What problems could you *not* find out about from these pictures?
b What kinds of evidence would you need to examine in order to discover this information?

4 What are the strengths and weaknesses of pictures such as these, as evidence for historians trying to find out about the past?

EX The slave trade

Look at pages 42–43 of *In Search of History 1714-1900*. These give you an overview of the slave trade in the British Empire. Here are two questions historians sometimes ask about it:

◆ Why did the slave trade start in the first place?

◆ Why did the slave trade come to an end?

To answer these questions you need to do more than just describe how slaves were treated and what work they did. You need to look at all the different events which combined to cause change over time.

Flow diagram showing why the slave trade started

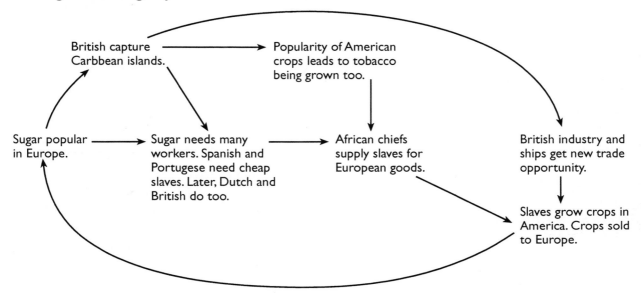

THE BEGINNING OF THE SLAVE TRADE

The slave trade forced Black Africans to go to America to work there. But the first settlements in America did not rely on slaves. They used White people from Europe. Many of these were free. Some were called indentured servants. These people signed an agreement saying they would work for a person for a certain period of time. They then had to keep to this agreement. They could not leave the work until the time was up. Some American Indians also worked on White farms.

This was first changed by the Spanish and the Portuguese in the 16th century. They had started growing sugar in Brazil and on the islands of the Caribbean. They suddenly needed huge numbers of workers. This was because it takes a lot of people to plant and harvest sugar.

The Spanish and Portuguese had already used African slaves to work for them elsewhere. The changes in America encouraged them to bring African slaves to work there.

They were helped by the fact that in West Africa some African rulers already used slaves and were willing to sell them. In return they got hold of goods from Europe which they found useful. African slave hunters travelled far into Africa, down rivers and along the coast to capture people to sell to Europeans. The slave trade became a great network of capturing, selling and using slaves. It was a system started by the Spanish and Portuguese and continued by the Dutch, but which really grew to a huge size under British control from the 17th century.

Keeping the system going

Once the system started, there were lots of people who wanted to keep it going.

◆ White owners of great farms (called plantations) wanted the Black workers.

◆ Black African rulers wanted the goods they received for selling slaves to White traders.

◆ People in Europe liked the things – sugar, rum, tobacco – which were grown in America using slaves as workers. Using slaves kept these goods cheap.

◆ Slave traders and ship owners in Britain made a lot of money from taking slaves to America. Between 1690 and 1807, about 11 000 British ships were used to take Black slaves to America.

◆ British industries made huge amounts of money: goods from these industries were sold to African slave traders and to the plantation owners in America to feed and clothe their slaves.

Europeans liked the things produced in America so much that more and more were grown in America. By 1680 the British island of Barbados was full of sugar plantations. In 1655 the British captured Jamaica from the Spanish. This island was used to grow sugar too. Soon the islands of the Caribbean were sending thousands of tons of sugar to Britain. During the 17th century tobacco began to be grown by the British on the east coast of America. Slaves were then used there too.

The slaves in the tobacco plantations soon began to have children, and fewer slaves had to be brought from Africa. But on the sugar plantations of the Caribbean islands, the work was even harder. Thousands of slaves died, and more were to be brought from Africa to replace them. About 70 per cent of all slaves brought to America went to work on the sugar plantations. In total, about 11 million Black Africans landed in America. Many others died on the journey. We will never know how many men, women and children died in this way.

The Black people forced to go to America had a great impact on the development of America. Most of the money made by White people from America was only possible because of the hard work of Black slaves. They made up a huge amount of the working population.

Bar chart to show the population of the Americas in 1820

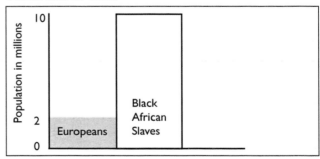

INVESTIGATION

❶ Using the evidence you have seen so far, explain in your own words why the slave trade started and continued. You will need to:

◆ Write an introduction, explain what the slave trade was.

◆ Then write paragraphs which:
a identify what caused it to start, and why this led to the transportation of slaves;

b explain how the situation in Africa help provide the slaves that were wanted;
c explain how Britain became involved, and how this encouraged the slave trade;
d show how, once it had started, a variety of different factors kept the trade going.

◆ Conclude saying what you think was the main reason it started and continued.

THE END OF THE SLAVE TRADE

The slave trade had a huge impact on America and Europe. Even people who had never seen a slave might find themselves linked to the slave trade. They might eat, drink or smoke something grown using slave labour. They might produce something which was sold to an African slave-trading chief or to a plantation owner.

What is surprising is how quickly the slave trade came to an end in the British Empire. This happened for a number of reasons. One extremely important reason was the work of Christian anti-slavers such as William Wilberforce. They held public meetings and drew the attention of people to the brutal treatment of slaves. But there were many reasons why the slave trade ended.

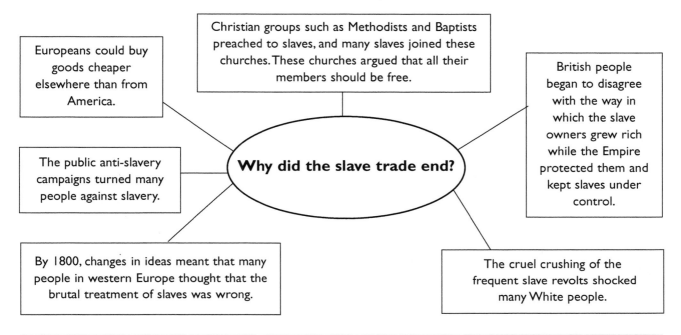

Europeans could buy goods cheaper elsewhere than from America.

Christian groups such as Methodists and Baptists preached to slaves, and many slaves joined these churches. These churches argued that all their members should be free.

British people began to disagree with the way in which the slave owners grew rich while the Empire protected them and kept slaves under control.

The public anti-slavery campaigns turned many people against slavery.

Why did the slave trade end?

By 1800, changes in ideas meant that many people in western Europe thought that the brutal treatment of slaves was wrong.

The cruel crushing of the frequent slave revolts shocked many White people.

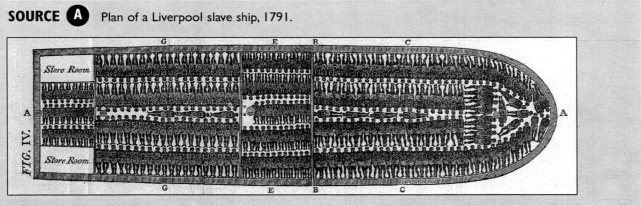

SOURCE A   Plan of a Liverpool slave ship, 1791.

INVESTIGATION

❶ Look at Source A. This plan was actually published by an anti-slavery organisation. How might it have used this in its attacks on the slave trade?

❷ 'It was broad economic and social changes which undermined slavery in the British colonies.' (Professor Jim Walwin, *The British Empire* 1997). Use the information on this sheet to explain how this was true. To help you: economic is to do with money and trade, social is about people's way of life and beliefs, colonies were lands in the British Empire.

EX Changing 19th-century Britain

During the 19th century, Britain changed in many ways. The following description of some of these changes was written in 1839. The writer was the Reverend Sydney Smith. He was a minister in the Church of England. He was in favour of many of the changes taking place in Britain during the 19th century. He was not one of those poorer people whose lives were badly affected by some of these great changes.

SOURCE A

" Gas was unknown: I groped about the streets of London in all but the utter darkness…

I have been nine hours in sailing from Dover to Calais before the invention of steam. It took me nine hours to go from Taunton to Bath, before the invention of rail roads, and I now go in six hours from Taunton to London! In going from Taunton to Bath, I suffered between 10,000 and 12,000 severe bruises, before stone-breaking Macadam was born.

I can walk, by the assistance of the police, from one end of London to the other, without molestation; or, if tired, get into a cheap and active cab, instead of those cottages on wheels, which the hackney coaches were at the beginning of my life.

I had no umbrella! They were little used and very dear. There were filthy coffee-houses instead of elegant clubs. Game could not be bought. Quarrels about Uncommuted Tithes were endless. The corruptions of Parliament, before reform, infamous. There were no banks to receive the savings of the poor. The Poor Laws were gradually sapping the life of the country; and whatever miseries I suffered, I had no post to whisk my complaints for a single penny to the remotest corners of the empire. "

Reverend Sydney Smith, 1839.

INVESTIGATION

1 Who was the 'stone-breaking Macadam' mentioned in lines 6–7? Why might Sydney Smith have thought he would stop him getting bruised on a journey?

2 What is 'Game' mentioned in line 12? Which of the inventions mentioned earlier might have made it easier to buy it in towns by 1839?

3 What were 'Tithes' (line 13)? What kinds of people might be quarrelling about them?

4 Which reform would have stopped the 'corruptions of Parliament' (line 13)?

Explain how it would have managed this.

5 Why might Sydney Smith have thought the Poor Laws were 'sapping the life of the country' (line 15)?

6 What changes does he *not* mention which you might have expected him to refer to?

7 Why might some people have *not* been as happy about some of these changes as Sydney Smith was? Which changes might some people not have liked? Explain why.

Interpretations of the past

Historians often have different views about the past. These differences of opinion are called 'interpretations'. They may disagree about:

◆ why something happened;

◆ what something led to;

◆ how important an event, or person, was;

◆ whether a person was good or bad.

These different interpretations happen for a number of reasons:

◆ Different primary evidence may give different views of a person, or event.

◆ Some historians may think that one piece of evidence is more important than another.

◆ There may be gaps in the evidence.

◆ Things modern historians believe in can affect the way that they think about events and people in the past.

◆ Historians may look at different areas of a person's life and get quite different views about that person, depending on what part of the person's life they look at.

One person who was very important in 19th-century Britain was Sir Robert Peel. He was a member of a political **party** called the Tory Party. In the 1830s they started calling themselves Conservatives. Historians disagree in their ideas about him.

◆ Some historians think he was a great man. They think he cared more for his country than for his political party. They think that was wise and good.

◆ Some historians think he was a bad leader of his party. They think he **betrayed** his party by doing things his party did not agree with.

◆ Some think he simply copied other people's ideas.

Before you look at these different interpretations on the part of historians, look at the main points in Peel's life in the box below. Then look at how people from his time had different views about him.

The main events in the life of Sir Robert Peel

1823:	He listened to advice from prison reformers and improved life in prisons.
1829:	He started the police force.
1829:	To stop violence in Ireland, he allowed Catholics more freedom. Many Tories were very angry. This split his party.
1830s:	He reunited the Tory Party and called it the Conservatives.
1841–45:	Peel was Prime Minister. He did a lot to make the British **economy** stronger.
1841–45:	He brought in laws to improve working conditions in factories and mines.
1846:	He got rid of the Corn Laws. These laws were to keep cheap foreign corn out of Britain. Many Conservative farmers were very angry. This split his party again!

DIFFERENT INTERPRETATIONS ABOUT PEEL FROM HIS OWN TIME

AGAINST PEEL:

SOURCE A

"I find that for between 30 and 40 years, he has traded on the ideas and intelligence of others. He is a **burglar** of other's **intellects.**"

Benjamin Disraeli, 1846. He was in the same political party as Peel. He did not like Peel because he thought Peel should have given him a job in the government. Disraeli hoped to become a famous politician himself and was keen to get rid of Peel.

SOURCE B (right)

This cartoon shows Peel riding the way he wants to go. The people in the carriage are members of his own party. This cartoon was drawn when Peel was trying to get rid of the Corn Laws. It says he ignored the views of people in his party who thought he was wrong to do this.

The sign says 'Free Trade'. This means making it easy for goods from other countries to come into Britain.

THE DEAF POSTILION.
A POLITICAL PARODY, AFTER GEORGE CRUIKSHANK.

FOR PEEL:

SOURCE C

"Oh there has never been such a noble **premier,**
As Robert Peel before in the nation.
In every way he carried the **sway,**
For the good of his country, God rest him."

A popular song, written shortly after Peel died in 1852. Songs like this were often sold in towns to working people. These people often liked Peel because they thought getting rid of the Corn Laws would make bread cheaper. These songs often made complex things sound very simple.

SOURCE D

A cartoon from 1850. It shows Britain happy and well-fed because Peel has got rid of the Corn Laws.

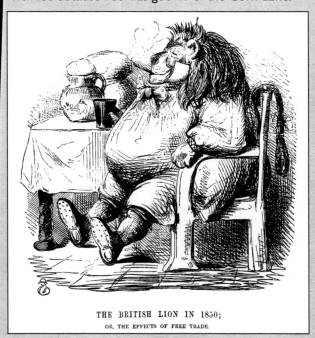

THE BRITISH LION IN 1850;
OR, THE EFFECTS OF FREE TRADE.

INVESTIGATION

1. Look at Sources A and B. What 'problem' with Peel does each one tell you about?

2. Look at Sources C and D. What 'good' things about Peel does each one tell you about?

3. Imagine you were a member of the Conservative Party in 1846. Which of these things about Peel might you like? Which might you dislike? Explain why.

4. Imagine you were not a member of the Conservative Party in 1846. Which of these things about Peel might you like? Which might you dislike? Explain why.

5. In 1856 a person wrote that Peel 'did not create his own ideas, he borrowed other people's.' Which of Sources A–D might this person have agreed with? Explain why.

6. a Look at the information about Sources A and C. What might make you unsure about how much you could rely on their opinion of Peel?
   b 'Even though these sources might not be reliable, they are still useful to a historian.' Explain why this is so.

7. 'It is sometimes very hard to get one clear picture of what a person in the past was like.' From what you have seen in these primary sources, explain why this is true about Sir Robert Peel. Start your answer with: 'It is hard to get a clear picture of what Peel was like because it depends on how you look at him. If you just think of him as the leader of his party, then …
   But if you think of him as leader of the whole country, then …'

THE DIFFERENT INTERPRETATIONS OF MODERN HISTORIANS

Now look at these modern interpretations of Peel. (Evidence produced after the period of history being studied is called a 'secondary source'.) They too are very different from one another. Read them. Think about:

◆ any differences;

◆ anything the same;

◆ what evidence the historians might have used to get their ideas.

SOURCE E

❝The proper contrast is between the **statesman** who does something he believes in at the right time and the **politician** who resists measures he knows to be just and necessary in order to please a particular group of people, or for personal spite, or ambition.❞

R. Grinter, Disraeli and Conservatism, 1968. He thought Peel had been a statesman.

SOURCE F

❝Whether he could have prevented the great split of 1846 must remain one of the great 'ifs' of history. It may be that no one could have preserved unity, but Peel set about the task in the worst possible way. Indeed one could argue that he never set about it at all.❞

R. Blake, The Conservative Party from Peel to Thatcher, 1985.

SOURCE G

"Peel himself was a 'dull' man, 'fitted to work and explain; he was not able to charm or amuse'. Shaftesbury [a Conservative] thought him an iceberg with a faint thaw on the tip. O'Connor [an Irish politician] said his smile was like the gleam on the silver plate of a coffin lid."

L.C.B. Seaman, Victorian England, 1973.

SOURCE H

"In spite of all his successes there was a lack of **vision** in Peel."

G. Kitson-Clark, Peel, 1936.

SOURCE I

"Financial stability had been achieved, trade revived. More than any other man he was the **architect** of the early Victorian age."

N. Gash, Sir Robert Peel, 1961.

INVESTIGATION

1 Look at Sources E–I. Then fill in the following table:

Secondary source	Does it give you a positive or a negative opinion about Peel?	What information does it give you?	Which of Sources A–D might this writer have used? If none say 'none'.
Source E			
Source F			
Source G			
Source H			
Source I			

📖 WORD BOX

architect person who plans something.

betrayed acted like a traitor.

burglar a thief.

economy how money is earned, how businesses are run.

intellect a person's ideas and thoughts.

party group of people who believe the same things about how a country should be run.

politician person who is a member of a political party and runs the country.

premier leader of a country.

statesman person who cares for the whole country, not just his party.

sway support.

vision clear ideas and beliefs.

How did ideas about farming change in the 18th century?

In the 18th century, there were great changes in ideas about farming. These changes were so big that they came to be called the Agricultural Revolution. The word 'agriculture' means 'farming'. The word 'revolution' means a 'big change'. On this sheet are some mix and match cards. On some cards you will find the name of a person. On other cards you will find new ideas about farming. You need to match the right name with the right idea.

To help you, look at pages 6–7 in the textbook *In Search of History 1714-1900*.

Jethro Tull – a farmer from Berkshire	**'Turnip' Townsend – a Norfolk farmer**	**Robert Bakewell – a Leicestershire farmer**
Robert Colling – a Durham farmer	**Thomas Coke – a Norfolk farmer**	**King George III – King of England**

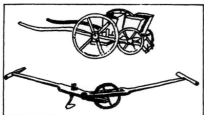

THE SEED DRILL PLANTED SEEDS IN STRAIGHT LINES. THE HOE GOT RID OF WEEDS.

GROWING TURNIPS GAVE CATTLE WINTER FOOD.

LETTING ONLY THE BEST SHEEP BREED LED TO BIGGER AND BETTER SHEEP.

LETTING ONLY THE BEST CATTLE BREED LED TO BIGGER AND BETTER CATTLE.

PUTTING MARL IN SANDY SOIL MADE IT GROW MORE CROPS.

THE KING LIKED FARMING, SO OTHER PEOPLE BECAME MORE INTERESTED IN IT TOO.

Now write an essay to answer the question:

> **How did new ideas change farming in the 18th century?**

Use the information from the boxes and anything else that you know which is relevant.

◆ Start your first paragraph with: 'New ideas are important because...'

◆ Start your second paragraph with: 'There were new ideas about making crops grow better...'

◆ Start your third paragraph with: 'There were new ideas about making animals bigger...'

◆ Start your fourth paragraph with: 'Famous people made other people interested in farming...'

F Changing industry

In the 18th century, there were tremendous changes in the way that cloth was made. This industry is called the 'textile industry'. 'Textile' is another word for 'cloth'. On this sheet is a timeline. In the boxes are:

◆ some of the inventions which caused the textile industry to change;

◆ the names of people who invented these new machines;

◆ ways that the industry changed.

1 Copy out the timeline onto a blank sheet of paper.

2 Put each machine in the right place on the timeline. Shade it in one colour if it was a 'spinning' machine. Shade it in another colour if it was a 'weaving' machine.

3 Put the right inventor with the right machine.

4 Then put the way the industry changed in the right place on the timeline. Each change will need to go after one of the inventions.

5 Did any of these changes lead to another machine being invented?

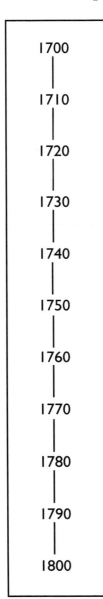

1700

1710

1720

1730

1740

1750

1760

1770

1780

1790

1800

The inventions:

Spinning Mule   Flying Shuttle

Water frame   Spinning Jenny

Power loom

The inventors:

John Kay   Samuel Crompton

Richard Arkwright   James Hargreaves

Edmund Cartwright

Ways the textile industry changed:

Weavers worked faster but were scared of losing their jobs.

After about 30 years, it stopped hand-powered weaving.

It made spinning faster and easier. Often used in homes.

It made good-quality thread quickly and cheaply.

It led to factories (mills) being built with these machines in them.

F Writing about the changes in making cloth

Look carefully at your timeline of changes in the making of cloth. Historians use evidence like this to explain why changes happened. These changes form a chain of things happening. Each link in the chain leads to something else. But writing about these changes can be confusing. To make it easier, here is a suggested way of doing it. Look at the way this is laid out and use it to write about how and why the making of cloth changed in the 18th century.

How and why did the making of cloth change in the 18th century?

1 Start your first paragraph like this: '*In the 18th century there were great changes in the making of cloth. A number of inventions led to these changes. The first invention was the Flying Shuttle...*' (Now write about who invented it and what it did. Say how it changed the making of cloth.)

2 Start your second paragraph like this: '*The weavers could now work faster. They needed more thread (yarn) to turn into cloth. This was made by spinners. The spinners were helped by another invention...*' (Now write about this invention, who invented it and what it did. Say how it changed the making of cloth.)

3 Start your third paragraph with: '*The way to make a lot of money was to build a bigger spinning machine and put lots together...*' (Now write about the next invention, who invented it and what it did. Say how it changed the making of cloth.)

4 Start your fourth paragraph with: '*The Water Frame made strong thread. But people wanted better quality thread than this...*' (Now write about the invention which made this possible. Say what it was and who made it. Say how it changed the making of cloth.)

5 Start your fifth paragraph with: '*The weavers now found the spinners were working faster than they were. An invention by Edmund Cartwright helped them catch up...*' (Now write about what this invention was and what it did. Say how it changed the making of cloth.)

6 Start your sixth paragraph with: '*All of these inventions changed the making of cloth. Cloth was made faster than before. Lots of it was made. It cost less to buy than before. These changes were important because...*' (Now say why you think these changes were so important. Think about it. Put down your own ideas.)

F The dangers of railways!

Railways were one of the great inventions of the 19th century. But at the time some people thought they were terrible things. Some of these people's feelings can be seen in cartoons made in the 19th century. By examining these cartoons, you can find out the messages these people wanted to put across to others. Look carefully at the cartoons. Write down who the people are, or what is happening. Then complete the sentence underneath each picture. Use information from the cartoon to help you do this.

SOURCE A A cartoon from 1830. This was after a member of the government had been run down by a train.

The person who drew this thought that railways were _____

_____.

SOURCE B Drawn in about 1850. An undertaker (person who arranges funerals) gives his business card to a passenger.

The person who drew this thought that railways were _____

_____

_____.

SOURCE C A cartoon showing stage coach drivers out of work because people are using railways.

The person who drew this thought that railways were _____.

Look at all these opinions. Explain how and why different people had different ideas about railways.

F Factory reform

Look at pages 60–62 of *In Search of History 1714–1900*. There you will see that work in factories slowly got better during the 19th century. Two things you need to understand are:

- why factory **reforms** did not always change things;
- the arguments for and against laws to make life better in the factories.

On the left side of this box are two laws. Listed alongside them are reasons why they did not always work. Using a pencil and a ruler, draw a line from the correct reasons to the right law. Ignore the reasons that are wrong. Then complete the sentences shown at the bottom of this box.

1802 Apprentices Act

- ◆ Magistrates and factory owners were often friends.
- ◆ Children wanted things to stay the same.
- ◆ There were very big fines if the law was broken.
- ◆ Fines were small. Factory owners could ignore the law.
- ◆ The law only applied to Wales.

1833 Factory Act

- ◆ It was hard to tell how old a child was.
- ◆ The law only applied to Scotland.
- ◆ The law only applied to mills making cloth.
- ◆ There were only four inspectors to check all the mills.
- ◆ The mills could only be checked on Tuesdays.

The law of 1802 did not work because…

There was another law in 1833 and this had problems too…

No reform…

Imagine you are a factory owner against reforming factories. Then imagine you are a person who wants reform. Explain what you believe. Choose the right ideas from the box below.

- ◆ Children are treated like slaves.
- ◆ What is good for our factories is good for the whole country.
- ◆ Factory life ruins people's health.
- ◆ Children get no education.
- ◆ We own the machines and the workers.
- ◆ If they don't like it, get another job.

Reform now…

 WORD BOX

reform to make something better.

Act a law agreed by Parliament. Laws say what people should do, how they should behave.

F A changing world

Between 1800 and 1900, many changes took place. Some of these changes made it easier to travel about. Other changes made it easier to send messages. It was as if the world was getting smaller. Some of these great changes are mentioned on pages 86–89 of *In Search of History 1714–1900*. Put the changes in the right-hand box in their correct place on the timeline.

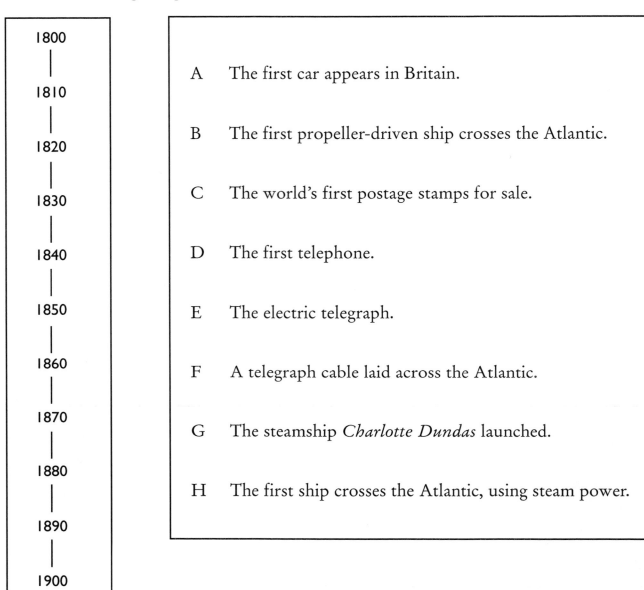

1800
|
1810
|
1820
|
1830
|
1840
|
1850
|
1860
|
1870
|
1880
|
1890
|
1900

A The first car appears in Britain.

B The first propeller-driven ship crosses the Atlantic.

C The world's first postage stamps for sale.

D The first telephone.

E The electric telegraph.

F A telegraph cable laid across the Atlantic.

G The steamship *Charlotte Dundas* launched.

H The first ship crosses the Atlantic, using steam power.

❶ Look carefully at your timeline. Which of these inventions do you think was the most important? Think about things like:

◆ Which invention changed ordinary people's lives the most?

◆ Which invention made other important changes happen later?

❷ Complete the following statement. Decide on your own reasons for your answer.

'The invention I think was the most important was _____ _____.'

'This is because _____ _____.'

Part V
The Twentieth Century World

TN The Twentieth Century World

As with Expansion, Trade and Industry (becoming Britain 1750–1900), the original Era of the Second World War was significantly altered by the revisions to the original National Curriculum. In many respects this produced a better fit with *In Search of History: The Twentieth Century World*. There were, however, exceptions, and these came primarily in the areas of 'depth' and in the coverage of the Second World War. Consequently, this area of the pack focuses on:

◆ the need for 'study in depth';

◆ an outline coverage of the Second World War;

◆ Foundation Sheets which complement the depth work but which also assist less-able students in dealing with some of the more complex content covered in the book.

Depth Study: The Western Front is a popular area of study and one which has a very brief coverage in the existing textbook. The aim of this Depth Study is to give students an opportunity to look at the events on the Western Front over a series of lessons and to build this into the outline work of the study unit. The first part of Chapter 2 in the textbook can be used as background to this Depth Study, covering as it does the causes of the First World War. The rest of the Depth Study is free-standing and moves from an overview to recruitment (with examination of propaganda), life in the trenches, case studies on two major battles and war poetry (again allowing for critical use of sources), and concludes with an overview of changes on the Western Front. The work on the recruitment posters could be extended by looking at other propaganda and recruitment posters, found via a trawl of other textbooks and library books. In addition, the Imperial War Museum, London, is an excellent source of reproductions. These could be subjected to the same critical enquiry as those provided in this pack. The imaginary letter from the trenches can be prepared through group work and whole-class discussion on the kinds of issues that might be mentioned and

how these issues might be approached. There is also a writing template to assist less-able students. Another opportunity for extended writing is provided within the examination of the Battle of Verdun and in the research work at the end of 'Changing weapons and tactics on the Western Front'. **Depth Study: The Nazi treatment of the Jews** is not an identified 'in depth' area within the revised National Curriculum but is clearly of tremendous importance and is identified as an area that should be covered within an outline study of the Second World War. The subject is so vast that no textbook handling of it can ever be sufficient. The main approach here is to examine the process by which Nazi anti-Semitism developed into the Holocaust.

Extension work focuses mostly on giving students an outline knowledge of the main events and issues of the Second World War, covered briefly in the second part of Chapter 8 in the textbook. (There is one sheet which gives an insight into the difficulties of redrawing the map of Europe after the First World War, and which could follow on from Chapter 3.) Regarding the Second World War, the main topics covered: **Blitzkrieg, The war on the Eastern Front, The war in the Far East, The dropping of the first atom bomb** and **Why did Germany lose the Second World War?** give students an overview of central areas, while research tasks give the opportunity for further independent study. The exercise on '**Why did Germany lose the Second World War?**' gives the opportunity for critical comprehension of an extended source.

The Foundation Sheets **Why did Hitler come to power?** and **What events caused a Cold War?** assist students in extracting and using information based on the existing textbook. The same is true of **The road to war**, and this exercise could be attempted instead of the first part of Chapter 8. These areas were all chosen as they are essential areas that students should understand but are, nevertheless, complex and demanding.

The Western Front

During the First World War, there was fighting in many areas of the world. These places where fighting happened are called **fronts**. This Depth Study is about fighting on the Western Front. The Western Front was in Belgium and France. Here the British, French and their **allies** were fighting the Germans from 1914 until 1918. This fighting is sometimes called **trench** warfare. This is because the soldiers dug trenches in the ground to get away from the bullets and bombs of the enemy. They lived in these trenches.

This Depth Study gives you an opportunity to explore one part of history in detail. You will be able to find out a lot about what it was like fighting on the Western Front.

The map on this sheet shows you where the Western Front was. It shows you where the lines of trenches ran. It shows you where and when the main battles were fought.

WORD BOX

allies countries on the same side.

ammunition bullets, shells, bombs.

artillery large guns which fire explosive shells.

bombardment firing explosive shells.

casualties people killed or wounded.

court martial an army court to punish soldiers who have done something wrong.

conscription being made to join the military.

front where the fighting is happening in a war.

operation an attack, a battle.

propaganda telling only your own point of view.

recruitment persuading people to join the military.

reserve trenches the line of trenches behind the front-line trenches.

shelling another word for 'bombardment'.

trench ditches which were dug to shelter soldiers from bombs and bullets.

volunteering freely deciding to join the military.

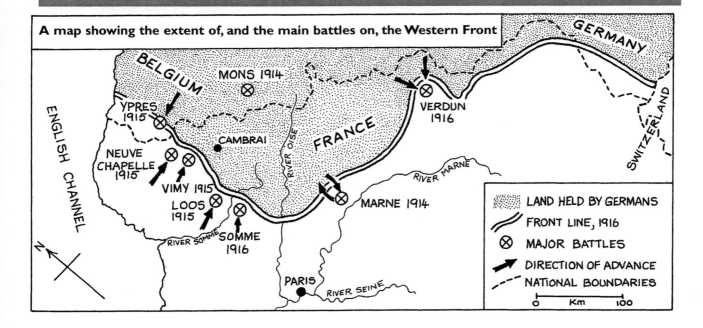

A map showing the extent of, and the main battles on, the Western Front

LAND HELD BY GERMANS
FRONT LINE, 1916
⊗ MAJOR BATTLES
DIRECTION OF ADVANCE
NATIONAL BOUNDARIES

RECRUITMENT AND PROPAGANDA

When governments of countries are fighting a war, they need to persuade their people to fight. They need them to join the armed forces. This is called **recruitment**. Governments use lots of different ways to try to encourage people to fight for them. Some examples can be seen on this page. These are all British posters from the first two years of the First World War. As this war went on, the British found that not enough men were **volunteering** to fight. In 1916 they made men join the army. This is called **conscription**.

In wartime, governments also try to control the information their people have about the war. This is because governments want their people to think that they are good and their enemies are bad. They want their people to think that they will win the war. They do not want their people to hear any bad news. Controlling information, so people only hear your own point of view, is called **propaganda**. There is often propaganda on recruitment posters.

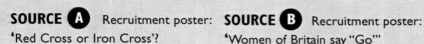

SOURCE A Recruitment poster: 'Red Cross or Iron Cross'?

SOURCE B Recruitment poster: 'Women of Britain say "Go"'

SOURCE C Recruitment poster: 'Daddy, what did *you* do in the Great War?'

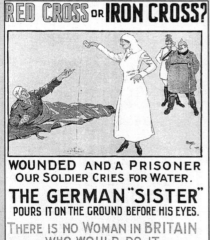

USING THE EVIDENCE

❶ Look carefully at each one of these sources. Each one of them uses a different way to put pressure on men to join the army. Explain how each poster tries to make men go and fight the Germans.

❷ Which one of these recruitment posters might be described as propaganda? Explain why – refer to what is shown on the poster.

❸ *Research*. Try to find four other examples of First World War recruitment posters. For each one:

◆ *describe* what is on the poster;
◆ *explain* how it tries to make men fight;
◆ *evaluate* how well you think it works.

WHAT WAS IT LIKE LIVING IN THE TRENCHES?

What it was like living in the trenches:

◆ Protected from enemy attacks by sandbags and barbed wire.
◆ Suffering from swollen 'trench feet' from living in trenches full of water.
◆ Living in rooms cut into the dirt walls – dug-outs.
◆ Having lice through not being able to keep clean.
◆ Shot at by snipers.
◆ Blown up by **bombardments.**
◆ Carrying out raids to capture enemy prisoners.
◆ Boring food – plum and apple jam again!
◆ Boring jobs – cleaning rifles, repairing the trench...
◆ Having to 'go over the top' to attack the enemy trenches in battles.
◆ 'No-man's-land' between the lines of trenches a sea of mud, destroyed houses, barbed wire, dead trees, dead people...

SOURCE A

66 My dug-out held 25 men tight packed. Water filled it to a depth of 1 or 2 feet, leaving say 4 feet of air. One entrance had been blown in. I nearly broke down and let myself drown in the water. Towards 6 o'clock, when, I suppose, you would be going to church, the **shelling** grew less intense and less accurate. 99

From a letter written by a soldier named Wilfred Owen, who fought on the Western Front.

SOURCE B

66 If you are in the **reserve trenches**, you will be carrying forward stores, **ammunition**, or supplies each night, unless you are patrolling, or raiding, or digging trenches for the next **operation**. By now you will have got used to that itching under the arms [lice]. 99

Written by General Farrar-Hockley, describing life for soldiers in the trenches. This was written in 1964. He did not fight in the First World War. He is a soldier and a historian who has used accounts written by soldiers about the war to write his book, The Somme.

● ● ● ● ● ● ● ● ● ● ● ● USING THE EVIDENCE ● ● ● ● ● ● ● ● ● ● ● ●

❶ Look carefully at Sources A and B. Make a list of what each tells you about life in the trenches.

❷ Imagine you are a soldier on the Western Front. Write an imaginary letter home. Explain what it is like living in the trenches and how you feel about it. Use the notes you have made for

Question 1 and the information box to help you decide what to mention.

❸ Source B was written 50 years after the First World War. Does this mean it is *not* a useful source for finding out about the war? Explain the reasons for your answer.

● ●

THE BATTLE OF VERDUN, FEBRUARY TO DECEMBER 1916

The Battle of Verdun was one of the bloodiest battles of the First World War. It lasted 10 months. The battle was fought around the French city of Verdun. It was fought between the Germans and the French. In the battle, it was the Germans who were attacking and the French who were defending Verdun. Most historians believe that the Germans lost the battle.

> ## Why did the Germans lose the battle of Verdun?

To answer this question, you must first understand what the aim of the German attack was.

> ## What was the German aim in attacking Verdun?
>
> The Germans knew that the French forts at Verdun were very famous. They believed that the French would be ashamed if Verdun was captured. The Germans hoped that the French would lose so many men defending Verdun that they would not be able to go on with the war.

The main events of the Battle of Verdun

From the beginning, the Germans did not stick to one aim for the battle. They were supposed to make sure that they did not lose too many men. They wanted the French to lose huge numbers of men. The German commander hoped that as the battle went on people in France would become so tired of the battle they would make the French government end the war. But in January the German commander ordered his soldiers to attack and keep on attacking until they won. The German commander then decided that his soldiers would attack in a smaller area than had first been planned. This helped the French hold up the attack.

The French were taken by surprise by the huge German bombardment which started on 21 February. This smashed the

French trenches and barbed wire. One French fort, called Fort Douaumont, was captured because its drawbridge was left down.

The French sent Marshal Petain to lead the army at Verdun. He was determined that Verdun would not be captured. The German attack began to slow down. They desperately threw in more men to try to break through. The French lost huge numbers of men but so did the Germans. This had not been part of their plan. It was the French who were meant to be 'bled white' by the battle! The French **artillery** destroyed many of the German guns and in March blew up the German store of **shells** which contained 450 000 powerful shells.

The German commander Falkenhayn had other problems. One of the officers under him was the Crown Prince, the son of the German ruler, the Kaiser. He was powerful because he was the Kaiser's son. Falkenhayn found it hard to control him. The Crown Prince was determined to defeat the French at Verdun. He argued that more German soldiers should be sent into the battle.

Falkenhayn let him do this, and German **casualties** rose even more.

In July the British attacked the Germans in the Battle of the Somme. No new German troops could be sent to Verdun, as they were needed to fight the British. The German attack on Verdun ground to a halt. In the autumn, the French recaptured much of the land they had earlier lost to the Germans. By December, the Battle of Verdun was over.

Number of French soldiers killed during the Battle of Verdun, by August 1916:	Number of German soldiers killed during the Battle of Verdun, by August 1916:
315,000	261,000

Number of artillery shells fired during the whole Battle of Verdun:
40 million shells were fired. 200 shells for every soldier killed in the whole battle on both sides (French and German).

USING THE EVIDENCE

1 Look at Source A. Using this source and the other information, explain in your own words what the Germans aimed to do in the Battle of Verdun.

2 Look at Source B. Do you think that the Germans would have been pleased, or disappointed by this French commander's response to the German attack on Verdun? Give the reason for your answer. Remember to think about what the German aim was for the battle.

3 Historians often have to decide whether people in the past succeeded or failed in doing what they aimed to do. Make a list of the ways that the Battle of Verdun would have had to be fought to make it fit the German aim. Think about:

◆ how long the battle should last;
◆ how the French should act;
◆ how many French soldiers should be killed (a few, quite a lot, very many);
◆ how many German soldiers should be killed (a few, quite a lot, very many);
◆ how the battle should end.

4 'For Germany, Verdun was a failure', according to Jay Winter and Blaine Baggett in the book *1914–1918 The Great War and the Shaping of the 20th Century* (1996). Do you agree or disagree with this view?

◆ What questions will you need to ask about the battle in order to decide? Make a note of your questions.
◆ Using these sheets, and other evidence you have researched, identify relevant information to help you answer your own questions.
◆ Decide why a historian might have the view that the Germans failed. Make a note of the possible reasons.
◆ On the basis of your investigation of the evidence, decide whether you agree, or disagree with the above point of view.

THE FIRST DAY OF THE BATTLE OF THE SOMME, 1 JULY 1916

The Battle of the Somme started at 7.30 a.m. on the morning of 1 July 1916. The battle was a British attack on the German trenches. There were some French soldiers helping too, but most of the attack was carried out by soldiers from Britain and from the British Empire.

The British hoped to make a hole in the German lines. This would be a terrible defeat for the Germans. This would stop the Germans from attacking the French at Verdun. This was important as the British were the allies of the French and wanted to help them. The British also hoped that they would be able to 'get the war moving again'. They hoped that if they broke through the German trenches, then British cavalry (horse soldiers) could pour through the gap and drive back the Germans. This would stop the terrible trench warfare which was killing so many people and dragging on without an end in sight.

The British plan went terribly wrong. On the first day, the British lost about 20 000 killed and 40 000 wounded. The Germans lost about 6 000 killed and wounded. To understand why, you first need to look at what the British planned to happen. Then you need to look at the evidence which tells you what actually happened. We can use this to:

◆ look at why things happened the way that they did in the past (you know by now that historians call this 'cause' and 'consequence');

◆ explain why 'aims' are not the same as how things really turn out;

◆ use sources of evidence to find out what events in the past were really like;

◆ compare this evidence with how things were planned to be and understand what is similar and what is different between plans and reality.

The British plans for the first day of the Battle of the Somme

BRITISH ARTILLERY WILL BOMBARD GERMAN TRENCHES FOR A WEEK, BEFORE ATTACKING. THIS WILL DESTROY GERMAN BARBED WIRE, MACHINE GUNS, TRENCHES AND FRONT-LINE SOLDIERS....

HUGE MINES WILL BE PLANTED UNDER GERMAN TRENCHES...

BRITISH SOLDIERS WILL ATTACK AFTER DAWN AND WALK SLOWLY ACROSS NO MAN'S LAND. ALL THE GERMANS WILL BE DEAD...

THE CAVALRY WILL THEN ADVANCE.

How did the first day of the Battle of the Somme really turn out?

Look at these sources to see what really happened on 1 July 1916. As you are reading them, think about which of the British plans for the day failed. Think about why these plans failed. Think about how this made the first day of the battle turn out the way that it did.

SOURCE A

"Suddenly we were in the midst of a storm of machine-gun bullets and I saw men beginning to twirl round and fall in all kinds of curious ways as they were hit – quite unlike the way actors do it in films."

Private Slater, of the 2nd Bradford Pals' regiment.

SOURCE B

"At 9 o'clock I was in a dug-out when someone shouted to me in an amazed voice 'the Tommies [British] are here'. I rushed up and there, just outside the barbed wire, were ten or twenty English soldiers with flat steel helmets. We would have had to surrender but then the English artillery began to fire at our trench; but a great deal of the shells were too short and hit the English and they began to fall back."

Felix Kircher, of the German 26th Field Artillery.

SOURCE C

"The task of the artillery was two-fold; to destroy the enemy trenches and to cut the barbed wire in front of them. For all the effort made, heavy guns were too few. Also the existence of the deep bunkers was not known and even where the trenches were smashed the defending troops had a fair chance of survival. Many guns were worn which wrecked their accuracy [so they could not cut the barbed wire] and the quality of the ammunition was poor; far too many shells failed to explode"

M. M. Evans, The Battle of the Somme *(1996).*

USING THE EVIDENCE

1. Look carefully at Sources A and B. Describe how the first day of the Battle of the Somme was different from the British plans for the day. You will need to look back at how the day was meant to be.

2. **a** Using all the sources, make a spider diagram to explain why the British plans for the first day failed.
   b Then briefly explain why each of these reasons caused a problem. You might not find all the answers to this in the sources, so think about why there would have been problems.

3. Which do you think was the most important reason why the British plan failed? Explain why you think this was more important than any of the other reasons. You will need to write about the other reasons too and say why they are less important.

WAR POEMS

There are many sources of evidence that tell us about the Western Front:

◆ official descriptions of battles written by the government and the army;

◆ soldiers' descriptions of what life was like, written in letters at the time and in books written afterwards, looking back;

◆ photographs, taken by photographers working for the government;

◆ army maps of the trenches;

◆ objects like rifles, tanks, planes;

◆ the remains of trenches and shell holes that can still be seen in Belgium and France;

◆ poems written by soldiers on the Western Front.

Some of the most unusual evidence from the Western Front is in the form of poems written by soldiers. Many writers and poets volunteered to fight, or were made to fight in the war. As the war dragged on, they wrote about it. Their poems are evidence for how some soldiers felt about the war. You can read some of them here.

SOURCE A

❝If I should die, think only this of me:
That there's some corner of a foreign field
That is for ever England. There shall be
In that rich earth a richer dust concealed;
A dust whom England bore, shaped, made aware,
Gave, once, her flowers to love, her ways to roam,
A body of England's, breathing English air,
Washed by the rivers, blest by suns of home.❞

'The Soldier', by Rupert Brooke. Although this poem was famous during the First World War, Rupert Brooke actually died in the Middle East in 1915. This was away from the trench warfare of the Western Front in France and Belgium. He died before the horrors of the Battles of Verdun and the Somme.

SOURCE B

❝'Good-morning, good-morning' the General said
When we met him last week on our way to the line.
Now the soldiers he smiled at are most of 'em dead,
And we're cursing his staff for incompetent swine.
'He's a cheery old card,' grunted Harry to Jack
As they slogged up to Arras with rifle and pack.
But he did for them both by his plan of attack.❞

'The General', by Siegfried Sassoon. Siegfried Sassoon fought on the Western Front. He survived the war and died in 1967.

" Bent double, like old beggars under sacks,
Knock-kneed, coughing like hags, we cursed through sludge,
Till on the haunting flares we turned our backs
And towards our distant rest began to trudge.
Men marched asleep. Many had lost their boots
But limped on, blood shod. All went lame; all blind;
Drunk with fatigue; deaf even to the hoots
Of tired, outstripped Five-Nines that dropped behind.

Gas! GAS! Quick boys! – an ecstacy of fumbling,
Fitting the clumsy helmets just in time;
But someone still was yelling out and stumbling
And flound'ring like a man in fire or lime…
Dim through the misty panes and thick green light,
As under a green sea, I saw him drowning.

In all my dreams, before my helpless sight,
He plunges at me, guttering, choking, drowning.

If in some smothering dreams you too could pace
Behind the waggon that we flung him in,
And watch the white eyes writhing in his face,
His hanging face, like a devil's sick of sin;
If you could hear, at every jolt, the blood
Come gargling from the froth corrupted lungs,
Obscene as cancer, bitter as the cud
Of vile, incurable sores on innocent tongues –
My friend, you would not tell with such high zest
To children ardent for some desperate glory,
The old Lie: Dulce et decorum est
Pro patria mori. "

'Dulce et decorum est', by Wilfred Owen. Wilfred Owen fought in the trenches and was killed in 1918. In this poem, the title and the last line mean, 'It is sweet and right to die for your country'. It was the kind of slogan which encouraged people to join the army.

USING THE EVIDENCE

① Look at Source A. What view of war do you get from this poem written by Rupert Brooke? Explain how he uses language to give you this view.

② Do Siegfried Sassoon (Source B) and Wilfred Owen (Source C) have a similar or a different view of war to Rupert Brooke? Explain how you decided. To do this:

◆ explain the view of war put forward in Sources B and C;

◆ describe the kind of language used in Sources B and C;
◆ show how these are similar to, or different from, the ideas and language used by Brooke.

③ The kinds of experience a person has can affect the ideas that they have. Look at the information about each of the three poets. Then explain how their experiences may have caused them to write in the way that they did.

CHANGING WEAPONS AND TACTICS ON THE WESTERN FRONT

The fighting on the Western Front was a new kind of warfare. Few soldiers had expected the war to turn into bloody attempts to break through lines of trenches. As the war dragged on, new weapons were invented, or used, to try to overcome the problems. New ways of fighting (tactics) were developed to use these new weapons. (See the box below.)

The problems to be overcome

◆ Machine guns killed huge numbers of attacking soldiers.

◆ Barbed wire made it hard to get to enemy trenches.

◆ Deep trenches meant soldiers could hide from artillery.

◆ It was hard to discover what was happening behind the enemy trenches.

◆ Mud made it hard to cross No Man's Land.

NEW WEAPONS

The tank. First used by the British in September 1916 in the Battle of the Somme. Armour gave protection from machine guns and barbed wire. But artillery bombardments churned up mud, and tanks often got bogged down.

Aircraft. Used to check where the enemy was and to tell artillery where their shells were falling.

Gas. First used by the Germans in April 1915 in the Battle of Ypres.

Submachine gun. First used by the Germans in 1918. It helped attacking infantry hit back at enemy machine gunners.

NEW TACTICS, USED BY 1918

Small groups of well-armed soldiers penetrated enemy trenches and attacked strong points.

Aircraft attacked from the air and gave information about enemy positions.

No long artillery bombardment warned the enemy of an attack. Instead, a mixture of shells were used containing explosives, gas, smoke and shrapnel. Headquarters and communications, as well as trenches, were hit. Tanks could then be used as the ground was not churned up.

• • • • • • • • • • • USING THE EVIDENCE • • • • • • • • • • •

❶ Look at the problems to be overcome. Explain which of the problems each of the new weapons and tactics were designed to overcome and how they were meant to do this.

❷ *Research.* Find out about one of the new weapons described in the tinted box

above. Decide on what questions you want your research to explore. Carry out your research and decide how successfully you answered your original questions. Keep a record of books, videos and CD-ROMs used and how useful they were.

DS The Nazi treatment of the Jews

Hitler and his followers, the Nazis, hated Jewish people. The Nazis said they hated Jews because:

◆ They said that it was Jews who had made the German government surrender at the end of the First World War, in 1918.

◆ They said that it was Jews who had started communism and who had made Russia become a Communist country after 1917.

◆ They said that rich Jews controlled the banks and many industries and became rich by making German people poor.

◆ They believed that Jews were not fully human. They called them 'inferior' and 'sub-human'.

◆ They said that the Germans were superior people, the 'Master Race'.

◆ They believed that Jews across the world were trying to rule the world and to destroy Germany.

The things that the Nazis said were not true. The person who started communism – Karl Marx – was a Jew and some rich business people were Jews, but they were not part of a worldwide plot to rule the world. Many Jews were very poor. Jews just wanted to get on with their own lives in the countries in which they lived. Germany had lost the First World War because it had been beaten in battle. The Nazi ideas were based not on facts but on hatred and fear.

Many people, though, believed the Nazis. These people wanted someone to blame for the problems in their lives. They knew that for hundreds of years many people in Europe had blamed the Jews for any problems that occurred. There was a tradition of blaming the Jews. The Nazis were part of this. They wanted someone to hate.

When Hitler became ruler of Germany, in 1933, the Nazis began to persecute the Jews. By the end of the Second World War, in 1945, the Nazis had murdered about six million Jewish people. Historians ask the question:

> **Did the Nazis plan this from the beginning, or did their plans for the Jews change over time?**

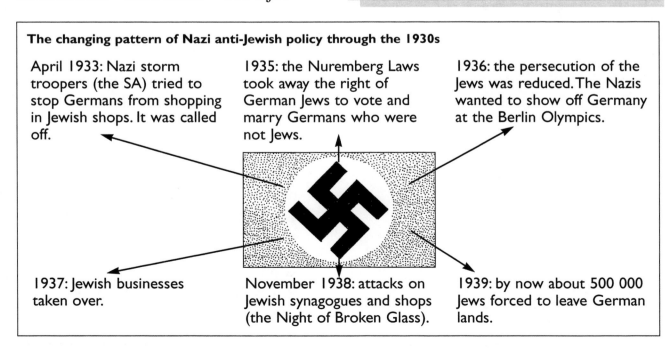

The changing pattern of Nazi anti-Jewish policy through the 1930s

April 1933: Nazi storm troopers (the SA) tried to stop Germans from shopping in Jewish shops. It was called off.

1935: the Nuremberg Laws took away the right of German Jews to vote and marry Germans who were not Jews.

1936: the persecution of the Jews was reduced. The Nazis wanted to show off Germany at the Berlin Olympics.

1937: Jewish businesses taken over.

November 1938: attacks on Jewish synagogues and shops (the Night of Broken Glass).

1939: by now about 500 000 Jews forced to leave German lands.

SOURCE A Nazi anti-Jewish poster. It dates from 1937. It makes Jews look violent (holding a whip) and greedy (holding money).

DER EWIGE JUDE

GROSSE POLITISCHE SCHAU IM BIBLIOTHEKSBAU DES DEUTSCHEN MUSEUMS ZU MÜNCHEN · AB 8. NOVEMBER 1937 · TÄGLICH GEÖFFNET VON 10-21 UHR

SOURCE B

❝Perhaps a million German lives would have been saved if 12,000–15,000 Jews had been killed with poison gas at the start of or during the war.❞

Written by Hitler in his book Mein Kampf *(My Struggle) in 1924. He was writing about the First World War. He blamed the Jews for Germany losing this war.*

SOURCE C

❝The Jew must get out of Germany, yes out of the whole of Europe. That will take some time yet, but will and must happen.❞

Hitler to another Nazi leader, Goebbels, in November 1937.

USING THE EVIDENCE

1 Look carefully at Sources A, B and C. Explain what each one tells you about Nazi attitudes towards the Jews.

2 Study the information in the box on the previous page. Some historians think that in the 1930s the Nazi treatment of the Jews, though always horrible, varied and did not follow a clear plan. Does the information here make you agree or disagree with this point of view? Write what you think, explaining why you think as you do.

3 Look at Source B. Why might some historians think that this is evidence to show that Hitler always had his own plan for what would happen to the Jews? To do this, you will need to find out yourself what happened to Jews in

the Second World War. This will also be useful preparation for what you will be exploring next.

4 *Research*. On these past two pages there has been information about a number of people or things connected with the Nazi Party. Look at the list below. Carry out your own research. Find out who or what these were. How important were they in Nazi Germany? What part did they play in the Nazi persecution of the Jews?

- ◆ Storm troopers (the **SA**)
- ◆ Joseph Goebbels
- ◆ *Mein Kampf*
- ◆ Nuremberg Laws, 1935
- ◆ The Night of Broken Glass (called *Kristallnacht* in German – 'Crystal Night').

HOW DID THE NAZI TREATMENT OF THE JEWS CHANGE IN THE EARLY YEARS OF THE SECOND WORLD WAR, 1939–41?

In September 1939, the Second World War started. By the summer of 1940, the Germans had conquered, or dominated, all the major countries of western, northern and eastern Europe. These countries stretched from France in the west to Poland in the east of Europe. Many Jews lived in these countries and now found themselves living under Nazi rule. Between 1939 and 1941, the Nazi treatment of these Jews changed.

How did Nazi treatment of the Jews change?

◆ Forcing Jews to leave land ruled by the Nazis stopped.

◆ In Poland, Jews were forced to move into special areas of some cities. These overcrowded areas were called ghettos.

◆ Healthy Jews were forced to work in labour camps.

◆ A plan to force Jews to go to the island of Madagascar, near Africa, was talked about but abandoned.

◆ Nazi leaders in Poland began to suggest ways of getting rid of Jews. There were ideas like **sterilising** Jews and working them to death.

Why did Nazi treatment of the Jews change?

◆ In wartime it was not possible for the Nazis to arrange for people to leave Europe.

◆ Instead of getting Jews out of Nazi territory (as they had done in the 1930s), the Nazis now found they had many more Jews in the lands they ruled. There were three million Jews living in Poland alone.

◆ The Nazis did not care what other countries thought of them anymore.

◆ It was easier to keep their treatment of the Jews secret in wartime.

◆ There was overcrowding and outbreaks of diseases in the Polish ghettos.

The turning point: the invasion of the USSR

In 1941 Hitler invaded Russia. He had always hated communism, and now he hoped to destroy Russia totally. He believed that Russia was run by Jews. There were nearly five million Jews living there. His attack on Russia gave him the chance to destroy both communists and Jews there. Then, by the end of 1941, it became clear that Germany might not be able to beat the Russians. So the Nazis turned their hatred and frustration on the Jews in even more terrible ways. They were determined that if they lost the war, no Jews would survive in Europe.

As the German army advanced into Russia, it was accompanied by special units of the **SS**. These were called the *Einsatzgruppen*. They had the job of killing Jews. Between June 1941 and April 1942, they murdered about 750 000. In the next year, they killed 1.5 million more.

USING THE EVIDENCE

❶ Look at the ways in which Nazi treatment of Jews changed between 1939 and 1941. Explain why it changed.

❷ How did the invasion of Russia begin a new way of treating Jews? Explain possible reasons why this happened.

THE FINAL SOLUTION

In January 1942, an important meeting took place on the edge of Berlin. It was called by a high-ranking SS officer called Reinhard Heydrich. He had been given the job of organising the murder of all the Jews still alive in Europe. The meeting is called the Wannsee Conference. It planned what the Nazis came to call 'the Final Solution to the Jewish problem'. Over the next year they planned and experimented with different ways to carry out the murder of all the Jews in Europe.

The Final Solution begins

◆ The mass shooting of Jews in eastern Europe continued. In the autumn of 1941, the Nazis began to transport German, Austrian and Czech Jews to the east to shoot them. They had been shooting Russian Jews since the summer.

◆ Special vans were used to gas Jews.

◆ Finally, gas chambers were set up in special extermination camps. The largest was at Auschwitz, in Poland. Most Jews died in these camps.

SOURCE A

❝I request you further to send me, in the near future, an overall plan covering the organisational, technical and material measures necessary for the accomplishment of the final solution of the Jewish question which we desire.❞

An order sent by Hitler's deputy, Göring, to Reinhard Heydrich in July 1941.

SOURCE B

❝This is a glorious page in our history and one that has never been written and can never be written. For we know how difficult we would have made it for ourselves if, on top of the bombing raids, the burdens and the **deprivations** of war, we still had Jews today in every town as secret **saboteurs**, agitators and troublemakers.❞

From a speech by the commander of the SS, Heinrich Himmler, to SS leaders in 1943. He is trying to justify the extermination of the Jews.

USING THE EVIDENCE

❶ Read Source A. What was the 'final solution' mentioned by Göring? Explain what it was and how it was carried out.

❷ Why do you think that in Source B Himmler said that the killing of the Jews was something that 'can never be written'?

❸ In this source, what excuse does Himmler make for murdering the Jews?

In the factories of death...

The extermination camps were factories of death. In them, millions of people were murdered. Thousands of trains took Jewish people from all over Europe to these extermination camps. They were carried in cattle trucks. The journeys took days. The people in the trucks had no food or water. Many died on the journey. Those that survived arrived at the camps exhausted and terrified.

When they arrived, the SS separated off those who could work. They were then taken away and worked to death in factories in the camps. The rest – the old, sick, women and little children – were gassed. Their bodies were burnt in great ovens called crematoria.

How did the Nazis manage to get people to go into the gas chambers? Look at the evidence on this sheet and you will begin to understand how they carried out these terrible crimes.

SOURCE A

"Particular efforts were made to reassure the arriving Jews. It was designed to look as far as possible like a normal station with a clock, ticket office, and timetables. There was also a large notice at the entrance to the camp: 'Attention Warsaw Jews! You are entering a **transit** camp from which you will be transported to a labour camp.'"

The extermination camp at Sobibor, Poland, described by the historians J. Noakes and G. Pridham.

SOURCE B

"The instruction was that everyone should take a bath and then go and get **disinfected**. Everyone bundled their clothing together and – **culmination** of the **illusion** – hung it up on a numbered peg. From there they went stark naked into the gas chambers."

An eyewitness remembers Auschwitz.

 WORD BOX

culmination the final thing.

deprivation not to have the things you need to live.

disinfected cleaned of germs.

illusion pretending something, to trick people.

SA a group within the Nazi Party.

saboteurs people who damage things.

SS Nazis who controlled the police and the camps.

sterilise treat people to stop them having children.

transit a place to stay for just a short time before moving on.

USING THE EVIDENCE

1 Look carefully at Sources A and B. Explain how they help you understand how the Nazis were able to make people do what they wanted them to do when they arrived at the camps.

2 What does Source B mean by 'culmination of the illusion'?

 # Redrawing the map of Europe, 1919

At the end of the First World War, the victorious allies redrew the map of central Europe. Many people who had once been ruled by the Austrians, Germans and Russians were given their own countries. But it was very hard deciding on the boundaries of these new countries. On this sheet you can draw your own boundaries for the new country of Czechoslovakia. The Czechs had once been ruled by Austria. Look at the map and follow the instructions.

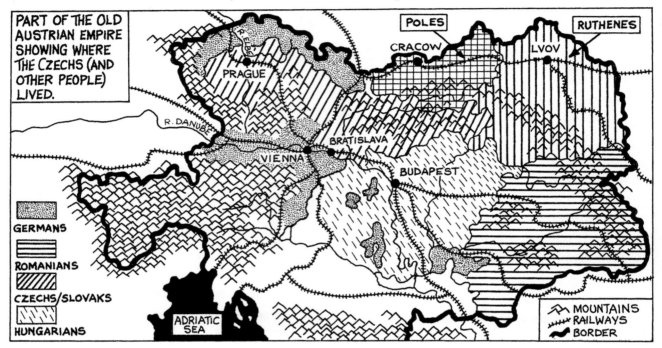

PART OF THE OLD AUSTRIAN EMPIRE SHOWING WHERE THE CZECHS (AND OTHER PEOPLE) LIVED.

GERMANS

ROMANIANS

CZECHS/SLOVAKS

HUNGARIANS

MOUNTAINS
RAILWAYS
BORDER

You will need this sheet, tracing paper, a pencil and rough paper to record your decisions. Lay the tracing paper on the map and decide on the 'best' boundaries for the new country of Czechoslovakia. When you are doing this, you must bear in mind the 'issues' below. You must decide which you think are the most important. Perhaps you can find a way to cover all of them. Perhaps you will decide that some are more important than others. However, you cannot completely ignore any of them. When you have drawn your boundary, give your work to a neighbour. They can mark you according to how well you have met all the 'issues'. Now you can see how hard the job was in 1919!

INVESTIGATION

Issues:

1 All Czechs and Slovaks must live in one country. Score 1–5.

2 Try not to include people other than Czechs or Slovaks in Czechoslovakia. Score 1–5.

3 Your country must be defended by frontiers running up to and including mountains. Score 1–5.

4 Your country must have an effective transport system, including railway junctions (where railway lines meet) and rivers. Score 1–5.

5 You must avoid having any part of your country that could easily be cut off by an enemy (e.g. if the country was too thin in the middle). Score 1–5.

A new kind of war: Blitzkrieg

Between 1939 and 1941, the Germans had many great victories in the Second World War. This was mainly because they used a new way of fighting a war.

This was called the Blitzkrieg. This is a German word, meaning 'Lightning War'. Look at the diagram on this sheet to see how it worked.

The Blitzkrieg (Lightning War)

STAGE 1. BOMBERS DESTROY THE ENEMY AIR FORCE ON THE GROUND.

STAGE 2. BOMBERS ATTACK MILITARY TARGETS. PARATROOPS LAND BEHIND ENEMY LINES.

STAGE 3. LIGHT TANKS AND SOLDIERS IN LORRIES RACE DEEP INTO ENEMY TERRITORY. THEY AVOID DEFENDED AREAS.

STAGE 4. DIVE BOMBERS ATTACK ADVANCING ENEMY SOLDIERS.

STAGE 5. HEAVY TANKS ADVANCE, AVOIDING CITIES AND DEFENDED AREAS.

STAGE 6. FOOT SOLDIERS, HELPED BY ARTILLERY, DEAL WITH FORTS OR CITIES STILL HELD BY THE ENEMY.

SOURCE A

❝Most people were still thinking of war in terms of trench lines, artillery bombardments, and infantry advances. The speed of the German advance, the precision with which the Panzer [tank] divisions sliced the Polish defence into pieces, was a terrible shock. Added to the armoured thrust was the air support in the shape of the Stuka dive bomber.❞

Ian V. Hogg, The Weapons that Changed the World (1986).

INVESTIGATION

1 Using the diagrams and Source A, explain what the Blitzkrieg was, how it worked and why it was so successful.

2 *Research.* Find out how the Blitzkrieg was used in the battle for France (1940) or in the invasion of Russia (1941). Whichever you choose, look at how the attack was planned and carried out, how people tried to oppose the Germans and how successful the Germans were.

The war on the Eastern Front

On 22 June 1941, Hitler launched an attack on Russia. Hitler hated communism and thought that the people of eastern Europe were inferior to the Germans. On top of this, he wanted land in eastern Europe for German people to move into and rule. He called this *lebensraum* (living Space). To get this, he planned to destroy Russia and enslave its people.

Hitler believed that Russia would collapse under the terrible force of a quick German victory. He was wrong. The fighting, on what was called the Eastern Front, became a savage and terrible war which eventually caused Germany to lose the Second World War.

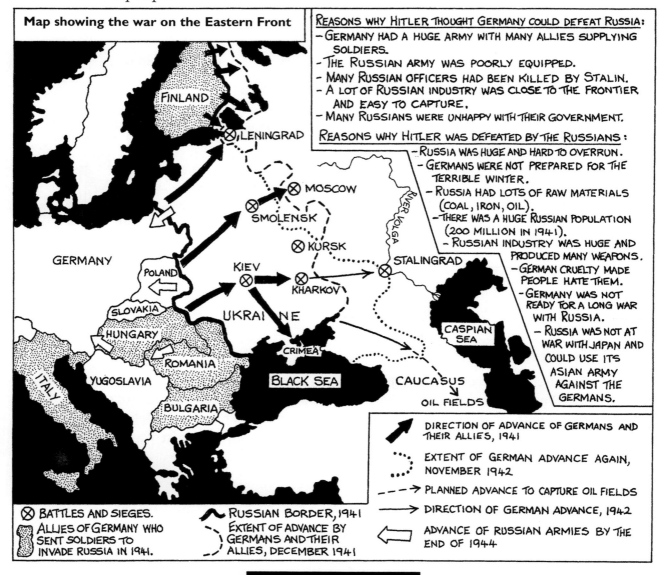

Map showing the war on the Eastern Front

REASONS WHY HITLER THOUGHT GERMANY COULD DEFEAT RUSSIA:
- GERMANY HAD A HUGE ARMY WITH MANY ALLIES SUPPLYING SOLDIERS.
- THE RUSSIAN ARMY WAS POORLY EQUIPPED.
- MANY RUSSIAN OFFICERS HAD BEEN KILLED BY STALIN.
- A LOT OF RUSSIAN INDUSTRY WAS CLOSE TO THE FRONTIER AND EASY TO CAPTURE.
- MANY RUSSIANS WERE UNHAPPY WITH THEIR GOVERNMENT.

REASONS WHY HITLER WAS DEFEATED BY THE RUSSIANS:
- RUSSIA WAS HUGE AND HARD TO OVERRUN.
- GERMANS WERE NOT PREPARED FOR THE TERRIBLE WINTER.
- RUSSIA HAD LOTS OF RAW MATERIALS (COAL, IRON, OIL).
- THERE WAS A HUGE RUSSIAN POPULATION (200 MILLION IN 1941).
- RUSSIAN INDUSTRY WAS HUGE AND PRODUCED MANY WEAPONS.
- GERMAN CRUELTY MADE PEOPLE HATE THEM.
- GERMANY WAS NOT READY FOR A LONG WAR WITH RUSSIA.
- RUSSIA WAS NOT AT WAR WITH JAPAN AND COULD USE ITS ASIAN ARMY AGAINST THE GERMANS.

⊗ BATTLES AND SIEGES.
▨ ALLIES OF GERMANY WHO SENT SOLDIERS TO INVADE RUSSIA IN 1941.
∿ RUSSIAN BORDER, 1941
⌒ EXTENT OF ADVANCE BY GERMANS AND THEIR ALLIES, DECEMBER 1941

→ DIRECTION OF ADVANCE OF GERMANS AND THEIR ALLIES, 1941
⋯ EXTENT OF GERMAN ADVANCE AGAIN, NOVEMBER 1942
--→ PLANNED ADVANCE TO CAPTURE OIL FIELDS
→ DIRECTION OF GERMAN ADVANCE, 1942
⇦ ADVANCE OF RUSSIAN ARMIES BY THE END OF 1944

INVESTIGATION

1 Look carefully at the information shown on the map. Explain why Hitler thought that Germany and its allies could defeat Russia.

2 Again using the map information, explain why Germany was defeated.

EX The war in the Far East

The Second World War really was a 'world war': it was fought in Europe, Africa and Asia and on the seas of the world. In Asia, the war was fought between Japan and its allies on one side and Britain and the USA and their allies on the other. The war in Europe started in September 1939. In Asia it did not start until December 1941. But for China it had started much earlier, as Japan had attacked China in 1931. The war in Asia, like that in Europe, ended in 1945. In that year, Japan finally surrendered.

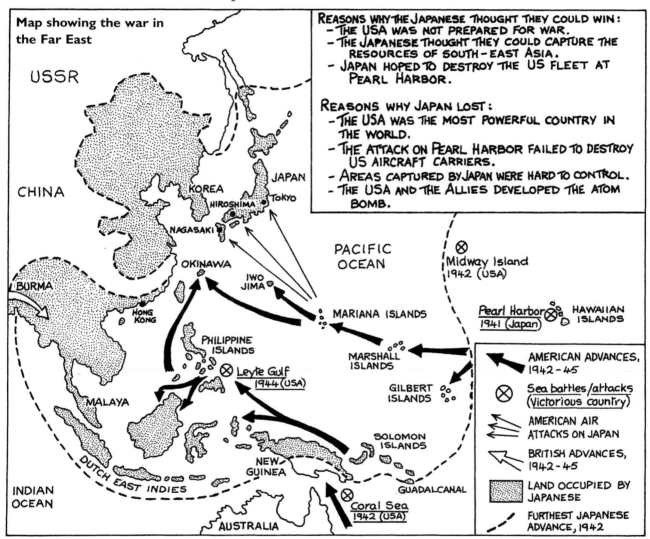

Map showing the war in the Far East

REASONS WHY THE JAPANESE THOUGHT THEY COULD WIN:
- THE USA WAS NOT PREPARED FOR WAR.
- THE JAPANESE THOUGHT THEY COULD CAPTURE THE RESOURCES OF SOUTH-EAST ASIA.
- JAPAN HOPED TO DESTROY THE US FLEET AT PEARL HARBOR.

REASONS WHY JAPAN LOST:
- THE USA WAS THE MOST POWERFUL COUNTRY IN THE WORLD.
- THE ATTACK ON PEARL HARBOR FAILED TO DESTROY US AIRCRAFT CARRIERS.
- AREAS CAPTURED BY JAPAN WERE HARD TO CONTROL.
- THE USA AND THE ALLIES DEVELOPED THE ATOM BOMB.

USSR

CHINA

KOREA

JAPAN

HIROSHIMA Tokyo

NAGASAKI

OKINAWA

IWO JIMA

BURMA

HONG KONG

PHILIPPINE ISLANDS

Leyte Gulf 1944 (USA)

MALAYA

DUTCH EAST INDIES

INDIAN OCEAN

NEW GUINEA

AUSTRALIA

Coral Sea 1942 (USA)

PACIFIC OCEAN

Midway Island 1942 (USA)

Pearl Harbor 1941 (Japan) HAWAIIAN ISLANDS

MARIANA ISLANDS

MARSHALL ISLANDS

GILBERT ISLANDS

SOLOMON ISLANDS

GUADALCANAL

AMERICAN ADVANCES, 1942-45

Sea battles/attacks (Victorious country)

AMERICAN AIR ATTACKS ON JAPAN

BRITISH ADVANCES, 1942-45

LAND OCCUPIED BY JAPANESE

FURTHEST JAPANESE ADVANCE, 1942

INVESTIGATION

1 To attack the USA seems to have been inviting defeat. Why did the Japanese think they could win the war that they had started?

2 Describe the course of the war in the Far East and explain why, in the end, it was Japan which was defeated.

3 *Research.* Find out about one of the major battles shown on the map. Decide what questions you wish to explore. Carry out your research. Explain how successful you were in answering your questions. Make a list of the sources of information you used and how useful they were to you.

The dropping of the first atom bomb

At 8.15 a.m. on 6 August 1945, the US bomber *Enola Gay* dropped the first ever atomic bomb on the Japanese city of Hiroshima. This was called Operation Centreboard, and it caused the deaths of 80 000 people, as well as injuring 35 000. Later, many more died, and the final number of people killed was about 138 890. Many of these died from radiation sickness caused by this new weapon.

Still Japan did not surrender. At 11.02 a.m. on 9 August, another US bomber, called *Bock's Car*, dropped a second atom bomb. This time it was dropped on the Japanese city of Nagasaki. In total, some 48 857 people were killed then, or in the years to come, from their injuries and from radiation sickness.

Ever since these attacks took place, people have argued whether these weapons needed to be used to stop the war with Japan. Look at the arguments and decide what you think.

The case for dropping the atom bombs:

◆ It would quickly end the war with Japan which had dragged on since 1941.

◆ The Japanese had fought so hard and suicidally on Pacific islands such as Luzon and Okinawa that the USA thought an invasion of Japan could cause the war to last another year at the cost of a million US lives.

◆ From July 1945, Japan began to train an army of suicide soldiers to attack US ships if the USA invaded Japan.

◆ On 30 July the Japanese rejected Allied demands for surrender.

◆ The cities attacked were military targets. Hiroshima was an industrial centre, Nagasaki an important port.

◆ Ordinary bombing raids were as bad. A firebomb raid on Tokyo on 9 March 1945 had killed 83 000 people.

The case against dropping the atom bombs:

◆ Japan was almost ready to surrender before the bombs were dropped. On 30 July the Japanese Prime Minister had only meant to say that Japan was not ready to reply to Allied demands for surrender. His words were mistranslated by the Allies.

◆ The USA and Britain really wanted to drop the atom bomb to frighten the Russians. They feared that after the war Russia would be a threat.

◆ No city is just a military target. To destroy a whole city must mean the slaughter of many unarmed civilians.

◆ The Allies made it difficult for Japan to surrender by a call for 'unconditional surrender'.

◆ It was probably Russia declaring war on Japan on 8 August which caused Japan to surrender on 15 August.

INVESTIGATION

Prepare a debate on the issue of whether the atomic bombs should have been used against Japan. Use this sheet and carry out your own research on the atomic attacks. Look at the moral (right and wrong) arguments as well as the military ones.

Take one side of the argument and argue the case for it, while others in the class argue for the other side. Afterwards, write about both points of view, ending with your own opinion based on all the evidence examined.

EX Why did Germany lose the Second World War?

In the summer of 1941, Germany looked to have almost won the Second World War. Yet by the summer of 1945 Germany had been completely defeated and divided up amongst the victorious Allies (Britain, Russia, USA and France). History students are often asked to examine small chunks from the writings of historians to try to understand their opinions. This is an opportunity to practise your skills on a much longer piece of writing. It is also an opportunity to compare ideas found in school textbooks with more detailed secondary sources written by historians.

SOURCE A

66 By the beginning of 1945 the accumulation of Germany's reverses had produced disintegration. Hitler no longer had an army capable of sustaining the fight, he had so little fuel that his soldiers had orders to siphon off the fuel in a disabled tank before abandoning it, he scarcely had an air force at all, his anti-aircraft units were manned by a mixture of regulars, prisoners-of-war and teenagers down to sixteen, and his secret weapons had not worked the miracles that were expected of them.

After 1942 the Luftwaffe [German air force] formations were outnumbered, its airfields bombed and its new types and new weapons failed it. The HE177 four-engined bomber appeared in 1943 but in small numbers only and after Germany's chance to affect the issue by heavy bombing had passed; the Luftwaffe was never able to drop the super-bombs which were dropped by its enemies on German cities.

During 1942–3 the Luftwaffe had been called upon to fight on four fronts. It was not strong enough to do so. Great numbers of aircraft were drawn into battles in which the Luftwaffe was gradually ground out of existence. In 1944 a new front was added in the west. This was the last straw.

Germany did not manage to produce the Second World War's most startling new weapon – the nuclear bomb. On the main fronts the German armies were overwhelmed by superior numbers and material. 99

P. Calvocoressi and G. Wint, Total War (1972).

INVESTIGATION

❶ Construct a spider diagram of the reasons suggested in this source for the defeat of Germany.

❷ If you can find any links between these various reasons, show them with dotted lines. Explain what these links are.

❸ Which do you think seems the most important of these reasons? Explain how you decided by referring to the other reasons as well.

❹ Look in your school textbooks or library books. What reasons do they give for Germany's defeat? In what ways are they similar to/different from Source A?

F Letter from the trenches

In the Depth Study on the Western Front, you will find a sheet telling you what it was like in the trenches. On that sheet you are asked to write an imaginary letter home. In your letter, you are telling people at home about life in the trenches. You can use this sheet to help you write that letter.

Letter home from the trenches

Dear..............

We are living in trenches. These are like ditches in the ground [mention and explain 'dug-outs', 'sandbags', 'barbed wire', 'lice', 'trench foot']...
....
....
....
....

Life can sometimes be boring [mention 'plum and apple jam', 'cleaning your rifle', 'repairing the trench']......................................
....
....
....

It is very dangerous here [mention 'snipers', 'bombardments']
....
....
....

Sometimes we have to leave the trench [mention 'raids','battles', 'No Man's Land']..
....
....

I wish I was home. Perhaps I will get some leave soon. Then I will come home for a few days.

Love..

F The first day of the Battle of the Somme

Use this sheet to help you organise your answers to the questions on the first day of the Battle of the Somme which can be found in the **Depth Study: The Western Front.**

1 Cross out the wrong words each time you come to a choice:

◆ Source A shows that lots of men were **killed/frightened/deafened** by **planes/ machine guns/rockets.** This was not supposed to happen because the **British/American/Chinese** hoped that their **ships/artillery/tanks** would have smashed the German **planes/machine guns/rockets** before the battle even started.

◆ Source B shows that German soldiers were still **dead/alive/asleep** because they had sheltered in **trees/dug-outs/ houses.** The British had thought they would all be **dead/alive/asleep.** Then the English **warships/artillery/planes** began to kill their own men. This was not meant to happen. They were meant to kill only **Russians/ Germans/Georgians.**

2 Choose the right problems from the Options Box and put them on the arms of the spider diagram. Put one problem on each arm.

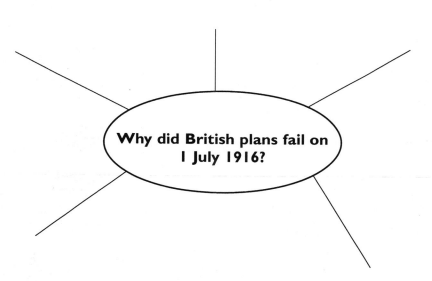

Why did British plans fail on
1 July 1916?

Options Box:

◆ Germans hid in dug-outs. They were not killed.
◆ Too few British.
◆ British shells hit own men.
◆ Ground too muddy.
◆ Too few heavy guns.
◆ Germans used gas.
◆ Secret plans captured by the Germans.
◆ Shells did not explode.
◆ Weather too cold.
◆ Barbed wire not destroyed.

Things which may help you answer questions 2b and 3 in the Depth Study section:

◆ Barbed wire made it hard for British soldiers to reach the German trenches.
◆ German machine guns had the power to kill thousands of British.
◆ Deep German dug-outs kept Germans safe from British bombardment.
◆ British bombardment could not cut barbed wire or hit some German targets.
◆ Attacking after dawn meant the Germans could see the British.

 # Why did Hitler come to power in Germany in 1933?

In 1933, Hitler became the ruler of Germany. He was the leader of a group of people called the Nazi Party (the German National Socialist Party). Historians often ask the question:

> **Why did Hitler come to power in Germany in 1933?**

To answer this important question, historians need to:

◆ find out all the different reasons;

◆ decide which are long-term reasons and which are short-term reasons;

◆ decide what things Hitler did to get power and what things were done by other people, or events;

◆ explain how these different reasons worked together;

◆ decide which were the most important reasons.

On this sheet you will find help with answering this important question. But before you do this, look at pages 28–29 of *In Search of History, The Twentieth Century World*. These pages will explain what happened in Germany between the end of the First World War and Hitler becoming ruler of Germany.

'Why did Hitler come to power in Germany in 1933?'

First, write an introduction:

'This essay is about…' (Write what the essay is about. Write what you are trying to do. Explain that you will look at different kinds of causes. Explain that you will look at things Hitler did to get power and things done by other people and events. Finish by writing that you will try to decide which are the most important causes.)

Then, the main part of the essay:

'There are lots of different reasons why Hitler came to rule Germany. Some are long-term reasons…' (Write about how angry and worried Germans were in the 1920s: fights between rival political groups, having to pay for the damage caused in the First World War, prices going up in the great inflation.) *'These reasons made many Germans want a strong leader to sort out their problems and make Germany powerful again.'*

'Hitler did things to make people notice him…' (Write about how he tried to arrange a march on Berlin. How he was put in prison. How he wrote his ideas in a book called *My Struggle*.) *'Despite this, not many people voted for him…'* (Mention how things began to get better in Germany in the middle 1920s, so the Germans did not want a strong leader. In 1928 less than a million Germans voted for Hitler and the Nazis.)

'In this difficult time, Hitler was helped by powerful people…' (Write about businessmen giving him money as he was against communism. A printer printed his book for nothing.)

'The short-term reasons he came to power were that Germany had lots of problems after 1929…' (Write about the Wall Street Crash. Lots of Germans became unemployed. Germans were desperate – they turned to Hitler, hoping he could sort out the problems.)

Last, write a conclusion:

'There were lots of reasons why Hitler came to power…' (Say which you think were the most important.)

F The road to war, 1935–39

In 1939, the Second World War started. Historians sometimes call the events which led to the Second World War 'the road to war'. Some historians think that if Britain and France had acted differently Hitler might have been stopped.

In the diagram on this sheet you will see 'the road to war'. At certain points, there are important events. By each event are listed different things that Britain and France could have done. Decide what you would have done.

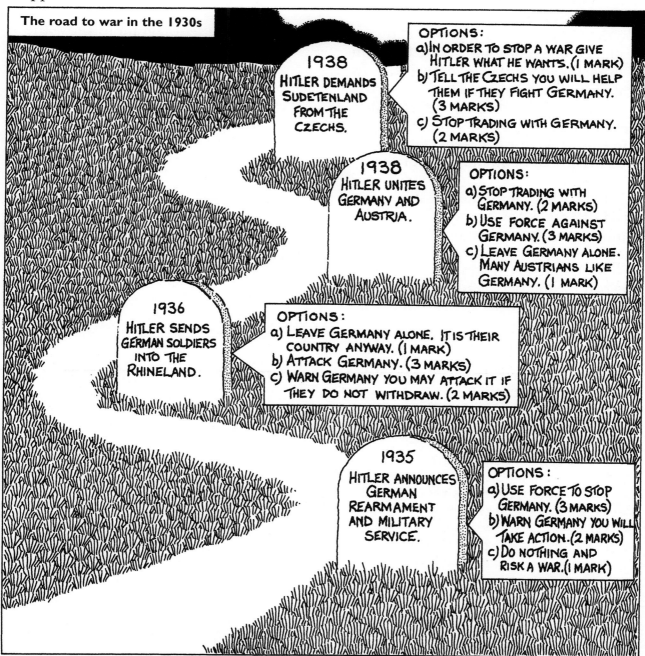

What did you choose? Add up your marks:

4–6 marks   You gave Hitler what he wanted. You did not stop the Second World War.
7–9 marks   You threatened Hitler. You might have stopped the Second World War.
10–12 marks   You stood up to Hitler. You had a small war but stopped the Second World War.

What events caused a 'Cold War' to start after the Second World War?

During the Second World War, Russia had fought Nazi Germany and had been an Ally (a friend) of Britain and the USA. Once Nazi Germany was beaten, this friendship quickly came to an end. The USA feared that Russia wanted to make all of Europe and the whole world communist. In communist countries, only the Communist Party was allowed to rule. People did not have the freedom to complain about the government. This is called a 'dictatorship'. The USA and its friends thought this was wrong. They were 'democracies'. In a democracy, people can vote for different political parties. They *can* complain about the government.

On the other hand, the Russians feared that the USA wanted to destroy communism. Russia had been invaded twice in the 20th century and did not trust the countries in western Europe. This bad feeling between the USA and Russia became known as the 'Cold War'.

Look at pages 42–43 of *In Search of History, The Twentieth Century World* to get an overview of how this 'Cold War' started. It mentions five events which happened between 1947 and 1955 which caused bad feelings between the USA and Russia.

1 Make a spider diagram to show the five main events. To help you, they are also printed in the box below. But be careful. There are some events in the same box which are wrong. Only choose the right events to put on your spider diagram. A sixth event (mentioned on page 44 of your textbook) has already been put on the spider diagram, to help you.

2 Look at all the events that you have put on your spider diagram. Briefly explain how each one of them might have led to bad feelings between the USA and Russia.

Events:

- 1947: Communists look as if they might take over Greece. Start of Truman Doctrine.
- 1948: France attacks Russia.
- 1947: USA starts Marshall Plan.
- 1950: USA explodes first atom bomb.
- 1949: Russia invades Italy.
- 1947: Russia sets up Cominform.
- 1951: Britain makes friends with Russia.
- 1949: Western countries set up NATO.
- 1954: NATO attacks Russia.
- 1953: War between Greece and Spain.
- 1955: Russia sets up the Warsaw Pact.

1948: Russians try to force USA and its Allies out of Berlin

What events caused a 'Cold War' to start after WW2?

Avenue
London to P

CW00664359

sus**trans**
JOIN THE MOVEMENT

JOIN THE MOVEMENT

2 Cathedral Square
College Green
Bristol
BS1 5DD
0117 926 8893
www.sustrans.org.uk

First edition printed 2013, reprinted 2014

ISBN 978-1-901389-88-3

Front cover photo: Notre Dame, Paris
© Jean-Pierre Dalbéra
Rear cover photo: Westminster Bridge, London
© Richard Peace
Frontispiece: Traffic-free on the Avenue Verte near Forges-les-Eaux
© John Grimshaw

CONTENTS

INTRODUCTION..4

IN THE UK

159 km / 99 miles
LONDON - HORLEY 53 km / 33 miles..14
HORLEY - GROOMBRIDGE 39 km / 24 miles...32
GROOMBRIDGE - NEWHAVEN 67 km / 42 miles..42

IN FRANCE

TO THE ROUTE SPLIT 82 km / 51 miles
DIEPPE - NEUFCHÂTEL-EN-BRAY 37 km / 23 miles...54
NEUFCHÂTEL-EN-BRAY - GOURNAY 45 km / 28 miles.....................................64

WESTERN OPTION
120 km / 74 miles
GOURNAY - THE VEXIN 60 km / 37 miles...74
THE VEXIN - ST-GERMAIN 60 km / 37 miles..84

EASTERN OPTION
184 km / 114 miles
GOURNAY - BEAUVAIS 39 km / 24 miles..94
BEAUVAIS - SENLIS 67 km / 42 miles...102
SENLIS - L'ISLE ADAM 37 km / 23 miles...112
L'ISLE ADAM - ST-GERMAIN 41 km / 25 miles..120

AFTER THE ROUTE OPTIONS REJOIN
ST-GERMAIN - PARIS 37 km / 23 miles...128

ROUTE TOTALS
WESTERN OPTION 398 KM 247 MILES
EASTERN OPTION 462 KM 287 MILES

The Avenue Verte - London to Paris by Bike

The route

Launched in summer 2012, the Avenue Verte cycle route connects two iconic sights, the London Eye and Notre Dame cathedral, letting you pedal between the hearts of both cities on traffic-free routes and quiet roads, taking in some fantastic landscapes along the way.

In England the route threads its way out of London on the leafy Wandle Trail before crossing the classic English countryside of the Downs and Weald, with their half-timbered villages and ancient churches. It then skirts along the beaches of the south coast, finally arriving at the Newhaven-Dieppe ferry.

In France, you pick up the superbly surfaced Pays de Bray Avenue Verte all the way to Forges-les-Eaux through the rolling Bray countryside in rural Normandy.

The route then splits, the western option following a traffic-free path down the Epte valley before minor roads and tracks take you across the sleepy, rolling countryside of the Vexin, a protected regional park which cosies up to the edge of the greater Paris urban area.

The longer eastern option passes through the wonderful cathedral city of Beauvais and the splendidly ancient towns of Senlis and Chantilly, then heads over to the pretty river Oise for a final stretch along the river.

The route options rejoin for the final 60 km (40 miles) to Notre Dame,

© Sue Nottingham

Along the Epte Valley

much of it traffic-free, taking in lovely sections of the River Seine, once the haunt of the Impressionist painters. In Paris itself you follow cycle paths along the Saint-Denis and Saint-Martin canals before cycling along quiet streets to the river Seine and France's most revered and famous building, Notre Dame cathedral.

Background

The Avenue Verte project has involved East Sussex, West Sussex and Surrey County Councils, Transport for London (TfL) and Sustrans, in partnership with Le Departement Seine-Maritime in France.

The idea for this iconic route had long been planned on both sides of the channel, but the catalyst came with the 2012 London Olympics which seemed an opportune moment to turn plans into reality.

Whilst the initial route contains some sections that are of interim standard, the route retains its initial stated aims of creating an 'alternative, car-free, gentler route between London and Paris for walkers and cyclists and especially for families.'

The route will continue to be developed on the French side especially, to include more traffic-free sections and greenways.

Sustrans and the National Cycle Network

 Sustrans are a leading UK charity enabling people to travel by foot, bike or public transport for more of the journeys they make every day. Sustrans are behind many groundbreaking projects including the National Cycle Network, over 14,000 miles of signed cycling and walking routes, on traffic-free paths and quiet roads across the UK.

Created from one of the first ever National Lottery grants in 1995, the popularity of the Network has grown enormously and it now carries over a million walking and cycling journeys daily and passes within a mile of 57% of the population (for examples of signs you will see when cycling on the National Cycle Network see overleaf).

The maintenance and the development of the National Cycle Network and Sustrans' other projects rely on the kind donations of Sustrans supporters. **Make your move and support Sustrans today!** Visit www.sustrans.org.uk or call 0845 838 0651 to find out more.

Route surface and signage

Most of the route shown in green on the following maps is traffic-free and suitable for new and returning cyclists and families.

There are some short sections of the route that use bridleways where the route surface is variable and can be rough; these are not suitable for road bikes (they are mainly on the western route option in France as it crosses the Vexin). There are on-road route alternatives here though.

At the time of writing around 40% of the route is traffic-free. The traffic-free proportion will increase over time.

The Avenue Verte uses a mix of established National Cycle Network routes 2, 4, 20 and 21 as follows:

Route	From	To
NCN 4	London Eye	Chelsea Bridge
NCN 20	Wandle Trail at Earlsfield	Merstham, north of Redhill
NCN 21	Merstham	Crawley
NCN 20	Crawley	Crawley
NCN 21	Crawley	Polegate
NCN 2	Polegate	Newhaven

Note that Avenue Verte logos may only be provided intermittently on some sections and are often provided as 'patch' signs on existing, larger NCN signs but you will have the reassurance of more continuous NCN signing in between.

The Avenue Verte also follows sections of local route in London: Cycle Superhighway 8 very briefly across Chelsea Bridge and past Battersea Park, and London Cycle Network Routes 5 then 3 from Battersea Park up to Clapham and Wandsworth Commons then joining NCN 20, the Wandle Trail, near Earlsfield train station. There is also a local route link between NCN 20 and 21 in Crawley.

You will see two official Avenue Verte logos (left) on signs in both the UK and France. Yellow and black signs mean a temporary route.

Avenue Verte logos will often appear together with National Cycle Network signs (right)

In France the full Avenue Verte logo signing appears more often along with the widespread green and white cycle route signing that can be found in many places across the country. Signs for temporary sections of the Avenue Verte are yellow, as above. Until 2012 France lacked a plan for a national signing system and green and white signage will probably remain the most frequently encountered type for some time to come, but there are also many local variants. However, from 2013 there are plans to standardise French cycle signage creating a national network from the many fine routes that already exist on the ground and which will be added to in future.

Eurovelo routes are those which run across European boundaries and bear the familiar yellow stars on blue background logo. National routes within France will be designated as *Véloroutes* and have their own consistent signage. The system however, is in its infancy.

How long does it take?

This guide splits the route into chapters each based around a reasonably comfortable day's ride, with eight chapters on the western option and ten on the eastern. These are based on distances an average leisure rider would find comfortable. Allow extra riding time for the urban sections at either end as they involve more complex navigation and present a plethora of sightseeing opportunities.

If you want to tackle slightly bigger daily mileages the western option is easily squeezed down into a week by combining the first two days' riding in France, going straight from Dieppe to Gournay, as some 47 km (29 miles) of this 82 km (51 miles) section are on a superb, fast, traffic-free tarmac path. Tackling the eastern option in seven days is a bit more of a challenge but a sensible option could be achieved by going straight from Dieppe to Gournay in a single day's ride with subsequent days as follows:

Gournay → Senlis 106 km (66 miles)

Senlis → Conflans-Sainte-Honorine 66 km (41 miles)

Conflans-Sainte-Honorine → Paris 58 km (36 miles)

Further information online

www.francevelotourisme.com

A new French organisation promoting use of the developing network of long distance cycle routes, and a very useful source of English language information about the route, including maps, stage information and accommodation.

www.avenuevertelondonparis.com

This dedicated website has been put together in French and English. There are wonderful, detailed zoomable route maps showing accommodation options and many other services as well as lots of advice on the practicalities of tackling the route.

www.sustrans.org.uk

Founders of the UK's National Cycle Network and charitable campaigners for sustainable transport in general. See page 5 for more information.

www.eurovelo.org.uk

EuroVelo is the European cycle route network. It is a project of the European Cyclists' Federation (ECF) that aims to develop a network of high-quality cycling routes that connect the whole continent.

Practical Information

Preparing for the ride

Before you go, check your bike is in good condition - make sure the tyres are pumped up and the seat and handlebars are set to the right position. Also check brakes and lights are in good order and tightly secured, gears are changing smoothly, and gear and brake cables aren't rusty or frayed. Wheel quick releases should be in the closed position and the chain should be clean and lubricated.

What to wear

You shouldn't need to invest in lots of specialist clothing or footwear to enjoy the Avenue Verte. Wear thin layers which you can easily add or remove as you go, and choose light, breathable fabrics. Take a waterproof, hat and gloves (your extremities are more exposed when cycling), and if you're going to be cycling at night, take a bright, reflective top. Padded shorts can be helpful for extra comfort when riding too.

Useful kit list

- Puncture repair kit & pump
- Tyre levers & spare inner tubes
- Water bottle
- Bike oil or lubricant
- Bike lights
- Bike 'multi-tool' or Allen keys & adjustable spanner
- Bike lock, bungee cords & panniers to carry luggage

Bike accessories

A bike bell is a must for any cyclist as it lets you warn pedestrians of your approach. Wearing a helmet is not compulsory in France or England so the decision is ultimately a question of individual choice – however although helmets can't prevent accidents from happening they can protect you if they do occur and are especially recommended for young children.

Comfortable clothing and hybrid bikes are ideal for exploring the Avenue Verte. Here the route approaches Paris by the river Seine.

Much of the Avenue Verte is ideal for leisure cycling; here at Parc Pierre Lagravère approaching Paris

Cycling with children

The Avenue Verte is generally easygoing cycling and even when you do pass through hills the gradients tend to be reasonably gentle. It also has a good amount of traffic-free riding, all of which make it well suited to cycling with children.

If cycling with a family, remember to keep children in front of you on roads (or in between if there are two of you), and take special care at road junctions. Plan day stages carefully with plenty of refreshment stops, and remember to keep toddlers wrapped up so they don't lose heat when you're pedalling.

What kind of bike?

The best bike to tackle the Avenue Verte on is a hybrid bike, rather than a racer, due to the small sections with a rough surface. However you can use any bike.

Good cycling code

- Always follow the Highway Code, or French Code de la Route
- Cycle at a safe and responsible speed
- Give way to pedestrians
- Remember that some people are hard of hearing and visually impaired. Don't assume they can see or hear you
- Where there are wheelchair users or horse riders please give way
- Ring a bell or call out to warn of your approach – acknowledge people who give way to you
- Follow the Countryside Code; in particular respect crops, livestock and wildlife and take litter home
- Take special care at junctions, when cycling downhill and on loose surfaces
- Always carry food, water, a puncture repair kit, a map and waterproofs
- Keep your bike roadworthy; use lights in poor visibility
- Consider wearing a helmet and high visibility clothing

Cycling in France

It is simply a pleasure. France is a cycling nation and accords cyclists status on the road and some great facilities, from wonderful off-road riding to city centre automated bike hire. If you're unfamiliar with cycling in France here are a few handy tips.

You will no doubt know to ride on the right hand side of the road, path or track you are on. However, there is an old rule of the road called priority from the right which is still a consideration. In the absence of all other signs this rule still applies - it means traffic joining from the right has priority - even if on a seemingly minor road. If, though, your road has yellow diamonds on white background signs you have priority, until you come to one with a black line through. Side roads often have stop or give way markings and roundabouts also usually have give way systems so this rule won't apply here. However, this is not always so, and in any case it's wise to make a habit of treating traffic coming from the right with extra caution as some drivers may still adhere to the old law!

In France traffic lights go directly from red to green but do go to amber between green and red. A red light accompanied by an amber flashing arrow pointing to the right means you can turn right as long as you give way to other vehicles. A green light replaced by a flashing yellow light means you may proceed but have to give way to crossing traffic and pedestrians.

Where a cycle path is indicated by a white bicycle on a circular blue background, it is obligatory to use it in preference to the road. Where it is on a rectangular background, it is optional.

Vélib bike hire Paris

Travel information

Bikes on UK trains

Bikes are carried free of charge on most UK trains, but spaces are usually limited and reservations are sometimes required, especially on intercity services. You can reserve a space for your bike when you book or by calling the train operator. There are normally no restrictions on folding bikes. For full UK travel information visit **www.nationalrail.co.uk** or call 08457 48 49 50

Eurostar

You have three options for taking bikes on Eurostar:

1. Full sized bikes taken on the same train as you. These must be booked in advance (i.e. at the same time as booking your ticket) and cost £30 per bike one way. Allow time before boarding to take it to the baggage office, a little distance from the boarding area at both London St Pancras International and Paris Gare du Nord.

2. As registered luggage, travelling on a separate train to passengers and arriving within 24 hours of the passenger. Bagged bikes of length 85-120cm cost £10 per bike. The costs rises to £25 per bike if the bagged bike is over 120cm long or if fully assembled and not bagged. This service can be booked on the day of travel.

3. As hand luggage on the train with you. The bike must be bagged and not more than 85cm in length (in practice this usually means folders only). Eurostar is at **www.eurostar.com** or telephone 08705 186 186.

French train operators

French railways (SNCF) will carry, free and as normal luggage, folding bikes or bagged, dismantled bikes to a maximum of 120cm x 90cm.

Many French trains will carry fully assembled bikes. This service is generally free of charge but on TGV high-speed trains bike spaces, if available, must be booked in advance.

Along the Avenue Verte you may want to make particular use of trains in and around Paris and express trains are great for getting your bike into and out of central Paris in one short hop:

(RER) (A) RER services are recognisable by an RER logo plus line logo and there are five lines, A to E, operating in the greater Paris area. **www.ratp.fr/en**

Transilien services run within the Île de France area and, like RER services, carry bikes outside of morning and evening rush hours.

French rail tickets can be booked online from the UK - Rail Europe can give you details of the current system of doing this and can also sell you your train tickets direct.

www.sncf.com is the website for French trains. **www.sncf.co.uk** and **www.raileurope.co.uk** offer similar online booking services.

Rail Europe can be contacted on 08708 371 371 or in person Monday to Saturday at 178, Piccadilly, London.

Ferry

Going as a foot passenger between Newhaven and Dieppe you usually have to board with the motor vehicles and lash your bike to the deck side or elsewhere as directed by crew. When booking you should include your bike (which needs booking on even if there's no charge for it; bike space is limited) LD Lines run two ferry crossings a day from Newhaven to Dieppe (and vice versa), taking around four hours.

For more information visit **www.ldlines.co.uk** or call 0844 576 8836

European Bike Express

This is easy and efficient travel specifically for cyclists. Stops in Northern France for 2013 include Calais, St-Witz north of Paris (so handy for a UK return after cycling the Avenue Verte - take RER line D to Survilliers Fosses and St-Witz is about 2.5 km / 1.5 miles from here), Thionville, Nancy, Nemours and Auxerre. Their air conditioned coaches have reclining seats and pull a purpose-built trailer capable of carrying bikes and bike trailers. Runs throughout the summer serving western France on an Atlantic route and central, Alpine and Mediterranean France (and even into Spain) on other routes. Single or return journeys. UK pick-up points down the eastern side of England between North Yorkshire and Kent, with an M62 / M6 feeder service on certain dates.

www.bike-express.co.uk
3, Newfield Lane, South Cave. HU15 2JW   01430 422111

© Nick Lazar

Travel in style between Newhaven and Dieppe

Booking accommodation in Paris should be done in advance as it can be tricky to find hotels with storage for bikes. Here the Avenue Verte passes Porte-St-Martin in the heart of Paris.

Accommodation listings and contacts

The listings in the guide shown with blue numbering ❶ have been chosen because they are both near the route, not too highly priced and usually quite near the beginning or end of the day sections.

This is of course just a cross-section of what is available and by travelling a little further off the route plenty more accommodation opportunities open up. There are several national organisations that also offer accommodation or listings services that might prove useful:

UK

Beds for Cyclists **www.bedsforcyclists.co.uk**
Camping and Caravanning Club **www.campingandcaravanningclub.co.uk**
Visit Britain **www.visitbritain.com**
Youth Hostels Association **www.yha.org.uk**
Independent Hostel Guide **www.independenthostelguide.co.uk**

France

France Velo Tourisme **www.francevelotourisme.com**
FVT manage the Accueil Velo (Cyclists Welcome) scheme and details of accredited providers will soon be shown on their route maps with an orange logo.
FUAJ (French YHA equivalent) **www.fuaj.org**
Avenue Verte official website **www.avenuevertelondonparis.com**

The Avenue Verte passes
right by Westminster near
the route start

London ~ Horley

Your start is the River Thames; 'liquid history' as one writer on London called it. The route start at the London Eye means you get the chance to survey one of the most famous views in the world, along the river from Westminster Bridge. You are soon threading your way through the heart of London, then across the green expanses of Clapham and Wandsworth Commons, busy with relaxing Londoners at weekends, before escaping motor traffic completely along the leafy Wandle Trail. Quiet minor roads lead over the beautiful, gentle North Downs.

Route Info

Distance 53 kilometres / 33 miles

Terrain & Route Surface After negotiating some traffic in central London you soon find yourself on the tarmac cyclepaths over Clapham and Wandsworth Commons. Joining the Wandle Trail near Earlsfield train station, you are initially on a crushed stone and earth path, but tarmac sections become much commoner as you head south and are interspersed with short, well-signed road sections.

The trail gradients are easy and there are plenty of refreshment stops en route. Leaving the trail at Carshalton, you are mainly on minor suburban roads, now encountering your first real hills, before a lovely minor road crossing of the North Downs. The easy pedalling final section uses a series of beautiful tiny roads and tracks through Nutfield Marsh to Redhill centre before minor roads and pavement cycle lanes lead to Horley.

Off-road 31% traffic-free on a variety of surfaces but often tarmac or good quality crushed stone. Some rough surfaces.

Profile

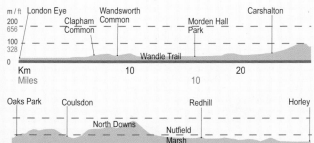

What to See & Do

• **Cycling** is a growing trend in London and the ever-expanding **National Cycle Network** in the capital has played its part, along with such developments as public hire bikes ('Boris bikes' after the mayor of London). There are plenty of green, traffic-free escapes suitable for family cycling in the heart of the city, whether it's a cross-town jaunt on the Regent's Canal, a spin around Hyde Park or an exploration of East London along the Greenway. Sustrans champions many of these routes through its London Greenways projects.

• **Westminster** is much more than the Houses of Parliament and the Abbey; the area around the start of the Avenue Verte holds plenty of hidden treasures too. Seek out Victoria Tower Gardens by the south-west corner of the Houses of Parliament, a lovely green space with great views and an interesting mix of sculptures and monuments. To the west of these gardens lies a picturesque maze of quiet streets clustered around Smith Square.

• It's a fine traffic-free ride with wonderful river views along the **Chelsea Embankment**, from the fine suspension bridge (Chelsea Bridge) to Albert Bridge and back to the Avenue Verte. This is easily combined with a spin around **Battersea Park** with its children's zoo, boating lake and the Peace Pagoda.

• Although the Avenue Verte heads west from the Thames' south bank at Westminster Bridge, **National Cycle Network Route 4** is a great way to explore the Thames' attractions to the east. These include Tower Bridge, the Cutty Sark, Greenwich Park and the Thames Barrier. East of Tower Bridge the majority of the route is traffic-free; quite an achievement in the heart of the capital.

• It's a splendid ride on a nice tarmac path over **Clapham Common**, passing the wonderful Italian cafe La Baita. There are also eating opportunities as you cross lovely Wandsworth Common.

The lovely La Baita cafe on Clapham Common

The Avenue Verte as it enters Morden Hall

• **The Wandle Trail** is a cycling and walking route following the river Wandle from Wandsworth, where it flows into the Thames, to Carshalton 15 km (9 miles) upstream at the river source. Once more than 90 mills lined its banks, making the River Wandle the most industrial in England. Today, parks largely replace the industry, and are the oasis of NCN 20 in London.

• **Wimbledon** boasts the history of tennis at the Wimbledon Lawn Tennis Museum (www.wimbledon.com) and local heritage at Wimbledon Windmill Museum. **Merton Abbey Mills** craft village is nearby with plenty of eateries.

• **Deen City Farm** is a community project with riding stables, pet farm and good priced cafe. www.deencityfarm.co.uk

• The National Trust Property at **Morden Hall** is well worth putting aside time for; it combines 125 acres of lovely parkland and its distinctive and characterful footbridges with the imposing hall itself, as well as preserved watermills (where tobacco was once ground), Morden cottage and a huge variety of landscapes, from rose gardens to marshland. A choice of cafes awaits too. www.nationaltrust.org.uk

• It's hard to believe that **Farthing Downs**, crossed by the Avenue Verte along Ditches Lane, is still within Greater London. These North Downs chalk grasslands are a Site of Special Scientific Interest. You also pass through pretty Chaldon with a centuries old mural in the church.

• **Mercers Park**, just by the route north of Redhill at Merstham, is noted for the interesting bird population and watersports.

• The splendid landscaped grounds of **Gatton Park** lie to the north of Redhill and make a fine bike ride. www.gattonpark.com

• Historic **Reigate** lies about 2.5 km (1.5) miles west of the Avenue Verte as it passes through Redhill. Attractions include a conservation area, Priory Park and windmills.

17

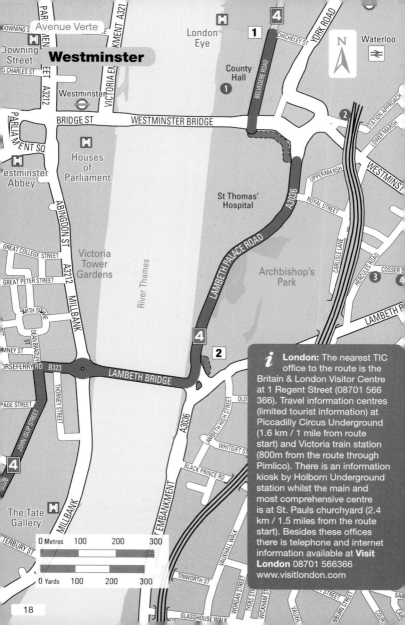

Westminster

Avenue Verte

Downing Street

Downing S

Downing Street

G CHARLES ST

London Eye

County Hall **1**

Waterloo

N

Westminster

BRIDGE ST

WESTMINSTER BRIDGE

PARLIAMENT SQ

Houses of Parliament

Westminster Abbey

ABINGDON ST

GREAT COLLEGE STREET

GREAT PETER STREET

SMITH SQUARE

DEAN BRADLEY

RNEY ST

ORSEFERRY RD

AGE STREET

THORNEY STREET

JOHN ISLIP STREET

TERBURY ST

The Tate Gallery

Victoria Tower Gardens

River Thames

MILLBANK

A3212

B323

LAMBETH BRIDGE

4

2

St Thomas' Hospital

Archbishop's Park

LAMBETH PALACE ROAD

A3036

ROYAL STREET

UPPER MARSH

CARLISLE LANE

HERCULES ROAD

COSSER S

LAMBETH P

3

Waterloo

STATION APPROACH

LOWER MARSH

WESTMINS

YORK ROAD

CHICHELEY ST

BELVEDERE ROAD

4

1

2

A3036

LAMBETH HIGH ST

WHITGIFT ST

BLACK PRINCE RD

OLD

EMBANKMENT

VAUXHALL WALK

TINWORTH ST

WORGAN ST

THYERS ST

WICKHAM ST

GLASSHOUSE WALK

i **London:** The nearest TIC office to the route is the Britain & London Visitor Centre at 1 Regent Street (08701 566 366). Travel information centres (limited tourist information) at Piccadilly Circus Underground (1.6 km / 1 mile from route start) and Victoria train station (800m from the route through Pimlico). There is an information kiosk by Holborn Underground station whilst the main and most comprehensive centre is at St. Pauls churchyard (2.4 km / 1.5 miles from the route start). Besides these offices there is telephone and internet information available at **Visit London** 08701 566366 www.visitlondon.com

0 Metres 100 200 300

0 Yards 100 200 300

18

Directions

1 The route begins outside the iconic London Eye – the first of many landmarks you will see on your journey to Paris along the Avenue Verte. Set off on Belvedere Road and head south until the junction with Westminster Bridge, cross the road on the toucan crossing, then turn left onto the shared use pavement and follow the road around to the right. Cross Lambeth Palace Road using the toucan crossing and rejoin the road, heading along the cycle lane. NB From Westminster to Chelsea Bridge follow NCN 4 signs.

2 At the roundabout at Lambeth Bridge head into the 'channelled' cycle lane in the middle of the road then across the bridge. On the other side, head straight over the roundabout, and take the second left onto Dean Ryle Street. Continue straight on to John Islip Street.

© Robert Scarth Creative Commons

Lambeth Palace

Accommodation

1 PREMIER INN
London County Hall, Belvedere Road SE1 7PB
0871 5278648   www.premierinn.com

2 THE WALRUS BAR AND HOSTEL
172, Westminster Bridge Road SE1 7RW
0754 5589 214   www.walrussocial.com
Mainly mixed-sex dormitory style accommodation

3 THE STEAM ENGINE
41-42, Cosser Street SE1 7BU   020 79280720
www.bestplaceinnwaterloo.hostel.com
Mixed sex dormitories

4 DAYS HOTEL LONDON WATERLOO
54, Kennington Road SE1 7BJ
020 79221331   www.daysinn.co.uk

OTHER LONDON ACCOMMODATION
YHA Hostels nearest the start of the Avenue Verte are St. Paul's and Oxford Street, both just over 2 km (around a mile) away. Neither has a cycle store. St. Pancras and London Central, each about 3.5 km (2 miles) away, have cycle stores, as do Earl's Court and Thameside, each about 5.5 km (3.5 miles) away.

Dover Castle Hostel
6, Great Dover Btreet, Borough SE1 4 XW
020 7403 7773   www.dovercastlehostel.com
Mixed sex dormitories. 2 km (1.25 miles) away.

A CRYSTAL PALACE CARAVAN CLUB SITE
Crystal Palace Parade SE19 1UF 020 8778 7155
www.caravanclub.co.uk   Non-members and tent campers welcome. Open all year. 8 km (5 miles) east of the route as it passes through Wimbledon.

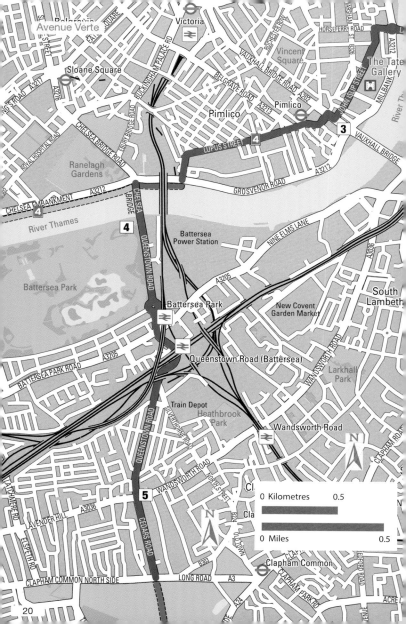

3 At the end of John Islip Street turn right onto Vauxhall Bridge Road, then immediate left onto Drummond Gate using the slip road. When the road forks, continue straight on into Lupus Street. Follow the road for its length, curving left, and when you reach the river turn right onto the cycle path on the pavement on the far side of the road (Battersea Power Station across the river). Continue on this path to the junction with Chelsea Bridge, rejoin the road and turn left onto this beautiful bridge.

Battersea Power Station

4 Once on the other side, continue straight on along Queenstown Road (on Cycle Superhighway route 8). At the roundabout head straight on (second exit) - cycle the roundabout or use the segregated cycle lane around the edge before rejoining the road. Continue straight on over the junction and follow Queenstown Road for its full length (**take care - busy at rush hour**).

5 Continue straight on onto Cedars Road until you reach Clapham Common, where the route heads straight on into the park at the traffic lights, and you join a segregated cycle path through the Common. Keep an eye out for the Victorian bandstand on your right – it remains the largest in London and was recently restored.

There are rail stations dotted along virtually the whole route out to Horley, itself around 45 minutes from London Bridge or London Victoria.
Stations are serviced by the following companies, with bikes on trains policies described (note folding bikes generally carried on all services at all times free of charge):

Southern Bikes free of charge. Reservations not required. Restrictions Mon - Fri:
• 7-10 am and 4-7 pm on any train due to arrive into London
• 4-7 pm on trains due to depart from London.
08451 27 29 20 www.southernrailway.com

First Capital Connect
Bikes free of charge. Reservations not required. Restrictions Mon-Fri:
• On trains arriving at any central London station between 7-10 am
• On trains departing any central London station between 4-7 pm.
0845 026 4700 www.firstcapitalconnect.co.uk

Gatwick Express Bikes free of charge. Reservations not required. Two cycle spaces per train.
Restrictions Mon - Fri:
• 7-10 am on any train due to arrive into London Victoria
• 4-7 pm on any train due to depart from London Victoria.
0845 850 1530 www.gatwickexpress.com

London Underground Folded bikes are allowed on anywhere, any time.
Non-folders allowed on some lines, free of charge, but not between 7.30-9.30 am and 4-7 pm. The most useful of these for accessing the Avenue Verte is the District Line, which has several stations on or near the route, including Westminster, Victoria and Wimbledon. For full details including a downloadable PDF 'bikes on the tube' map see www.tfl.gov.uk

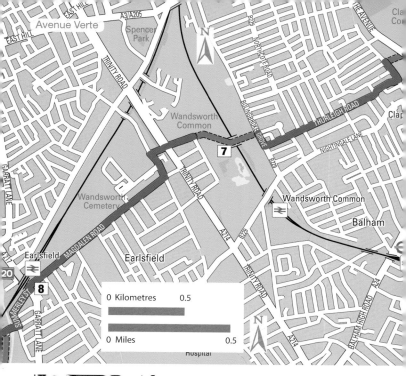

0 Kilometres 0.5

0 Miles 0.5

The Wandle Trail's 'waterwheel' signing

6 On the south side of Clapham Common turn right onto Windmill Drive, cross The Avenue, then follow the path west through the park until you reach Clapham Common West Side, where you'll need to turn left. Head along the cycle cut-through and turn right onto Thurleigh Road. At the end turn right onto Bolingbroke Grove. At the crossing, where the route turns left into Wandsworth Common, go onto the segregated path. Follow this until you reach the bridge over the railway lines.

7 On the other side of the railway take the path stretching diagonally across the Common to Dorlcote Road. Follow this road and cross Trinity Road using the toucan crossing, and head straight on, onto Alma Terrace. Turn left onto Lyford Road then right onto Magdalen Road at the mini roundabout.

8 Follow this road until you reach Garratt Lane at the traffic lights, where you turn left (a permitted movement for cycles only). Once on the high street take an immediate right turn onto Summerley Street (take care high street often quite busy).

The Wandle Trail

9 Follow Summerley Street south, and turn right at the end onto Trewint Street, a narrow road that leads onto a bridge over the River Wandle. From here follow signs for the Wandle Trail / NCN20. On the other side of the bridge turn left onto the riverside path and follow it south.

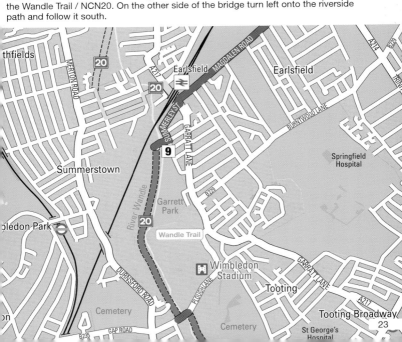

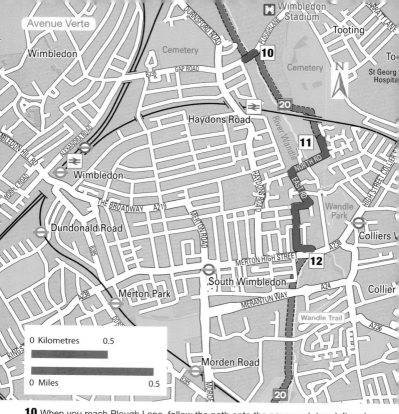

Avenue Verte

Wimbledon Stadium

Tooting

Wimbledon

Cemetery

Cemetery

To
St Georg
Hospita

10

GAP ROAD
B235

Haydons Road

20

River Wandle

11

Wimbledon

NORTH RD

EAST RD

Wandle Park

Colliers

THE BROADWAY A219

Dundonald Road

MERTON ROAD

MERTON HIGH STREET

12

A238

Merton Park

South Wimbledon

Collier

MERANTUN WAY

A24

Wandle Trail

A236

| 0 Kilometres | 0.5 |
| 0 Miles | 0.5 |

Morden Road

20

10 When you reach Plough Lane, follow the path onto the pavement, turn left and cross using the toucan crossing, before continuing south onto the riverside path.

11 At the southern end of the path head straight on to Chaucer Way. Follow it until you reach the junction with North Road, turn right and head across the bridge. Continue straight on to the mini roundabout. Turn left down East Road. When you reach the width restriction turn right onto All Saints Road, and then left onto Hanover Road. Follow this until you see the dead end, and turn left into Holmes Road.

12 Cross Merton High Street using the toucan crossing. On the other side turn right onto the traffic-free path. When the path ends, cross the car park and head through the stone arch to the toucan crossing over Merantun Way. Cross over the road and join the traffic-free path straight ahead. The ruins of Merton Abbey are located just to the east of the path.

Tram at Morden

Morden Hall

13 Continue along the Wandle Trail to Deen City Farm and cross over the small wooden bridge then the tram line level crossing. Take care crossing (trams can be quiet and approach without warning). Follow the path and take the left hand option where you see the signpost heading into Morden Hall Park, crossing over the river using the small footbridges. Head left over the ornamental bridge then take the right hand path and follow it to Morden Road.

14 At Morden Road turn right onto the pavement and use the toucan crossing. Turn right along the small residential road soon turning left into Ravensbury Park, following the segregated path along the river.

15 Turn right up the wooden walkway to the road, onto the shared use pavement along Bishopsford Road. Continue up the hill along the path, and cross the road where the green segregated cycle lane ends.

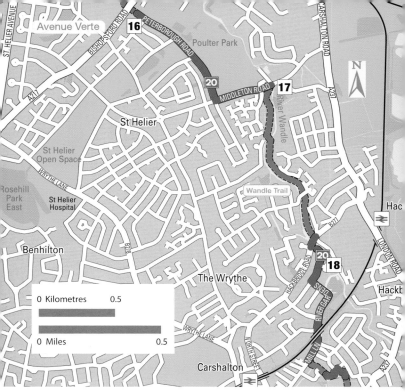

16 Once over Bishopsford Road head straight on, into Peterborough Road (cycle cut-through) and follow until the junction. Turn left onto Middleton Road.

17 At the traffic lights, turn right into the cycle path and follow the path to the river, crossing it at the spiral barrier, continuing on to Culvers Avenue, which you cross to stay on the riverside path. When you reach Hackbridge Road, cross the road with care and continue westwards along it, before turning left onto the shared space and into The Causeway.

18 Head along The Causeway then turn left into River Gardens, which turns into Mill Lane. After the junction with Butter Hill, turn left into the segregated cycle path that runs along the river.

19 Soon turn left onto the bridge, and continue on the path until Arcadia Close. Follow the road to the left, turn right onto Parkfield Close then head straight onto the path that runs around the edge of the sports centre. At the end of the path turn left onto Westcroft Road towards the High Street (Carshalton).

20 At the High Street turn left, then turn immediately right onto Park Lane. Head up the hill as the road turns into Boundary Road, at the end of which you will see a country lane that you should head straight onto.

Carshalton

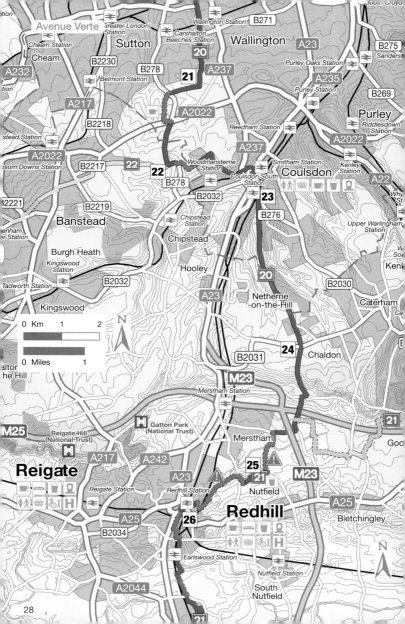

21 Continue straight on, having left Boundary Road, until you reach a tarmac road, where you turn right down the hill, enjoying the fantastic views. At the bottom turn right onto Woodmansterne Road, and then take a left when you see the Oaks Park sign, into the car park. Head through the park, turning left when you reach the club house. Head straight on through the wood and turn right onto the toucan crossing over Croydon Lane. On the other side, head left onto the cycle track and follow it down past the lavender fields until you reach Carshalton Road. Turn right onto it (can be busy).

22 At the junction turn left onto Rectory Lane, and head downhill before turning left at the sign for Hatch Lane (a narrow country path) on the left hand side. Carry on up the steep hill on the bumpy track. It eventually joins The Mount, a residential road. At the junction with The Grove turn right and continue straight on at Woodcote Grove Road onto The Avenue. Head downhill and turn right onto Brighton Road. Follow the traffic to the left, before heading onto the shared use pavement just before the roundabout.

23 Follow this path around, crossing the arm of the roundabout using the toucan crossing, and rejoin the road as you head up the hill of Marlpit Lane (busy, take care). Soon take the second road on the right (Downs Road) then fork left onto Ditches Lane. Follow this quiet road through Farthing Downs, which on a clear day has beautiful views of London and Surrey. Past a church fork right onto Church Lane.

24 Continue along Church Lane to cross over the main road in Chaldon onto Hilltop Lane as it runs steeply downhill. This road eventually turns into Warwick Wold Road that runs over the M25. Turn right onto Bletchingley Road and continue under the M23. After 400 metres turn left onto a path leading to a metal gate on your left. Head down this path through the nature reserve until it eventually meets Nutfield Marsh Road. Turn left and immediately right past the attractive Inn on the Pond.

25 Continue past the cricket ground into Chilmead Lane to Cormongers Lane. Turn right onto a narrow path behind the hedge. Turn left onto a traffic-free path through The Moors, the last open countryside before Redhill. The path emerges at a railway bridge, where you turn sharp right. Continue downhill, over a footbridge across Redhill Brook, then left into Noke Drive.

Tranquil Nutfield Marsh © Nick Macneil Creative Commons

26 At the traffic lights turn right under the railway bridges and past the train station, with services to London, Gatwick and Brighton. Turn left at the roundabout into Marketfield Way (cycle lanes). At another railway bridge join the shared footway beside the A23 Brighton Road. Turn left into Brook Road, still on the shared footway. At the T-junction turn left to pass under the railway line again. Leave the footway and turn right into Earlsbrook Road.

Avenue Verte

© Gareth Roberts Creative Commons

Gatton Park north of Redhill

5 BROMPTON GUEST HOUSE
6, Crossland Road, Redhill RH1 4AN
01737 765613 www.bromptonguesthouse.com

6 PREMIER INN REDHILL
Brighton Road
Salfords, Redhill RH1 5BT
0871 527 8930 www.premierinn.com

7 CAMBRIDGE HOTEL GATWICK
19, Bonehurst Road, Horley RH6 8PP
01293 783990
www.gatwickcambridgehotel.co.uk

8 THE AMBERS GUEST HOUSE
7, Vicarage Lane, Horley RH6 8AR
01293 785649 www.theambersgatwick.com

9 SOUTHBORNE GUEST HOUSE
34, Massetts Road, Horley RH6 7DS
01293 820112 www.southbornegatwick.com

10 THE LAWN GUEST HOUSE
30, Massetts Road, Horley RH6 7DF
01293 775751 www.lawnguesthouse.co.uk

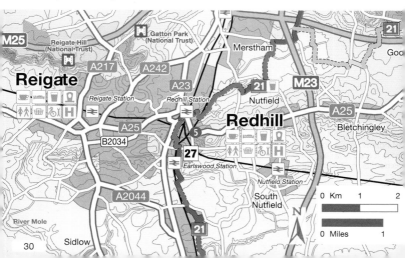

27 Continue straight ahead at the junction into Prince's Road, then right into Asylum Arch Road. Just before the arch under the railway, turn left onto an attractive tarmac path through woodland, parallel to the railway. To your left you will catch glimpses of the infamous "Asylum for Idiots" which closed in 1997 and is now private housing. Passing the modern East Surrey Hospital to the left, cross the busy road at the signal crossing and continue into the unmade track White Bushes.

28 Join Bushfield Drive, following roads through White Bushes housing area, bending left then turning right and right again. At the local shops turn left into Green Lane (a byway), into open countryside, leaving Redhill behind. After a short section between hedges, this becomes a concrete farm road through open fields.

29 Cross Honeycrock Lane, past a business park into another byway, which continues gently downhill through pleasant woodland to Cross Oak Lane. After a short distance on the old road, join the busy road and turn right with care into Lake Lane.

30 Follow Lake Lane into Horley. At the edge of town cross a road onto a cycleway, which emerges onto a residential road. Turn right and at the T-junction, right again into Smallfield Road. Cross the main road into Station Road and take the subway under the railway line, where you will need to dismount at busy times. The subway leads directly into the High Street, ideal for a well-earned rest at one of the local cafes.

Memorial gardens, Horley

Ian Capper Creative Commons

Avenue Verte

*The Forest Way runs between
East Grinstead and Groombridge*

Horley ~ Groombridge

The phrase 'astounding contrasts' may be a guidebook cliche, but it really is the case here, as the route out of Horley brushes up against the main Gatwick runway, landing lights at the side of the tarmac cycle path, planes passing incredibly close overhead. After more modernity through Crawley you are soon in a timeless landscape, along the Worth Way, a wonderfully rural path along an old railway trackbed. After a brief urban interlude at East Grinstead there's more fine traffic-free riding along the Forest Way, dotted with prosperous, handsome villages such as Forest Row, Hartfield, Withyham and Groombridge, with their distinctive red tiled, half-timbered and lap-boarded architecture and ancient inns. The lovely country town of Royal Tunbridge Wells is a tempting 14.5 km (9 mile) there and back excursion from the main route.

Route Info

Distance 39 kilometres / 24 miles

Terrain & Route Surface The majority of this section is on the Worth and Forest Ways, unsurfaced traffic-free paths where mudguards are advisable, especially in the wet. Before this the going is mainly on tarmac, either minor urban roads or some surprisingly leafy and green cycle paths around Gatwick and Crawley. Although you climb gradually to East Grinstead the route evens out any sharp gradients and you are then able to coast down most of the way to Groombridge.

Off-road 43% traffic-free, mainly on the crushed stone, unsealed surface of the Worth and Forest Ways.

Profile

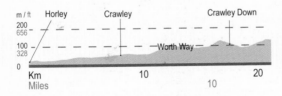

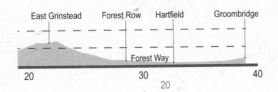

The Forest Way is dotted with attractive villages

What to See & Do

• Gatwick Airport may not be classed as a tourist attraction by many, but the route past here is certainly spectacular and there is a lift from the cycle path used by the Avenue Verte directly to the airport terminal.

• **Tilgate Park** lies just southwest of the route as it leaves Crawley. It's easily accessible via the traffic-free section of NCN 20 here and has a nature centre (including Meerkats!), a walled garden and cafe amongst much else.

• The historic local market town of **East Grinstead** has a lovely wide high street with half-timbered buildings. East Grinstead Museum is a small local history museum with free admission.

The town is particularly proud of the lovely Sackville College Almshouses and the National Trust property of Standen, which is famous for its Arts and Crafts associations.

• The steam powered **Bluebell Railway** has its northern terminus at East Grinstead, with a new station planned there for 2013. The southern terminus of Sheffield Park has a huge collection of old locomotives.
www.bluebell-railway.com

• At **Forest Row** you'll find a picturesque town in a lovely setting on a hill above the River Medway.

• **Hartfield** is an old village which was a centre for iron production in the nineteenth century and later the setting for Winnie The Pooh.

• Whilst **Groombridge** is an attractive village in its own right, its old centre clustered around a lovely green, it is for the **Spa Valley Steam Railway** that the village is best known. With small stations at Eridge and Groombridge, this extremely popular tourist railway crosses picturesque, traditional Kent and Sussex landscapes for nearly 8 km (5 miles) to end at Royal Tunbridge Wells West station. The train runs on weekends and holidays from April to October. As the railway allows bicycles on board a good option, if you wish to follow National Cycle Network route 18 linking Royal Tunbridge Wells to Groombridge, might be to cycle in one direction and take the steam railway in another.
www.spavalleyrailway.co.uk

Steam nostalgia is right by the route on the Spa Valley Railway

7715

© Glen Humble Creative Commons

Directions

1 In the centre of Horley, turn left onto busy Victoria Road. Where the main road rises to cross the railway, turn right then immediately left into The Drive. Turn right and continue to a large roundabout and take the first exit. Turn right, left and right again and at last reach the Riverside Garden Park, an attractive green space on the edge of Horley. The route closely follows the Gatwick Stream on a traffic-free path through the heart of Gatwick Airport.
Through the park pass under the A23 (long subway) emerging alongside the elevated shuttle train that links the North and South airport terminals. Pass under the shuttle building and follow the road directly alongside the railway platform. As you pass under the station and airport buildings, keep an eye out for the lift up to the terminal and the station if you need the facilities here. The path rejoins the Gatwick Stream, passing under the flight path. Ironically this is one of the greenest sections of the route.

2 You soon come back to modern life at City Place commercial development. Join the shared footway on the left hand side of Beehive Ring Road and continue on shared paths into Crawley, with signal crossings of Radford Road and Gatwick Road.
At a roundabout follow the footway right into Fleming Way, continue to the signal crossing and turn left into Newton Road. At the next major road turn right onto the footway and use the signal crossing to join the shared path. Join Woolborough Lane and pass under a major road (subway). Pick up the shared footway again; keep left then cross the road into an open space. Bear left and cross the road at a signal crossing. Turn left and immediately right to the junction of Routes 21 and 20 on North Road.

3 Route 21 continues ahead towards Three Bridges on Pond Wood Road, but the Avenue Verte follows Route 20 to the right on North Road. Bear left at the road junction and continue on North Road until it meets a T-junction. Turn left then right and right again, past playing fields. At the football ground turn left then right beside a major road. Continue beside the road for Crawley town centre and railway station. Cross the road at the signals to join Tilgate Drive cycle track, a green lane lined with trees and hedges.

4 Continue on this track until it meets St Leonards Drive, where you turn left. At the next junction Route 20 turns right into Rosamund Road towards Handcross, but we continue ahead on a tree-lined path, under the railway line to emerge next to Oriel School. Skirt the school and use the signal to cross into Maidenbower Drive. Cross the road to join an attractive bridleway through woodland to the left, eventually crossing the Gatwick Stream on a wooden footbridge. Turn right and immediately left, onto a path which climbs gently uphill to meet the old railway line, the Worth Way.

5 Pass under the Worth Way and turn right, climbing steeply to join the old railway. This is the start of a long section on former railways, a hugely attractive and largely traffic-free route all the way to the south coast. Pass under a subway, climb out of the railway cutting then turn right onto Church Road.

6 Turn left and just before the church bear left onto a wooded lane, which descends at first then climbs onto a substantial bridge over the M23. Leaving Crawley behind, enter open countryside on a wooded bridleway. At the next road turn left on a shared footway, then cross the road with care to rejoin the old railway towards Crawley Down.

7 Continue on the Worth Way until it emerges into Old Station Close, which as the name suggests was built on the site of the old station. Follow residential roads through Crawley Down to rejoin the old railway in Cob Close beside a pond.

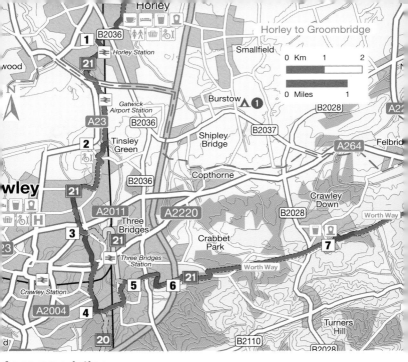

Accommodation

△ ❶ COPTHORNE SOUTHERN COUNTIES HISTORIC VEHICLE PRESERVATION TRUST
East Hill Lane Effingham Road, Burstow RH10 3HZ
01293 822014 www.campingandcaravanningclub.co.uk Members only but you can join at the site.
Small campsite about 5 km (3 miles) east of the route. Open all year. Own sanitation needed.

The leafy splendour
of the Worth Way

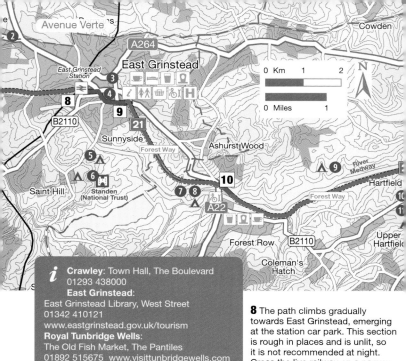

i **Crawley:** Town Hall, The Boulevard
01293 438000
East Grinstead:
East Grinstead Library, West Street
01342 410121
www.eastgrinstead.gov.uk/tourism
Royal Tunbridge Wells:
The Old Fish Market, The Pantiles
01892 515675 www.visittunbridgewells.com

8 The path climbs gradually towards East Grinstead, emerging at the station car park. This section is rough in places and is unlit, so it is not recommended at night. Cross the live railway on a narrow footbridge (steps on far side). Pass the station and cross a roundabout into Station Approach. At the next junction turn right into the town centre with numerous shops and cafes. Turn left into High Street with its attractive half-timbered buildings. Continue onto the Lewes Road.

9 Just before the A22 turn right to join the Forest Way to Groombridge. The Forest Way is another former railway, passing through the lovely High Weald with extensive views of rolling countryside. The path drops steeply to join the old railway alignment, crosses a road then passes through open countryside to Forest Row.

10 Forest Row village centre is worth the short detour off the Forest Way, with several interesting shops. Cross the A22 at the signal crossing and join the lane opposite, which leads to the old station site. Rejoin the old railway and continue down the upper River Medway valley past Hartfield and Balls Green.

2 PREMIER INN
London Road, Felbridge,
East Grinstead RH19 2QR
0871 527 8348 www.premierinn.com

3 CRANSTON HOUSE GUEST HOUSE
Cranston Road, East Grinstead RH19 3HW
01342 323609 www.cranstonhouse.co.uk
Secure cycle storage

4 GOTHIC HOUSE ACCOMMODATION
55, High Street, East Grinstead RH19 3DD
01342 301910 www.gothichouse55.co.uk
On the route

▲ **5** ASHWOOD FARM CAMPING
West Hoathly Road, East Grinstead RH19 4ND
01342 316129
http://woodlandcampingeco.wordpress.com

▲ **6** EVERGREEN FARM CAMPSITE
West Hoathly Road, East Grinstead RH19 4NE
01342 327720

7 BRAMBLETYE MANOR BARN
Brambletye Lane, Forest Row RH18 5EH
01342 826866 www.brambletyemanorbarn.co.uk

▲ **8** ROKO BIKERS AND HIKERS CAMPSITE
Brambletye Lane, Forest Row RH18 5EH
07977 223956   Just off the route

▲ **9** ST IVES FARM
Butcherfield Lane, Hartfield TN7 4JX
01892 770213 www.stivesfarm.co.uk
Around 1 km (0.6 miles) from the route

10 THE HAY WAGGON INN
High Street, Hartfield TN7 4AB
01892 770252 www.thehaywaggon.co.uk
0.5 km (0.3 miles) from the route

▲ **11** HARTFIELD – STAIRS FARM
Jib Jacks Hill, Hartfield TN7 4DQ
07526618841
www.campingandcaravanningclub.co.uk
Around 1 km (0.6 miles) from the route

There are rail stations at Gatwick Airport (served by First Great Western, Southern, First Capital Connect and the Gatwick Express), Crawley-Three Bridges (Southern and First Capital Connect) and East Grinstead (Southern). These are all close to the Avenue Verte.

Groombridge has no station itself but there is one at Ashurst (Southern) about 4 km (2.5 miles) to the north. Eridge, 4 km (2.5 miles) along the Avenue Verte to the south of Groombridge, has a station (Southern) which is also the terminus for the Spa Valley Railway heritage line, which runs up to Royal Tunbridge Wells and carries bikes.

Royal Tunbridge Wells main line station (Southeastern) is around 0.8 km (0.5 miles) from the Spa Valley Railway terminus.

Bikes on trains policies:

First Great Western
Reservation advised where possible   08457 000125   www.firstgreatwestern.co.uk

Southeastern
Peak hour restrictions on services to and from London, although no restrictions going south from Tonbridge 0845 000 2222   www.southeasternrailway.co.uk

The Pantiles, Royal Tunbridge Wells
© Tunbridge Wells Borough Council

11 At the old railway junction in Groombridge the path runs through fields alongside the live railway, emerging onto a lane to the south of the village.

The village centre is up to the left whilst the main route continues on minor roads to the right.

Groombridge has a couple of shops and a pub but the main attraction is the Spa Valley Railway, which runs to Tunbridge Wells.

The cycle ride on Route 18 is also attractive, passing woodland and the rock formations at High Rock **12**.

A good option is to take the steam train in one direction and cycle the other way. Tunbridge Wells is a large town with good facilities and the famous Georgian colonnaded walkway known as The Pantiles.

⚠ 12 MANOR COURT FARM
Ashurst, Tunbridge Wells TN3 9TB
01892 740279 www.manorcourtfarm.co.uk
Campsite and bed and breakfast about 2 km
(1.25 miles) from route

13 THE CROWN INN
Groombridge TN3 9QH
01892 864742 www.thecrowngroombridge.com
Around 1 km (0.6 miles) from the route

14 THE BEACON COUNTRY PUB
Tea Garden Lane,
Royal Tunbridge Wells TN3 9JH
01892 524252 www.the-beacon.co.uk
West of Royal Tunbridge Wells and convenient
for the link route

15 ALCONBURY GUEST HOUSE
41 Molyneux Park Road,
Tunbridge Wells TN4 8DX
01892 511279 www.alconburyguesthouse.com
Cyclists Welcome

16 THE RUSSELL HOTEL
80, London Road
Royal Tunbridge Wells TN1 1DZ
01892 544833 www.russell-hotel.com

17 40, YORK ROAD
Royal Tunbridge Wells TN1 1JY
01892 531342 www.yorkroad.co.uk
Centrally located bed and breakfast

18 THE BRICK HOUSE B & B
21, Mount Ephraim Road
Royal Tunbridge Wells TN1 1EN
01892 516517 www.thebrickhousebandb.co.uk

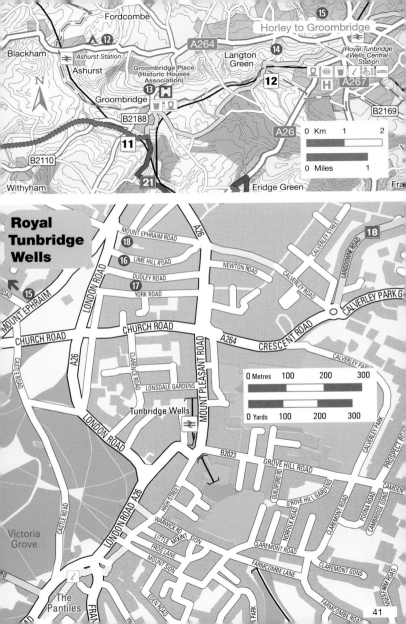

Royal Tunbridge Wells

Fordcombe
Blackham
Ashurst Station
Ashurst
Groombridge
Groombridge Place
(Historic Houses
Association)
Withyham
B2188
B2110
A264
Langton
Green
Horley to Groombridge
Royal Tunbridge
Wells Central
Station
A267
B2169
A26
Eridge Green

15
12
14
12
13
11
21

0 Km   1   2
0 Miles   1

MOUNT EPHRAIM ROAD
A26
LIME HILL ROAD
DUDLEY ROAD
YORK ROAD
MOUNT EPHRAIM
LONDON ROAD
A26
CHURCH ROAD
CHURCH ROAD
CASTLE ROAD
CLARENCE ROAD
LONSDALE GARDENS
NEWTON ROAD
CALVERLEY STREET
LANSDOWNE ROAD
CALVERLEY ROAD
CALVERLEY ROAD
CRESCENT ROAD
A264
CALVERLEY PARK G
CALVERLEY PARK
CALVERLEY PARK
PROSPECT R
Tunbridge Wells
MOUNT PLEASANT ROAD
B2023
GROVE HILL ROAD
HIGH STREET
GUILDFORD RD
GROVE HILL GARDENS
GROVE HILL ROAD
NORFOLK ROAD
CLAREMONT ROAD
FIONA ROAD
CLAREMONT ROAD
CAMBRIDGE GDNS
CAMDEN
LONDON ROAD
A26
WARWICK RD
MOUNT SION
FROG LANE
MOUNT SION
EDEN ROAD
CLAREMONT ROAD
FARMCOMBE LANE
CLAREMONT GDNS
FARMCOMBE R
NER FARM ROAD
Victoria
Grove
The
Pantiles
CASTLE ROAD
FRA

18
16
17
15
18

0 Metres   100   200   300
0 Yards   100   200   300

41

The Avenue Verte arrives at the
South Coast by Seven Sisters
Country Park

Groombridge ~ Newhaven

The fine villages of Rotherfield and Mayfield are found along the route, as you dip and climb on a minor road across the High Weald. Weald is the old English word for forest and this area still retains around a quarter of its original thick blanket of trees. At Heathfield you start a gentle 122 metre (400 feet) drop along the wide, excellently-surfaced tarmac of the Cuckoo Trail to Polegate. As well as being a former railway, the Cuckoo Trail is something of a haven for wildlife, including cuckoos. Your final descent to the English Channel and the ferry that awaits you at Newhaven takes you through a picturesque gap in the South Downs, the Cuckmere Valley and the south coast's famed chalk white cliffs at the Seven Sisters Country Park.

Route Info

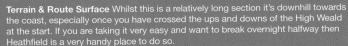

Distance 67 kilometres / 41.5 miles

Terrain & Route Surface Whilst this is a relatively long section it's downhill towards the coast, especially once you have crossed the ups and downs of the High Weald at the start. If you are taking it very easy and want to break overnight halfway then Heathfield is a very handy place to do so.
From Heathfield the going really couldn't be easier, as you follow the well-surfaced Cuckoo Trail, cross the Cuckmere Valley on quiet roads and finish on a traffic-free run along the coast into Newhaven. Off-road sections are mostly tarmac.

Off-road 43% mainly good quality tarmac. One short unsealed woodland track west of Polegate at the end of the Cuckoo Trail.

Profile

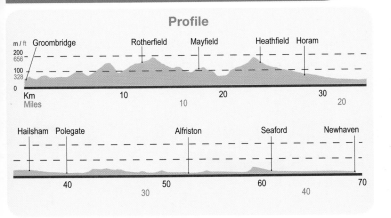

What to See & Do

• **The High Weald's rolling farmland and forests** provide some testing cycling, with short but stiff climbs. The reward is a succession of lovely country viewpoints and villages. **Mayfield** High Street, just off the route, is a wonderful opportunity to break in attractive surroundings. www.highweald.org

• It's particularly apt that **Heathfield** hosts an **Anglo-French market** every August Bank Holiday Monday. Just south of Heathfield on the Cuckoo Trail at **Horam** is the Sussex Farm Museum.

• **Knockhatch Adventure Park,** near Hailsham, boasts birds of prey, crazy golf, mini-quad and bungee trampolines amongst the many attractions of its 80 acres.

• **Michelham Priory**, some 4 km (2.5miles) west of the Cuckoo Trail at Hailsham is an impressive Augustinian priory with a watermill powered by the surrounding moat.

• The **Low Weald** is only around 8 km (5 miles) wide, extending from Polegate east to Ditchling and Hellingly. This broad, low-lying, gently undulating clay vale underlies a small scale intimate landscape with an intricate mix of copses and shaws, a patchwork of fields and hedgerows.

• **Drusillas Zoo** is a blend of action packed activities and a serious, conservation-minded zoo. They hold the studbook for rockhopper penguins and capybara (studbooks being important conservation documents).

The enticing Smugglers' Inn at Alfriston, complete with antique CTC sign.

NCN 2 to Brighton is a spectacular route option if you want to carry on cycling west of Newhaven.

• The **Long Man of Wilmington hill** figure can just be glimpsed from the route on the section near Drusillas Zoo. It is 69.2 metres (227 ft) tall, holds two "staves", and though formerly thought to originate in the Iron Age archaeological work has shown that it may have been cut in the 16th or 17th century AD.

• **Alfriston** is a beautifully preserved South Downs village, sheltering in the Cuckmere Gap. The **National Trust's Clergy House** is a medieval thatched cottage and was the first property they acquired back in 1896. A 14th century church and 15th century inn are also amongst Alfriston's fine collection of old buildings.

• Just south of Litlington a lovely view opens up across the Cuckmere Valley to National Trust owned Cradle Hill. Look out for the **white horse** cut into the chalk on the steep scarp there. It dates from 1836.

Also in the area is High and Over's dramatic river cliff which has been carved out of the soft chalk by the river below.

• The **South Downs National Park** was only granted its status in 2011 and is the UK's newest National Park. Known for stunning views from chalk ridges and cliffs it also includes the contrasting wooded countryside of the High Weald (see above) www.southdowns.gov.uk

• Situated just off the route as you approach the south coast, the **Seven Sisters Country Park** can certainly claim to have a landscape synonymous with Britishness; the sisters in question are towering chalk cliffs typical of the area. www.sevensisters.org.uk

• If you fancy continuing cycling west from Newhaven for nearly 16 km (10 miles) **NCN route 2** will bring you to **Brighton**. It is most famous for the Royal Pavilion, an extravagant Eastern-inspired construction and former palace. Also look out for The Lanes, a maze of shops, cafes and bars. NCN 2 is a fantastic ride, passing under white cliffs and entering Brighton alongside its expansive beach. Another option for seeing its attractions is to catch the train from Polegate and cycle back to Newhaven.

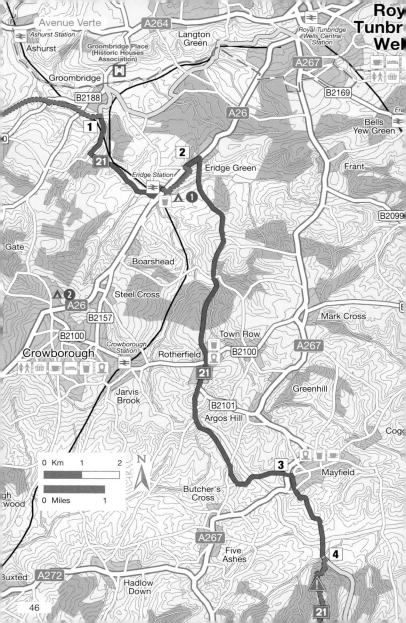

Directions

The next few miles between Groombridge and Heathfield cross the High Weald on quiet lanes, passing small woodlands and hilltop villages. There are no big hills, but several short steep climbs, meaning that this is the most physically demanding section of the route between London and Newhaven.

1 At the end of the Forest Way turn right then at the next junction turn left into Forge Road. Turn left past Eridge station, then right through a wooden gate at The Lodge and under the A26. Turn left and climb up a rough bridleway which runs alongside the main road.

2 The bridleway joins a length of old road, at the end of which turn right. The road undulates through woodland and pasture before climbing to the attractive village of Rotherfield with a few shops and a couple of pubs.
Continue from Rotherfield on the B2101 and where it bears left go straight on, onto quiet country lanes. At a fork in the road go left and drop steeply then coast almost all the way into Mayfield.

3 Outside the village carefully cross the A267 and climb steeply the other side to emerge close to the site of the old station. The route turns right, away from the village, but we recommend a short diversion along Station Road into the High Street, which has several shops and pubs. Leave the village on Newick Lane and after around 3 km (2 miles) there is a choice of route.

4 At Old Mill Farm, Route 21 turns right and follows a bridleway across a field and climbs up through woodland. The surface improves on higher ground, but can be muddy after rainfall and difficult with a loaded bicycle. The alternative route is to continue on Newick Lane, which climbs steadily up to the A265 main road.

Accommodation

▲ 1 FORGEWOOD CAMPING
Sham Farm Road, Danegate TN3 9JD
0772 029 0229 www.forgewoodcamping.co.uk
Adjacent to route

▲ 2 CROWBOROUGH CAMPING AND CARAVANNING CLUB SITE
Goldsmith Recreation Ground, Eridge Road
Crowborough TN6 2TN   01892 664827
www.campingandcaravanningclub.co.uk
90 pitch club site – non-members welcome
About 4 km (2.5 miles) from the route

There are no train stations on the route south of Eridge until you reach Polegate (Southern - see page 21 for bike carrying policy). Stations at Berwick and Southease are near the Avenue Verte. Seaford and Newhaven stations are on the route and are on a branch line. Newhaven has a town station and a harbour station, the town station being the one to use for the ferry port as it is pretty much adjacent to the ferry terminal.
Travel from London involves a change at Lewes (around 1 hour 20 mins from London Victoria), although you can travel direct to Brighton from London Victoria and London Bridge then ride the lovely NCN 2 to Newhaven which is around 16 km (10 miles).
The ferry service for Dieppe has a morning sailing and late night sailing and takes around four hours. Times vary according to the tide.
www.ldlines.co.uk See page 12 for more information on travelling by ferry.

5 Route 21 on Marklye Lane (the off-road option) emerges at A265 traffic lights, crossing straight over into Tower Street. The alternative route joins the A265 for a short distance, turning left into Tower Street. Follow residential roads through to the start of the Cuckoo Trail off Station Road. The centre of Heathfield is a short distance up the hill, with a full range of shops and services spread along the High Street. A short diversion to the old Heathfield Tunnel is worth the effort as it was restored and reopened to the public a few years ago. The tunnel runs under the High Street and leads to an attractive open space, a pleasant spot for a picnic.

3 BLACKBOYS YOUTH HOSTEL
The Glade, Gun Road
Blackboys, Uckfield TN22 5HU
0845 3719105 www.yha.org
About 7 km (4.5 miles) from the route

4 IWOOD BED AND BREAKFAST
Mutton Hall Lane, Heathfield TN21 8NR
01435 863918 www.iwoodbb.com
Secure storage for bicycles

5 HOLLY GROVE BED AND BREAKFAST
Spinney Lane, Little London
Heathfield TN21 0NU
01435 863375
www.hollygrovebedandbreakfast.co.uk

▲ **6** RUNT IN TUN
Camping and Caravanning Club Site
Maynards Green, Heathfield TN21 0DJ
01435 864284 www.runtintun.co.uk
By the route

▲ **7** HIDDEN SPRING CAMPSITE
Vines Cross Road, Horam TN21 0HG
01435 812640 www.hiddenspring.co.uk
Convenient for the route

▲ **8** HORAM MANOR TOURING PARK
Horam, Heathfield TN21 0YD
01435 813662 www.horam-manor.co.uk
About 1 km (0.6 miles) from the route

▲ **9** WOODLAND VIEW TOURING PARK
Horebeech Lane, Horam TN21 0HR
01435 813597

www.woodlandviewtouringpark.co.uk
Under 100 yards from the route

10 WIMBLES
Fords Lane, Vines Cross TN21 9HA
01435 810390 www.experiencesussex.co.uk
Cyclists Welcome bed and breakfast about 2 km
(1.25 miles) from the route

Easy riding on the Cuckoo Trail

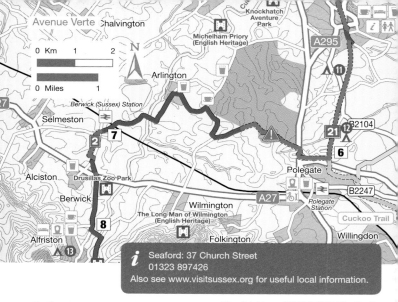

△ **11** THE HOMESTEAD
Ersham Road, Hailsham BN27 3PN
01323 840346
www.campingandcaravanningclub.co.uk
About 1 km (0.6 miles) from the route

△ **12** PEEL HOUSE FARM CARAVAN PARK
Sayerland Lane, Polegate BN26 6QX
01323 845629 www.peelhousefarm.com
Close to the route

△ **13** ALFRISTON CAMPING PARK
Pleasant Rise Farm, Alfriston BN26 5TN
Open all year About 1.5 km (1 mile) from the
route

14 ALFRISTON YHA HOSTEL
Frog Firle, Seaford Road, Alfriston BN26 5TT
0845 371 9101 www.yha.org.uk
Open all year Cycle Store

ALFRISTON ACCOMMODATION
Alfriston is about 8 kilometres from Newhaven
and has a number of options including April
Cottage (B & B with secure bike storage) 01323
870536, Dacres B & B 01323 870447, Chestnuts
Tearoom B & B 01323 870959, The George Inn
01323 870319, Highcroft B & B 01323 870553,

Riverdale House 01323 871038, The Star Inn
0843 7781972, Wingrove House 01323 870276,
Winton Fields 01323 870306 and the Deans
Place Hotel 01323 870248. There are also the
youth hostel and the campsite.

SEAFORD ACCOMMODATION
A good number of guest houses in Seaford which
is about 5 km (3 miles) from Newhaven. These
include The Silverdale 01323 491849, Malvern
House 01323 492058, The Avondale 01323
890008, Brecon Guest Accommodation 01323
892911, Cornerways 01323 492400, Cranleigh
House 01323 893113, Florence House 01323
873700, Hill House 01323 899759, Holmes
Lodge 01323 898331, The White Lion Hotel
01323 892473 and The Wellington Hotel 01323
899517. The Exceat Farmhouse 01323 870218
is in the Seven Sisters Country Park by the route
between Alfriston and Seaford.

AB FAB ROOMS BED AND BREAKFAST
11, Station Road, Bishopstone BN25 2RB
01323 895001 www.abfabrooms.co.uk
Just off the route about 3.5 km (2 miles) from
Newhaven

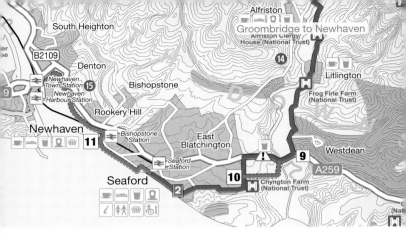

The Cuckoo Trail runs gently downhill to Polegate, passing through a number of towns and villages with several pubs and cafes to cater for travellers. Unlike the compacted stone surfaces of the Worth and Forest Ways, the Cuckoo Trail is tarmac most of the way. With the exception of two short on-road sections in Hailsham, the route follows the old railway line all the way to Polegate. Look out for the artworks along the Trail, including figures cut into the bridge parapets.

6 Just before the footbridge over the A27, turn right onto a path by the main road. Continue beside a minor road, under the A22, and follow round to the right. Turn left through a gate onto a bridleway, climbing through woodland (can be muddy in places after rain). At a crossing of tracks turn left and then join a tarmac lane. At the junction turn right and right again, then left at the next junction by the Yew Tree Inn in Arlington.

7 At the crossroads with Berwick station to the right head onto Common Lane then almost straight away turn left onto the Berwick Way, a path beside the road. At the end of the path join the road and continue to the roundabout on the A27. Use the signal crossing to join Alfriston Road past Drusillas Zoo Park.

8 Turn left just before entering the village, which is well worth a visit for its tea shops and thatched cottages. Cross the Cuckmere River and follow the valley down towards the coast, passing through tiny Litlington on the way.

9 At the A259 turn right onto the main road (narrow footway for those nervous of heavy traffic). The official route continues up the main road to the edge of Seaford where it turns left, but there is an alternative unsurfaced route across the fields. Cross the river at Exceat Bridge, then turn left at the Golden Galleon and join a rough track beside the river. Pass through a gate and turn right uphill over grass pasture. The underlying rock here is chalk, so the land is well drained and the going is reasonably good.

10 At the edge of Seaford, turn left into Chyngton Lane to rejoin the official route. Turn right onto Chyngton Way. At the corner of the golf course turn left uphill, then right into Corsica Road, which leads at last to the seafront with views over the Channel.
Turn right and follow the Esplanade through Seaford. Join the seafront cycle track at Dane Road, which leads to the town centre and the station.

11 Continue through Bishopstone and onto the excellent shared path beside the A259, with views over the Nature Reserve. Follow the path into Newhaven past retail parks and on to the entrance to the ferry port.

⑮ BARN OWLS SELF CATERING COTTAGES

Foxhole Farm, Seaford Road, Newhaven BN9 0EE
01273 515966 barn-owls.moonfruit.co.uk
Self catering and bed and breakfast about 1 km
(0.6 miles) from Newhaven, by the route

⑯ PREMIER INN

Avis Road, Newhaven BN9 0AG
0871 527 8810 www.premierinn.com

⑰ NEWHAVEN LODGE GUEST HOUSE

12, Brighton Road, Newhaven BN9 9NB
01273 513736 www.newhavenlodge.co.uk

⑱ THE OLD VOLUNTEER B & B

1, South Road, Newhaven BN9 9QL
01273 515204

YOUTH HOSTELS

There are YHA Hostels within about 5 km (3 miles) and 8 km (5 miles) of Newhaven. YHA South Downs at Beddingham BN8 6JS (0845 371 9574) halfway between Newhaven and Lewes, is open all year and is a 5 minute train ride north of Newhaven (Southease station). Telscombe BN7 3HZ (0845 371 9663), north of Peacehaven, has a cycle store.

BRIGHTON ACCOMMODATION

16 km (10 miles) from Newhaven, Brighton has a range of accommodation on offer. The centrally placed Kipps Hostel (01273 604182) offers both dormitory and private room accommodation and is one of a number of hostels in the town. There are chain hotels such as the Premier Inn (0871 527 8150), private ones small and large and many bed and breakfast guesthouses.

The Avenue Verte skirts the south coast at Seaford

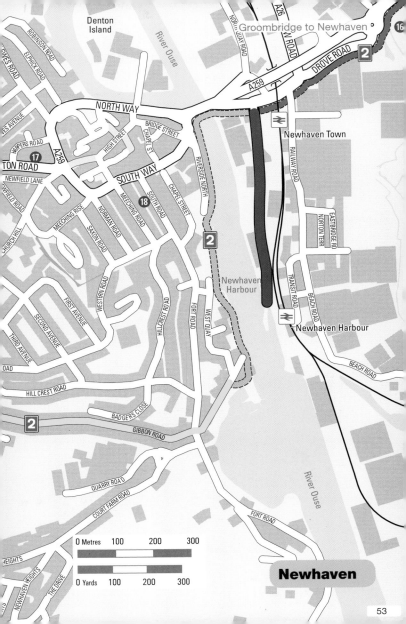

Denton
Island

River Ouse

A26

NORTH QUAY ROAD

N ROAD

DROVE ROAD

16

2

A259

Newhaven Town

ROBINSON ROAD

ELPHICK ROAD

YNES ROAD

ES AVENUE

NORTH WAY

BRIDGE STREET

CHAPEL ST

HIGH STREET

NAPERS ROAD

17

A259

TON ROAD

NEWFIELD LANE

SOUTH WAY

RIVERSIDE NORTH

RAILWAY ROAD

WFIELD ROAD

HURCH HILL

MEECHING RISE

NORMAN ROAD

MEECHING ROAD

SOUTH ROAD

CHAPEL STREET

18

SAXON ROAD

2

Newhaven
Harbour

EASTBRIDGE RD

NORTON TERR

BEACH ROAD

TRANSIT ROAD

WEST HILL ROAD

FIRST AVENUE

SECOND AVENUE

THIRD AVENUE

OAD

HILL CREST ROAD

HILLCREST ROAD

FORT ROAD

WEST QUAY

Newhaven Harbour

BEACH ROAD

2

BADGER'S CLOSE

GIBBON ROAD

QUARRY ROAD

COURT FARM ROAD

FORT ROAD

River Ouse

NEWHAVEN HEIGHTS

THE DRIVE

HEIGHTS

0 Metres   100   200   300

0 Yards   100   200   300

Newhaven

53

Dieppe's attractive harbour
welcomes you to France

Dieppe ~ Neufchâtel-en-Bray

Dieppe is a fine introduction to France; its lively harbour, packed in between dramatic cliffs, ensures a constant supply of fresh seafood to the restaurants that line it. Out of town you pass through attractive Arques-la-Bataille and its pretty, watery surroundings before joining one of the best cycle paths you'll find anywhere, the *Avenue Verte du Pays de Bray*, a wide, superbly surfaced path with nearby village services conveniently signed off the trail. There are long-term plans to extend the magnificent traffic-free section back into the heart of Dieppe. As well as the small-scale delights of village cafes and bars you should keep an eye out for the magnificent château at Mesnières.

Attractive Neufchâtel-en-Bray is a convenient and comfortable stopping off point, right by the trail and furnished with accommodation and plenty of bars and restaurants.

Route Info

Distance 37 kilometres / 23 miles

Terrain & Route Surface After negotiating the traffic of Dieppe's centre you are on the superb route along an old railway line that currently runs from Arques-la-Bataille to Forges-les-Eaux. The gradients are easy and there are plenty of charming villages right next to the route.

Off-road 77% traffic-free on wide, smooth tarmac.

Profile

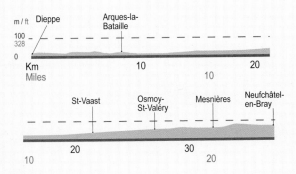

What to See & Do

• **Dieppe** has a reputation as one of the less industrial northern French ports and there's much to do and enjoy in this attractive small town. A climb to the small chapel of Notre-Dame-de-Bon-Secours lets you appreciate the dramatic setting of the harbour, packed between cliffs. The town museum in the Château de Dieppe just to the west of the front is also a great viewpoint. The lovely seafront lawns are a good place for a stroll, or those with younger cyclists might want to visit the aquariums of Cité de la Mer. Seafood dining is the main evening activity.

• **Arques-la-Bataille,** currently the start of a superb section of traffic-free route, has a handy cluster of shops, cafes and restaurants at its heart and also preludes some fine riding through the lakes of the Varenne outdoor and watersports centre, overlooked by the crumbling remains of a medieval castle.

Sedate traffic-free riding at Neufchâtel-en-Bray

A grand Norman residence near St-Vaast d'Equiqueville

• **Guy Weber Education Centre** at St-Aubin-le-Cauf is in a lovely riverside setting and home to various animals. Free entry. parcguyweber.free.fr

• It's hard to miss the **magnificent château** right by the route at **Mesnières-en-Bray**, around 6 km (4 miles) before the small, attractive town of Neufchâtel-en-Bray. Open to the public from Easter to 1st November.

57

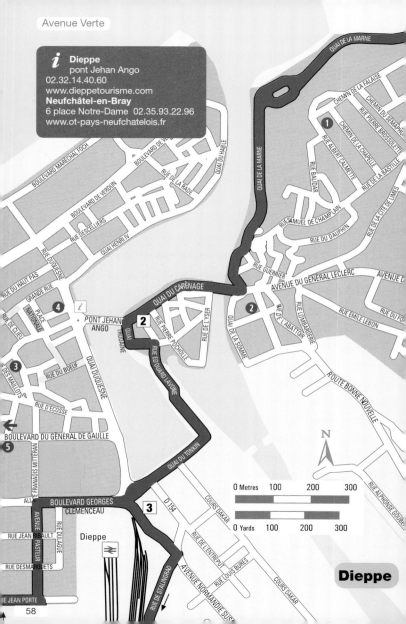

Dieppe

Accommodation

1 CHAMBRE D'HÔTES BALI-DIEPPE
2, chemin de la Falaise
76370 Neuville les Dieppe
02 35 84 16 84 www.lesvoilesdor.fr

2 VILLA DES CAPUCINS
11, rue des Capucins 76200 Dieppe
02 35 82 16 52 www.villa-des-capucins.fr

3 HÔTEL LES ARCADES
1 – 3, arcades de la Bourse 76200 Dieppe
02 35 84 14 12 www.lesarcades.fr

4 HÔTEL AU GRAND DUQUESNE
15, place Saint-Jacques 76200 Dieppe
02 32 14 61 10 http://augrandduquesne.free.fr

5 ÉTAP HÔTEL DIEPPE
6, rue Claude Groulard 76200 Dieppe
08 92 68 31 35 www.ibis.com

Plenty of hotels on the seafront too.

DIEPPE CAMPSITES
Camping La Source (02 35 84 27 04) and Camping Le Marqueval (02 35 82 66 46) are at Hautot-sur-Mer west of Dieppe. Camping Relais Motard (02 35 83 92 49), is on rue de la Mer about 1 km (0.6 miles) from the coast at Pourville-sur-Mer, west of Dieppe.

Directions

The hardest part is finding your way through Dieppe centre - a one-way system for bikes avoids the busy one-way system for cars. **Note:** There is a quieter, hillier, alternative route as shown in yellow on the map overleaf, but here we describe the quickest, busiest route. It will be much improved when the former railway from Dieppe becomes a cycle route.

1 From the ferry terminal follow signs for "Centre Ville" and cross the harbour on a metal swing bridge, the Pont Colbert

2 Before crossing a second bridge turn left and follow the signs through the harbour area. The road swings round to the right and brings you out opposite the railway station.

3 Turn left before the station into a multi-lane one-way road – remember to keep right and take the first right into another industrial area beside the railway tracks.

Sail and pedal - arriving in
Dieppe by bike is easy.

© Joël-Damase

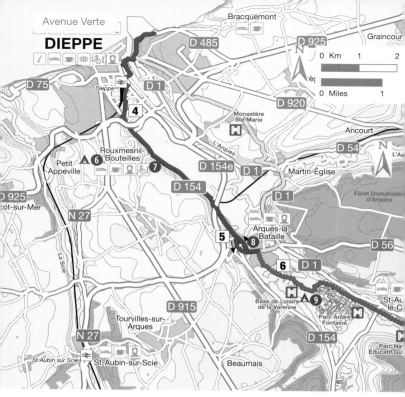

4 Having negotiated the route past Dieppe train station, pick up the cycle track and follow through the industrial estate, ending at a road where you turn right and cross a railway line at a level crossing. This is the old Dieppe to Forges-les-Eaux line, which is planned to become part of the Avenue Verte.

Turn left into rue General Chanzy and carry on for 7 km (4 miles) to Arques-la-Bataille, paralleling the old railway. You pass several cafes and hotels. The only thing to watch out for is a major roundabout where you may encounter some of the lorries coming from the ferry.

5 On entering Arques-la-Bataille there is a fork in the road with an imposing church in the background. Take the right option (D154) to Torcy. As you climb up a slight gradient into the centre of Arques, you will see the old château up on the hill above the village.

Straight ahead in the village centre then bear left at the end of the square to go downhill. Arques is an attractive village with plenty of bars, restaurants and shops. Continue on the main road until you see a level crossing but turn right before you reach it, onto the start of the superb traffic-free path.

6 The path winds through an attractive outdoor leisure park with many water-based activities, eventually joining the old railway beside a large industrial site.

▲ 6 CAMPING VITAMIN
365, chemin des Vertus 76550 Saint-Aubin-sur-Scie
02 35 82 11 11   www.camping-vitamin.com
Open March – October. About 1 km (0.6 miles)
from the route

7 HÔTEL L'EOLIENNE
20, rue de la Croix de Pierre
76370 Rouxmesnil Bouteilles
02 32 14 40 00 www.logishotels.com

8 CLEOME
23, rue de la Chaussée
76880 Arques-la-Bataille
02 35 84 16 56 www.cleomechambredhote.fr
On the route about 7 km (4.5 miles) from Dieppe

▲ 9 CAMPING DES 2 RIVIÈRES
76880 Martigny
02 35 85 60 82
www.camping-2-rivieres.com

The Avenue Verte near
Arques-la-Bataille

© Joël-Damase

Dieppe - Paris (St-Lazare) trains take around 2 hours 15 mins, with a change necessary at Rouen. Only selected trains from Paris carry bikes but most services on the 45 min journey from Rouen do.
After Dieppe there are no stations on or near this section of route.
www.voyages-sncf.com

Plenty of local signs on the traffic-free section

Continue for 24 km (15 miles) on the fantastic smooth tarmac surface all the way to Neufchâtel. You can do this very quickly, but we recommend that you take your time and visit some of the attractive villages along the route, most very close to the old railway, just a minute or two to bars, cafes and the all-important "boulangeries". Many of the local businesses have signs up at the many minor road crossings to entice you to try their wares.

7 One place worth a stop is the Guy Weber educational natural park just after the start of the railway path at St-Aubin-le-Cauf. This is free to enter and a great place for a picnic or a stroll beside the river Béthune .

Mesnières château

8 You will not miss the magnificent château at Mesnières, which is on your left. There is more to the village than the château and it is well worth spending a while here. Just before the village look out for a small sign for "lavoir" to the left, where a narrow path leads to an enchanting well and shaded rest area.

9 In Neufchâtel the old station has been converted into a public space and is a useful jumping off point for the town. The town centre is not immediately obvious – if in doubt head for the church spire. There is a wide range of shops and services on offer and some hotels too.

⑩ HÔTEL LE SAINT-PIERRE
15, grande rue Saint-Pierre
76270 Neufchâtel-en-Bray
02 35 93 02 12   Close by the route

⑪ LA BÉTHUNE
11, grande rue Saint-Pierre
76270 Neufchâtel-en-Bray
02 35 93 00 79 www.labethune.com
Hôtel restaurant close by the route

⑫ LE CHARDON BLEU CHAMBRE D'HÔTES
20, grande rue Fausse Porte
76270 Neufchâtel-en-Bray 02 35 93 26 64
http://wwwlechardonbleu.blogspot.co.uk
About 200 metres from the route

⑬ HÔTEL LE GRAND CERF
9, grande rue Fausse Porte
76270 Neufchâtel-en-Bray
02 35 93 00 02 www.grandcerf-hotel.com

⑭ LES AIRELLES
2, passage Michu 76270 Neufchâtel-en-Bray
02 35 93 14 60 www.les-airelles-neufchatel.com
Hotel and restaurant

⑮ CAMPING-SAINTE-CLAIRE
13, rue Sainte Claire
76270 Neufchâtel-en-Bray
02 35 93 03 93
www.camping-sainte-claire.com
By the route Cycle hire

FORGES-LES-EAUX ACCOMMODATION
If you want a longer first day on the French part of the route, Forges-les-Eaux is around 50 km (31 miles) from Dieppe and has a good amount of accommodation. For listings see pg 69.

Traffic-free, heading to Forges-les-Eaux

© Sue Nottingham

Neufchâtel-en-Bray ~ Gournay-en-Bray

The remaining part of the lovely, traffic-free *Avenue Verte du Pays de Bray*, continues past small Norman villages ending in Forges-les-Eaux, with its bustling centre grouped around the colourful town hall. Heading to the hills on minor roads the route passes through the *Pays de Bray*, a countryside of green, rolling hedge-lined dairy pasture and fruit farms dotted with half-timbered agricultural buildings making it ideal cycling country. Cheese gourmets should look out for Coeur de Neufchâtel. Gournay-en-Bray's attractive centre is dominated, on Tuesday and Friday mornings, by a wonderful market.

Route Info

Distance 28 miles / 46 kilometres
Terrain & Route Surface From Neufchâtel to Forges-les-Eaux, continuing along the traffic-free route is a flat, tarmac doddle. From Forges-les-Eaux you take to minor roads with quite a few fairly challenging (for more occasional riders at least) ups and downs.
Off-road 38% traffic-free on wide, smooth tarmac. The remainder on often moderately hilly minor roads.

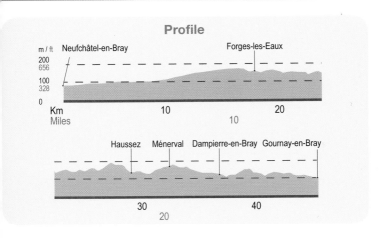

Profile

What to See & Do

• Bray landscape and food.
This section crosses the geological feature known as the 'Buttonhole' of the Bray Area, a fold in the earth's surface that has created a series of pretty hills whose ridges have eroded over time. Information boards have been put on the highest points in the area to allow a "reading" of these landscapes.
In particular you get a feel for this landscape as you climb and drop on minor roads between Forges-les-Eaux and Gournay-en-Bray.
Look out for the local Norman produce: cream, butter and dairy products, apples, pears, honey, vegetables, high quality meat and the well-known Neufchâtel cheese. Brayonne cooking combines local produce with fresh seafood and fish direct from Dieppe. Cider is a local speciality too.

The Avenue Verte greenway near Forges-les-Eaux

St-Saire

• **Forges-les-Eaux** is a spa town with pretty villas dating from the Belle Époque period of history at the end of the 19th century. Further back in history Louis XIII, Anne of Austria and Cardinal Richelieu all came to take the waters here. A 19th century casino (sitting opposite the large attractive Epinay park and lake Andelle) added to the town's reputation as a high class resort. Good collection of local museums, including the museum of the French Resistance and another featuring models of horse-drawn vehicles. Small attractive town centre clustered around the distinctive town hall.

• **Gournay-en-Bray** is a market town that suffered much destruction in World War II but has been attractively restored. Excellent market in the town centre Tuesday and Friday mornings.

Avenue Verte

D 1314

D 929

Neufchâtel-en-Bray D 929

A 29

Gare de l'Avenue Verte

A 28

1

D 1314

Neuville-Ferrières

Bouelles

D 1

Nesle-Hodeng

St-Saire

D 135

N

D 7

0 Km	1		2
0 Miles		1	

i **Forges-les-Eaux**
rue Albert-Bochet
02.35.90.52.10
www.forgesleseaux-tourisme.fr
Gournay-en-Bray
9 place d'Armes
02.35.90.28.34
www.ot-gournay-en-bray.fr

D 1314

2

Beaubec-la-Rosière

D 915

Sommery

Serqueux *Serqueux*

D 919

Forges-les-Eaux
i

3

Ancienne gare thermale

Le Fo

68

D 919 D 915

Directions

1 Continue on the traffic-free path away from Neufchâtel-en-Bray, climbing gradually up the Béthune Valley.

2 At Beaubec-la-Rosière, where the railway path comes to an end at the main line railway (trains from Serqueux to Rouen and Paris), the route continues on a traffic-free path, crossing under the live railway. This emerges onto a road on Serqueux's outskirts. Turn right and prepare for the first hill after leaving Dieppe! Pass over the railway again then turn left onto another path. Bear right where this becomes a narrow lane and cross over a main road into a byway. This soon leads into a zigzag ramp onto another short section of railway path.

You have crossed the watershed between the Béthune and Epte valleys, so this section is delightfully downhill into Forges (take care not to miss the yellow diversion signs for the town centre on the left). It is possible to continue to the end of the line where you will see an old station building and on your right the monumental gate of Gisors.

3 Back to the diversion, follow the yellow signs through quiet residential streets. Turn right at a school to pass the imposing church down to rue de la République, where you turn left for the town centre.

Numerous businesses have sprung up alongside the Avenue Verte. Here the former station of Nesle St-Saire south of Neufchâtel-en-Bray has been smartened up and converted into a cafe.

Accommodation

FORGES-LES-EAUX

If you want a longer first day on the French part of the route, Forges-les-Eaux is around 50 km (31 miles) from Dieppe and has a good amount of accommodation including the Forges Hotel (02 32 89 50 57), Hôtel le Continental 02 32 89 50 50), Hôtel la Paix (02 35 90 51 22), Hôtel le Colvert (02 35 09 70 40), Hôtel le Saint-Denis (02 35 90 50 70) and Hôtel Sofhotel (02 35 90 44 51). There's also a hostel (gîte d'étape), Le Relais du Chasse Marée (02 35 09 68 37) and a campsite, Camping la Minière (02 35 90 53 91).

The section from Forges to Gournay is very different to the railway path and younger children may find the ups and downs and twists and turns quite challenging. The route passes through an undulating landscape on minor roads. Although it does pass through a number of villages, there are very few facilities – the author did not see a single shop in 27 km (17 miles).

Ménerval

4 From the centre of Forges take the D915 for a short distance towards Gournay then turn left at Hôtel Le St Denis onto rue de la Republique (D919). Cross the old railway then immediately go right into a very quiet road passing fields and farmhouses. Continue beside the railway line until you come to a T-junction.

5 Turn right here, cross the railway then turn immediately left. This railway line is planned to form the extension of the railway path from Forges through to Gournay. At the next junction turn left onto the D61 and cross the railway again at La Bellière. Continue on the D61 through Pommereux, climbing steadily to a crossroads where you go straight ahead. At the next junction fork right for the D120 to Haussez (poor surface here, care required).

6 In Haussez turn right and right again, then under the railway bridge and immediately left on a very quiet lane. Cross the river Epte then climb steadily out of the valley to Ménerval, a small village with a huge church. Just before you reach the watertower turn left. This is one of the highest points on the route between Forges and Gournay and you can look forward to several kilometres downhill.

7 Keep an eye out for the Avenue Verte sign as there is a sharp right then left that is easy to miss as you pick up speed down the D16 towards Dampierre-en-Bray. If you do miss this turn you will pick up the route again after the loop through Dampierre. In the village centre turn right then left onto the D84.

8 Turn right at the roundabout onto the D16 for Gournay, then turn left after a short distance to Cuy-St-Fiacre.

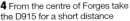 **1** CAMPING L'AVENUE VERTE
2, route de Villers Vermont
76220 Doudeauville
02 35 90 60 39
http://campingtipi.e-monsite.com
About 14 km (9 miles) from Forges-les-Eaux and about 11 km (7 miles) from Gournay-en-Bray.
Some 3 km (2 miles) from the route at Haussez.

2 LA FERME LES PEUPLIERS
1542 Le Long Perrier
76220 Dampierre-en-Bray
02 35 90 22 90
www.lafermelespeupliers.com
About 8 km (5 miles) before Gournay-en-Bray
Secure bike storage

3 CHAMBRES D'HÔTES "LA BRAYONNE"
167 chemin de la Vieuville
76220 Dampierre-en-Bray
02 35 90 10 99
www.chambresdhoteslabrayonne.com
About 8 km (5 miles) before Gournay-en-Bray

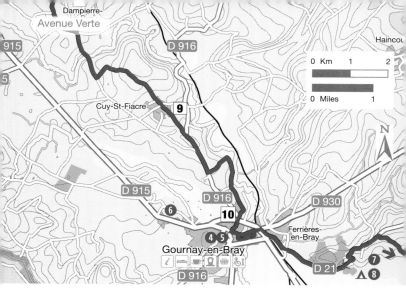

9 Carry on through Cuy-St-Fiacre until the road joins the D916 to Gournay. This is one of the main roads into the town and can be busy, so you are advised to turn left to Cité St Clair.

10 You will come to the signalled junction of the D916 with the N31 on the edge of the town centre. Proceed ahead on rue de l'Abreuvoir / rue des Bouchers to the attractive fountain in the centre. Look out for the sign pointing to Hailsham 196 km (122 miles) away. Hailsham in East Sussex is the twin town of Gournay and by happy coincidence is on the Cuckoo Trail, part of the Avenue Verte route in England.

4 HÔTEL LE CYGNE
20, rue Notre Dame
76220 Gournay-en-Bray
02 35 90 27 80
www.hotellecygne.fr

5 HÔTEL DE NORMANDIE
21, place Nationale
76220 Gournay-en-Bray
02 35 90 01 08

6 HÔTEL LE ST AUBIN
550, Chemin Vert
76220 Gournay-en-Bray
02 35 09 70 97
www.hotel-saint-aubin.fr
A good km (0.6 miles) from the route

7 LES CHAMBRES DE L'ABBAYE
2, rue Michel Greuet
60850 Saint-Germer-de-Fly
03 44 81 98 38
www.chambres-abbaye.com
Chambres d'hôtes on the route about 6 kilometres on from Gournay-en-Bray. Accueil Vélo (Cyclists Welcome). See map on page 78.

8 CAMPING LA RONFLURE
29, rue Paul Dubois
60850 Le Coudray-Saint-Germer
03 44 81 83 88
About 0.5 km (0.3 miles) from the route some 12 km (7.5 miles) on from Gournay-en-Bray (see map on page 97)

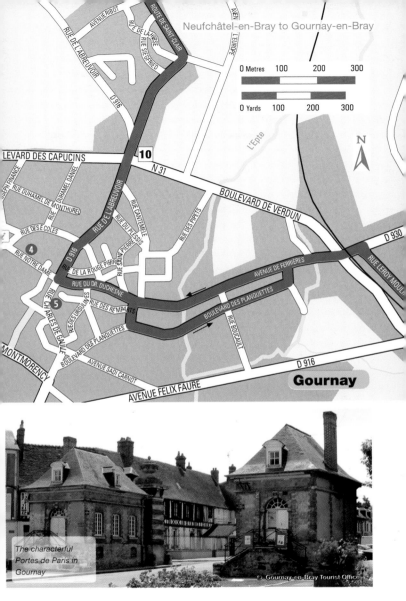

The characterful
Portes de Paris in
Gournay

© Gournay-en-Bray Tourist Office

Gisors' superb 11th century castle

Gournay-en-Bray ~ The Vexin

Shortly after Gournay-en-Bray, St-Germer-de-Fly is important in route terms as it's here you must choose between western and eastern options (see overview map on inside cover). However, it's an attractive place in its own right, the immaculately manicured centre with a cluster of handy shops grouped around the magnificent facade of the wonderful medieval abbey. Heading down the peaceful lanes of the Epte valley you reach Gisors, dominated by its fine Norman castle which faces the 12th century church of Saint Gervais-St. Protais and is a hugely picturesque breaking off point before some wonderfully easy cycling along the high quality Epte Valley Greenway (*Voie Verte de la vallée de l'Epte*).

Route Info

Distance 60 kilometres / 37 miles

Terrain & Route Surface There are two climbs on minor roads, one shortly after leaving Gournay and another longer one leaving St-Germer and climbing above the Epte valley before a long road descent to Gisors. Once on the hard-surfaced traffic-free route out of Gisors both gradients and navigation are easy all the way to the gateway to the Vexin region at Bray-et-Lû. As on the route south of Dieppe, villages just off the traffic-free path are signed (there are no real villages directly on this route section).

Off-road 31.5% traffic-free on wide, smooth tarmac.

Profile

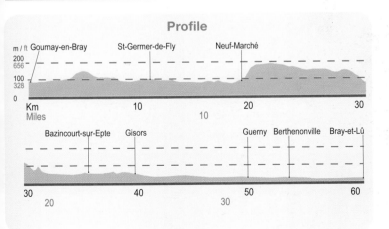

Avenue Verte

What to See & Do

• The highlight of tiny **St-Germer-de-Fly** is the Benedictine Abbey. It's hard to imagine a more peaceful scene today but it has a tortuous past; founded in the seventh century it was destroyed by the Normans, rebuilt in the twelfth century, and altered numerous times afterwards. The Chapel of the Virgin's stained glass copies Sainte-Chappelle in Paris. For cyclists it's the major route split on the Avenue Verte; head east for Beauvais and the Oise or south for Gisors and the Vexin.

• Sitting on the border of the Normandy and French Vexin areas, the town of **Gisors** was the focus of struggles between the Duchy of Normandy and the kingdom of France in medieval times. The castle stronghold overlooking the city, built in the eleventh century on a motte, according to legend housed the treasure of the Templars. It faces the equally impressive and imposing church of Saint Gervais-St. Protais, built in the twelfth century, which has the dimensions of a cathedral and a surprising mix of architectural styles.

View of Gisors from the castle

76

Traffic-free down the Epte Valley

• The **Epte Valley Greenway** is a joy to cycle, a high-quality, well-surfaced route along an old railway line. Dotted with small villages and ridgetop castle remains, it parallels the clear and tranquil waters of the Epte river.

• Should you feel like carrying on south of Bray-et-Lû to the end of the traffic-free trail you will find yourself in the small attractive town of Gasny. From there you can carry on using minor roads to **Giverny**, something of an international tourist attraction, hordes flocking in coach loads to Monet's house and garden as well as the associated Museum of American Art. Monet's garden, complete with water-lily pond, is indeed spectacular. You can return to Bray-et-Lû by bike or carry on to the attractive working town of Vernon with its plethora of cafes, restaurants and hotels. If you want to shortcut to Paris by rail Vernon offers a direct 50 minute train service with selected services carrying bikes. Bray-et-Lû to Vernon is 18 km (11 miles).

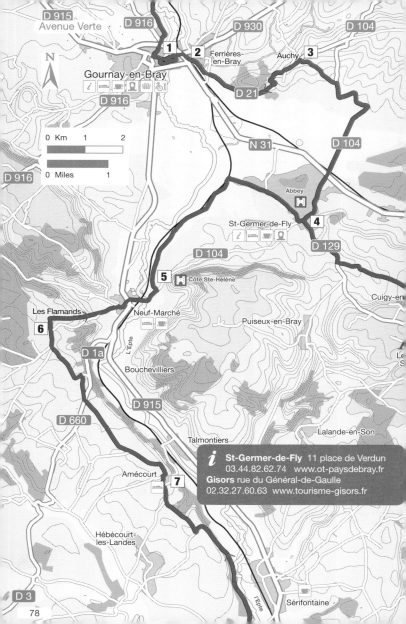

St-Germer-de-Fly 11 place de Verdun
03.44.82.62.74 www.ot-paysdebray.fr
Gisors rue du Général-de-Gaulle
02.32.27.60.63 www.tourisme-gisors.fr

Directions

1 From Gournay centre (also see map on page 73), which features an attractive square with fountains, take rue du Dr. Duchesne east towards Ferrières. When the road becomes one-way east to west, take a right into a cul-de-sac. This is a no through road for motors but bikes can use the delightful boulevard des Planquettes, a tree-lined avenue. This path crosses the Epte on a footbridge then rejoins rue du Dr. Duchesne by turning left and right. Beware – this section of the road is still one-way but bikes are allowed. Continue to the traffic lights at a busy intersection with the N31.

2 Cross the N31 and the railway line then immediately right on the D21. Continue past the Danone factory and you are soon in open countryside, with a steady climb through woodland to Bethel and Auchy opening up great views.

3 At Auchy look out for a sharp right towards Orsimont and St-Germer-de-Fly. Continue until you meet the D104 following this all the way to St-Germer. The road twists and turns and there are some short steep climbs until you coast into St-Germer, which is dominated by the imposing abbey. Take care crossing the N31 for a second time. Just before the N31 you will notice a short rise to meet the old railway line, which forms part of the long term plan for the Avenue Verte between Gournay and Beauvais.

Route options split at St-Germer-de-Fly

4 St-Germer is the junction for the two branches of the current Avenue Verte route – at the main square keep right for Gisors and Cergy (or turn left for the alternative route via Beauvais - see chapter Gournay - Beauvais). For Neuf-Marché don't be tempted to take the more direct route signed on the D104 but follow the Avenue Verte signs right at a small roundabout. You will be rewarded with a beautiful ride on quiet lanes heading close to the railway and the river Epte.

5 Just outside Neuf-Marché you pick up the D104 once again and follow this for a short distance into the village and the traffic lights at the crossing of the busy D915. Neuf-Marché boasts a château, the Collégiale St Pierre. After crossing the main road take the left fork signed to Les Flamands and Rouge Mare, which becomes a long steady climb past meadows and a wooded ridge. Do look back before you reach the top for a wonderful view down to Neuf-Marché and the Epte valley.

6 Continue through Les Flamands, taking the left fork, although you have the option of a short diversion of 500 metres if you continue towards the Rouge Mare memorial. This is a curious sculpture in a delightful woodland setting.

7 In Amécourt follow the road round to the right then turn left on the D660 out of the village, passing the tiny Chapelle Sainte-Anne. After a short distance fork left. At the next junction turn left and follow the road through woodland towards Sérifontaine. After Amécourt the road falls into the Epte valley, where it stays until Gisors.

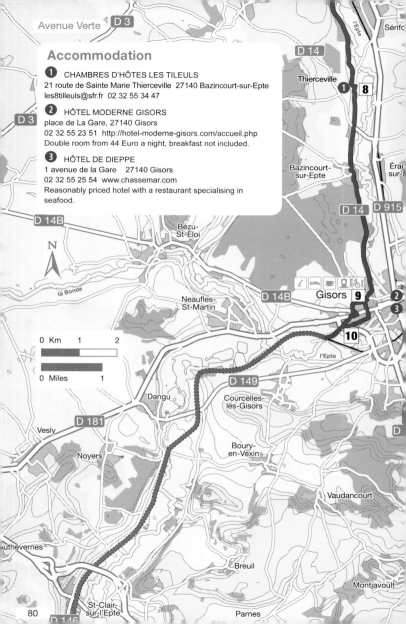

Avenue Verte D 3

Accommodation

1 CHAMBRES D'HÔTES LES TILEULS
21 route de Sainte Marie Thierceville 27140 Bazincourt-sur-Epte
les8tilleuls@sfr.fr 02 32 55 34 47

2 HÔTEL MODERNE GISORS
place de La Gare, 27140 Gisors
02 32 55 23 51 http://hotel-moderne-gisors.com/accueil.php
Double room from 44 Euro a night, breakfast not included.

3 HÔTEL DE DIEPPE
1 avenue de la Gare 27140 Gisors
02 32 55 25 54 www.chassemar.com
Reasonably priced hotel with a restaurant specialising in
seafood.

N

0 Km   1   2

0 Miles   1

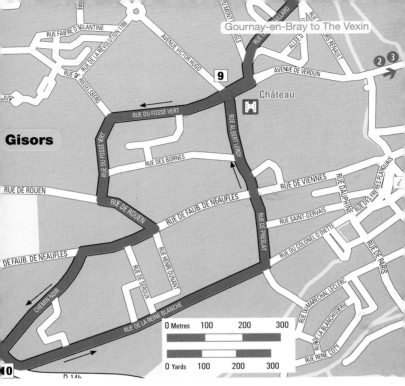

Gisors

At the bottom of the hill, don't be tempted to take the main road round to the left, but carry straight on and slightly right, up a gentle slope at the edge of the woodland. You may catch glimpses of the river Epte down to the left.

8 In Thierceville turn right at a fine country house. At the crossroads at the edge of Bazincourt continue straight ahead on the D14. In Bazincourt you will find a large number of fine old cottages and farm buildings. Carry on through the village and on towards Gisors, hugging the wooded edge of the Epte valley.

9 At the first major road junction in Gisors turn right. The official route goes straight ahead, but we recommend that you turn left for the classic Norman castle, which then offers fine views over the old town and the church and a good place for a picnic.

From Gisors town centre on rue de Viennes head south and you will soon pick up the Avenue Verte signs. Look out for the left turn into chemin Noir which is not easy to see and you join what appears to be a country lane.

10 Continue downhill until you meet the bypass and cross carefully into the road opposite, which runs alongside the river Epte. Soon turn right onto the "voie verte de la vallee de l'Epte" on the old railway line to Gasny. You can see the old tracks on the bridge over the Epte to the left.

The Epte Valley greenway is a fairly new path and is not as well developed as the original Avenue Verte south of Dieppe. There are very few villages directly on the traffic-free path down the Epte valley, but at each road junction you will find a helpful sign to the nearest village, with an indication of the range of services available. The railway path is naturally very easy to follow and passes through woodland and open fields and is never far from the river Epte.

11 On the approach to Bray-et-Lû you will notice the old zinc factory, dominating the village. The railway path is cut by the road and a roundabout, where you need to turn back sharp left and immediately right into the village. A channel of the river Epte passes under the factory, suggesting it may once have been water powered.

The peace and quiet of the Epte Valley traffic-free trail

© French Mystique Bike Tours

4 LA BUISONNIÈRE
19 rue Du Valcorbon 27630 Bus-St-Remy, Eure
02 32 52 33 09
Rural farmhouse with rooms from 65 Euros
http://la-buissonniere.over-blog.com/

5 DOMAINE DE LA GOULÉE
17, route de la Goulée 95510 Villers-en-Arthies
09 61 51 80 49 / 06 25 99 81 47
www.ledomainedelagoulee.com
Sumptuous countryside b & b with swimming pool, sauna, fitness room and garden. Around 2 km (1.25 miles) from the route.

6 LA PETITE FERME
2 route des Crêtes 95510 Chérence
01 34 78 23 18
http://www.cherence-lapetiteferme.com/
Rural bed and breakfast with rooms from 74 Euros pp a night, inc breakfast.
South of Bray-et-Lû

VEXIN ACCOMMODATION
The Vexin offers a number of luxury options too, offering the chance to stay in palatial style in an old château right next to the route:
Les Jardins d'Epicure, Bray-et-Lû
(01 34 67 75 87) and the Château de Maudétour at Maudétour-en-Vexin 06 13 24 77 04
www.chateaudemaudetour.com

 Gisors is the only train station on or near the route and is the terminus of a direct line to Paris St-Lazare, 1 hour 30 mins away.
Transilien services, linking Paris to its surroundings, accept bikes outside of rush hours. www.transilien.com

The surreal Axe Majeur at Cergy-
Pontoise - just off the route at
Vauréal

The Vexin ~ St-Germain

At Bray-et-Lû you head onto small roads and farm tracks across the Vexin, designated a *Parc Naturel Régional* so as to protect its gentle landscapes, architecture and wildlife. The museum of the Vexin is housed in a lovely château at Théméricourt. Soon after the Vexin things turn a little surreal as just off the route, between Cergy-Pontoise and Vauréal, is the gargantuan sculpture cum landscape feature known as the *Axe Majeur*, a startling sight and well worth the short detour. Heading across the river Seine things become very grand indeed, fine châteaux at Maisons-Laffitte and St-Germain, punctuated by lovely traffic-free riding through the forest of St-Germain and alongside the Seine itself.

Route Info

Distance 60 kilometres / 37 miles

Terrain & Route Surface The route across the rolling farmland and woods of the Vexin is a succession of minor roads and farm tracks of varying quality, some quite rough. The area has little traffic; indeed it struggles with problems caused by depopulation. From Cergy to St-Germain there is a real mixture of surfaces as road sections link a whole series of tracks and cycle lanes, some tarmac, some forest track (as on your approach to Maisons-Laffitte) and some good quality track by the River Seine on your final approach to St-Germain.

Off-road 32 % off-road comprising all kinds of surface from rough track to smooth tarmac.

Profile

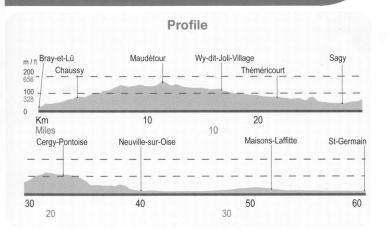

What to See & Do

• **The Vexin** is designated a Parc Naturel Régional with the aim of protecting its gentle landscapes, architecture and wildlife - as well as its human population who have been leaving the area steadily over the last few decades. You enter at Bray-et-Lû and head through the Parc Naturel's string of small, delightful villages using a mix of minor roads and tracks (dry weather only for the tracks at the time of writing - upgrading and new off-road routes were in the pipeline though).

The museum of the Vexin is housed in a lovely château at Théméricourt.
• **Villarceaux** is a beautiful country estate combining the ruins of a medieval fortified house, a sixteenth century mansion and an eighteenth century château set in sumptuous landscape gardens. The golf club restaurant is also open to the public and makes a classy lunch stop.
• The château at **Théméricourt** houses the museum of the French Vexin, showcasing its rare flora and fauna as well as local traditions.

Passing through the Vexin the Avenue Verte uses numerous tiny tracks and roads. This one is near Longuesse

The town of Maisons-Laffitte is surrounded by beautiful gardens

• Don't be tempted to keep pedalling past the modern surroundings of the Cergy area; it's home not only to a huge and attractive outdoor leisure park surrounding the ancient village of **Ham** but also the astonishingly grand **Axe Majeur walkway**. The walkway, just a short distance off the route, east of Cergy and Vauréal, is adorned with grand sculptures and in good weather opens up a lovely view to the area known as La Défense on the outskirts of Paris. It continues the grand avenue of viewpoints that crosses Paris, including the Arc de Triomphe and the Tuileries Gardens. The 3 km (2 mile) route starts at place des Colonnes Hubert Renaud at Cergy where the nearby bastide area and town clock are also worth a look.
• **Maisons-Laffitte** houses a grand château, acres of lovely forest tracks used for racehorse training and an attractive little town centre.
• **St-Germain** is altogether grander; not surprising as it was the summer residence of French kings from the 12th century onwards. The highlight of the current château is the terrace gardens, laid out by famous French landscape gardener Le Nôtre.

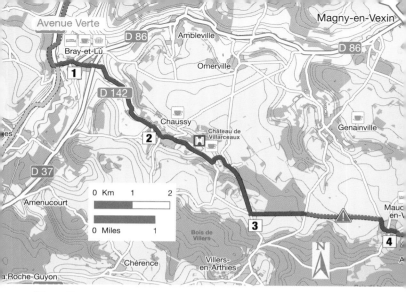

Directions

1 Having left the Epte Valley traffic-free path and headed through Bray-et-Lû centre go straight over a roundabout and start the steady climb out of the Epte valley. At the next junction continue straight ahead on the D142 to Chaussy and the Parc Naturel du Vexin. This is a protected landscape of rolling hills, meadows, woodland and villages.

2 You can't miss the church in Chaussy as it's built almost in the middle of the road! Continue up the valley to Villarceaux, where you catch glimpses of the château before it reveals itself. Turn left and climb steeply up the hill through woodland. At the top keep ahead and slightly right before descending gently. Continue uphill to a junction, now out of the Epte valley at a high point between Bray-et-Lû and Théméricourt.

3 Turn left onto an unnamed road, which runs straight as far as the eye can see. At the next junction the sign points ahead onto a rough track. This is not a mistake, it is the official route. It is passable on a road bike when dry, but likely to be difficult in the wet. Rejoin the road at Maudétour, where you turn right. Turn left at the church and pass the château on your right (a b&b).

4 The official route turns right down a grass track, but we strongly recommend you continue on the road to the north of this track, to Arthies.

Accommodation

1 CHAMBRES D'HÔTES LE PIGEONNIER
Château d'Hazeville 95420 Wy-dit-Joli-Village
01 34 67 06 17

2 CHAMBRES D'HÔTES LE CLOS DU SAULE
2 Grande Rue 95450 Gouzangrez
01 30 27 94 99 www.leclosdusaule.com

The Vexin offers a number of luxury accommodation options too, offering the chance to stay in palatial style in an old château right next to the route:
Les Jardins d'Epicure, Bray-et-Lû
01 34 67 75 87
Château de Maudétour at Maudétour-en-Vexin
06 13 24 77 04 www.chateaudemaudetour.com

5 Take the D159 to Wy-Dit-Joli-Village, which is a fast, gentle downhill stretch. Go straight ahead through the village, with a wiggle right and left. At the last junction in the village keep right and head out into open countryside. In Gadancourt go straight across the first junction and right at the second.

6 Another fast downhill leads to delightful Avernes. Unfortunately, the official route takes us away from the village centre, with a left turn at the Grande Rue and a right fork up rue de Clos Brigent. Continue straight ahead until the tarmac runs out and join a rough track. Take a left then right on farm tracks and continue until you meet tarmac roads in Théméricourt. You may prefer to take the D81 main road between Avergnes and Théméricourt to avoid these tracks. The Maison du Parc comprises an impressive château and an extensive public park. Not many facilities, but there are places to stay and at least one restaurant.

7 From the Maison du Parc (north entrance) in Théméricourt follow the signs through narrow streets, turning right then left onto the D81 towards Vigny.

i **Théméricourt** (Vexin) Maison du Parc 01.34.48.66.10
Maisons-Laffitte 41 avenue de Longueil 01.39.62.63.64
www.tourisme-maisonslaffitte.fr
Saint-Germain-en-Laye 38 rue au Pain 01.30.87.20.63
www.ot-saintgermainenlaye.fr

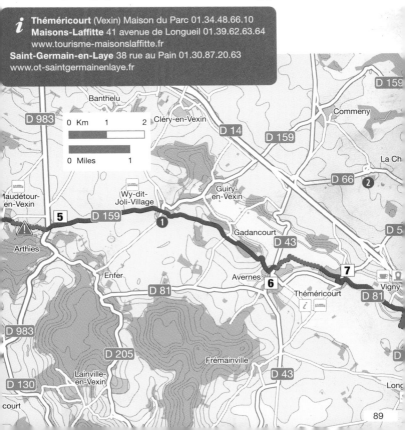

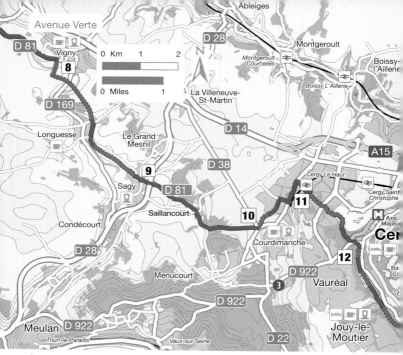

8 At the town sign in Vigny, turn right up a stone track beside a stone wall. If you are short of supplies you may want to continue into the town centre. Follow the track by the stone wall, cross a road (from the town centre) and continue onto another track, which climbs up and then down again into Longuesse. The surface is bumpy in places and you may prefer to take the D169 main road in the valley, especially in wet weather. Continue on-road then join another track, which has a compacted stone surface. Again there is a convenient on-road alternative nearby.

9 The village of Sagy is attractive with many old buildings and some recently restored or rebuilt. Turn right into the village centre with its artisan bakery (open early morning and evening). Turn left and cross the main road for Saillancourt. On leaving the village bear left at a roundabout, uphill. Continue to the edge of Courdimanche with its watertower.

10 At the roundabout bear left onto the cycle track. At the next junction turn left and join the road towards Cergy (new cycle tracks due on this section so exact directions may vary). Pass over two roundabouts then at traffic lights turn right, joining a bus lane for a short distance before turning left for the railway station and town centre on a contraflow cycle lane.

11 Turn right in front of the station and follow the ramp down to cross a busy road into the park opposite. The narrow path continues under a road bridge, winding through an attractively landscaped park and ending on a quiet road where you turn left. Continue downhill towards the Oise valley, crossing a busy road at traffic lights into the old town of Vauréal.

12 At a T-junction of narrow streets in Vauréal turn right and cross the road with the old church to your left. Now continue on a varied high level route with views across the Oise valley. There are few signs, but simply continue until you reach a major road, leading down to the bridge over the river. You are now in Neuville-sur-Oise, where the "Beauvais loop" rejoins the main route.

Note: For detailed mapping of the route around Cergy see pages 126-127

Sagy is typical of the many handsome villages in the Vexin

⇌ Numerous local Parisian trains (Transilien) and RER services (express trains), once you have crossed the Vexin, which has little if anything in the way of public transport: Cergy-le-Haut, Cergy-Préfecture, Neuville-Université, Conflans Fin d'Oise, Maisons-Laffitte, Sartrouville and St-Germain are all on RER line (A) and the latter four are also served by Transilien trains.

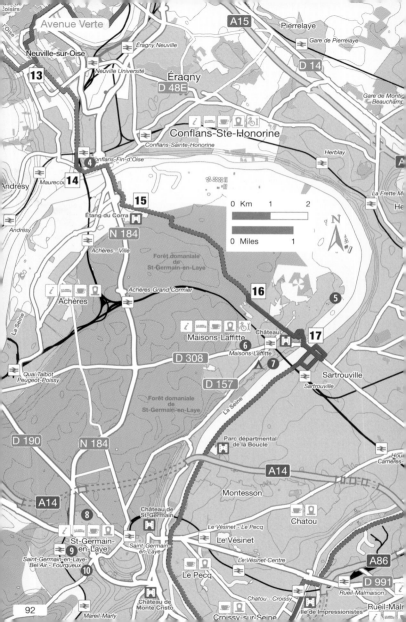

13 After crossing the bridge, turn right through a car park and join the riverside path under the big road bridge go straight ahead onto a narrow bumpy track, which emerges onto a tarmac road beside the water works.

14 Continue to the confluence of the major French rivers, the Oise and the Seine. At the railway bridge join the riverside path with large barges moored at the wharf. Pass under the road bridge and footbridge then sharp left and up the ramp to cross the Seine. Continue straight on up the old road, turn left between concrete blocks then right through a narrow gap into a housing estate. Continue on the road and just before the entrance gate turn right onto a cycle track. At its end turn left onto a crushed stone path alongside a stone wall, then turn right into the forest and left at the first junction.

15 Continue on the well surfaced forest track until you meet a wooden post at a confusing ten-way junction. Take the best surfaced track bearing right, signed route de la Vente Frileuse. At the road turn left onto another compacted stone track. Follow this down until you emerge through an old gateway into a housing area of Maisons-Laffitte.

16 Turn right onto the road, then left down the grand boulevard towards the magnificent château. Continue up to the château gates, turn left then right and right again at the main road. Follow to the roundabout on the north side of the bridge over the Seine.

17 Cross the river Seine on the main bridge opposite the château and take the first right into rue de la Constituante. Turn right again then left to join the riverside road. The tarmac gives way to a wide gravel path at the edge of Sartrouville. The path improves on the approach to Le Pecq, where a new surface has been constructed through the built-up area. The majority of this improved section is alongside a quiet road, which can be comfortably used by cyclists.

3 CHAMBRES D'HÔTES
François Lainée
10 rue de la Mairie 95000 Boisemont
01 34 66 87 32 (see map on page 90)

There is a cluster of reasonably-priced chain-style accommodation west of the route at Cergy, near the Oise route split. See pages 126-127

4 HÔTEL LE CLEMENCEAU
1 rue Georges-Clemenceau
78700 Conflans-Sainte-Honorine
01 39 72 61 30 leclemenceau@yahoo.fr

5 HÔTEL AU PUR SANG
2 avenue de la Pelouse 78600 Maisons-Laffitte
01 39 62 03 21

6 CHAMBRE D'HÔTE MSR HOFLEITNER
126 avenue du Général de Gaulle
78600 Maisons-Laffitte
01 39 62 86 49 http://chambre_a_paris.voila.net
Accueil Vélo member (the French version of Cyclists Welcome'). Double room in the same apartment block where the owners live.

△ 7 CAMPINGS INTERNATIONAL DE MAISONS-LAFFITTE
1 rue Johnson 78600 Maisons-Laffitte
01 39 12 21 91
www.campint.com

8 HAVRE HÔTEL
92 rue Léon Desoyer 78100 Saint-Germain
01 34 51 41 05 reservation@havre-hotel.com

9 HÔTEL DU COQ
45 boulevard de la Paix 78100 Saint-Germain
01 30 61 48 48 01 39 73 83 36
Good discounts on Friday and Saturday nights

10 CHAMBRES D'HÔTES LES CLÉMATITES
32 rue de Fourqueux 78100 St-Germain
09 53 33 61 83 http://chambredhoteclematite.com

A Beauvais street scene

© Peter Gutierrez

Gournay-en-Bray ~ Beauvais

This will remain one of the hilliest sections on the Avenue Verte until the old railway is converted to a traffic-free trail between Gournay and Beauvais. The hills make for some lovely panoramas across the rolling agricultural Bray countryside and the charms of the villages are low key and intimate; the characterful churches of Ons-en-Bray and Goincourt for example or the half-timbered buildings of the Bray countryside. There's also the usual very welcome accompaniment of a string of village bars and bakeries, providing ready fuel to climb the hills. Towards Beauvais the countryside changes, dominated by woods rather than farms, and on your final approach to the city you encounter the attractive Avelon and Thérain rivers, as cycle tracks and narrow back streets lead to the magnificent, dominating mass of the cathedral.

Route Info

Distance 39 kilometres / 24 miles

Terrain & Route Surface Plenty of hill-climbing on minor roads on perhaps the toughest section of the Avenue Verte, though a traffic-free link is planned for the near future. Remember the route splits at St-Germer-de-Fly between western and eastern options, this chapter covering the eastern option.

Off-road All on-road

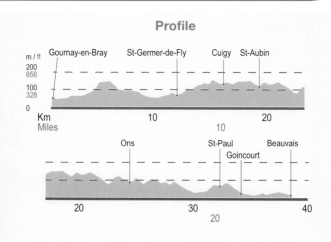

Profile

What to See & Do

• For details of **St-Germer-de-Fly** see page 76.
• A string of **attractive Brayon villages** line the route on minor roads between Gournay and Beauvais; Cuigy, St-Aubin, Ons and Goincourt all have their own unique, small scale charm.

Until the traffic-free route is continued from Forges-les-Eaux to Gournay, and eventually on to Beauvais, there are plenty of ridgetop rides and attractive views to be had on this section.

• The chief attraction of **Beauvais** is without doubt its **cathedral;** intended to be the greatest piece of Gothic architecture in France it was never finished, suffering from grandiose ambitions that saw various parts being built only to collapse soon after. Even today it remains without a nave. Despite past misfortunes it still dwarfs the centre of Beauvais and houses a couple of fascinating clocks, one medieval that has continued working for some 700 years. The other is a masterpiece made in the 1860s, comprising some 90,000 mechanical parts. When the hour strikes, 68 automatons come to life and a magnificent clockwork display unfolds.

Beauvais

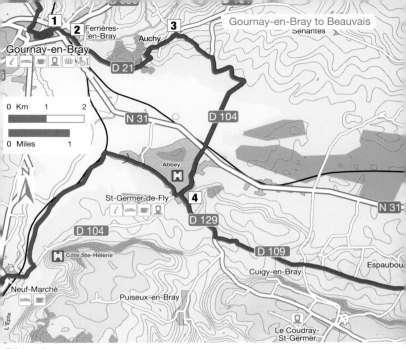

Directions

1 From the centre of Gournay, which features an attractive square with fountains, take the rue du Dr. Duchesne, heading east towards Ferrières. When the road becomes one-way east to west, take a right into a cul-de-sac. This is a no through road for motors but bikes can use the delightful boulevard des Planquettes, a tree-lined avenue. This path crosses the Epte on a footbridge then rejoins rue du Dr. Duchesne by turning left and right. Beware – this section of the road is still one-way but bikes are allowed.

2 Continue to the traffic lights at a busy intersection with the N31. Cross the main road and the railway line then immediately right on the D21. Continue past the Danone factory and you are soon in open countryside, with a steady climb through woodland to Bethel and Auchy. You are rewarded with extensive views across the valley and a pastoral scene with grazing cattle.

3 At Auchy look out for a sharp right towards Orsimont and St-Germer-de-Fly. Continue until you meet the D104 and follow this all the way to St-Germer. The road twists and turns and there are some short steep climbs until you coast into St-Germer, which is dominated by the imposing abbey. Take care crossing the N31 again (no traffic lights here). Just before the N31 you will notice a short rise to meet the old railway line, which forms part of the long term plan for the Avenue Verte between Gournay and Beauvais.

4 St-Germer is the junction for two branches of the current Avenue Verte route – at the main square turn left for Beauvais or keep right for the alternative route via Gisors and Cergy. Take the D129 towards Le Coudray and after a short distance turn left onto the D109 for Cuigy-en-Bray and St-Aubin-en-Bray.

5 The D109 climbs gradually out of the Epte Valley through the rolling countryside of the Pays de Bray region. Turn left 1.6 km (1 mile) after leaving St-Aubin-en-Bray then turn right. A steep descent and sharp climb bring you into the attractive village of Ons-en-Bray. Keep a close eye on the signs as the route takes some sharp turns through the village. Join the D2 as the landscape becomes more wooded and continue to La Barrière and turn left off the busier road. There follows a long descent through woodland, over the N31 bridge and down to the Avelon valley. To the left you catch sight of the Parc Saint Paul theme park, a good place for families to stop.

6 The route continues right on the busy D931 for a short distance before turning left on quieter roads towards Saint-Paul. Just after leaving the main road, cross the old railway between Gournay and Beauvais, which is planned to be part of the future Avenue Verte route. Follow the road round to the right and after 1 km (0.6 miles) turn left into Saint-Paul on a small hill. In the village centre bear right onto the rue de la Petite Fontaine. Continue up to the D626 and turn right towards Goincourt. Cross the D931 and soon enter the village with its attractive white painted church. Turn right and pass the church then cross the old railway for a second time.

7 Turn left onto the busy D981. In just over 1 km (0.6 miles), before the main road bears left, the route continues straight ahead on the D139, alongside the old railway. This soon leads to the first industrial area of Beauvais. As the centre of the city comes into view in a mixed industrial and residential area, turn left onto rue Tetard and cross the old railway once more.

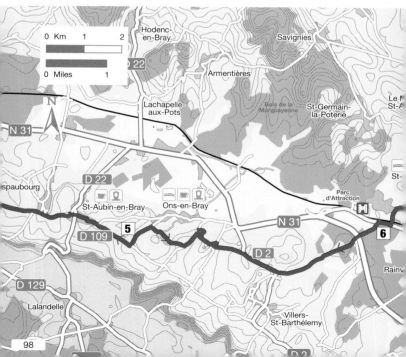

8 Follow round to the right and after a short distance turn left and cross the Avelon river on a footbridge (see town centre map overleaf also). This is the first time you get the sense of being in a large city, faced with the busy boulevard Saint-Jean.
The Avenue Verte has a one-way system through the city and heading east you turn left to follow an attractive cycle track between the Thérian river and the boulevard. Cross the boulevard at rue du Docteur Gerard and turn left into rue Saint-Nicholas. Before reaching the church on the corner of a parking area, turn right into a narrow street with an attractive old timber frame building on the corner. Turn immediately left into rue de l'École du Chant, another narrow street which emerges onto a wider road with the magnificent cathedral to the right. Turn right onto rue Saint-Pierre and pass the cathedral into the city centre.

Accommodation

1 LA GRANGE
1 rue du Marais 60000 Fouquenies
03 44 79 02 51
http://www.gaudissart.com
Hostel style accommodation for 15, some
4 km (2.5 miles) north of the route coming into
Beauvais

Numerous cycle carrying trains link Paris Nord station to Beauvais taking around 1 hour 30 mins.
There are very infrequent bike carrying services from Serqueux, on the Neufchâtel-Gournay section, changing at Abancourt, to Beauvais.

i **Gournay-en-Bray** 9 place d'Armes 02.35.90.28.34 www.ot-gournay-en-bray.fr
Beauvais 1 rue Beauregard 03.44.15.30.30 en.beauvaistourisme.fr

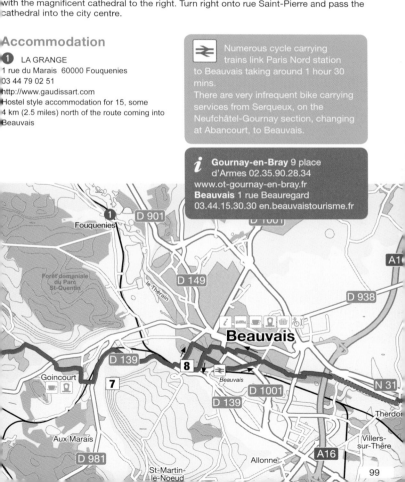

2 LE PALAIS BLEU
9 rue Saint Nicolas 60000 Beauvais
03 44 45 12 58
http://www.hoteldupalaisbeauvais.com
Rooms from 57 Euro, breakfast not included.

3 HÔTEL DU CYGNE
24 rue Carnot 60000 Beauvais
03 44 48 68 40 www.hotelducygne-beauvais.com

4 HÔTEL DE LA RÉSIDENCE
24 rue Louis Borel 60000 Beauvais
03 44 48 30 98   09 59 75 66 75
http://www.hotellaresidence.fr
Reasonable prices, about 1 km (0.6 miles) to the
north of the centre.

There is the usual collection of budget hotels
near avenue John Fitzgerald Kennedy around
2 km (1.25 miles) south of the route as it leaves
Beauvais, just north of Allonne, though they are
hemmed in by very bike-unfriendly trunk roads.

Beauvais's cathedral dominates the town

© Beauvais Tourisme

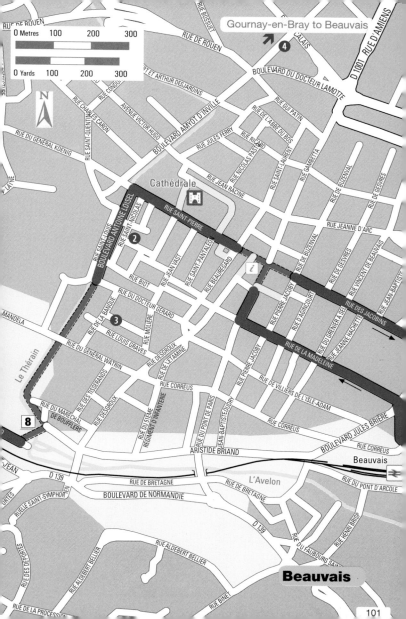

Beauvais

Cake stops and culture at Senlis

Beauvais ~ Senlis

This section uses part of the developing ambitious cycle network of the Oise area, which will eventually total some 240 km (149 miles) of cycle network. This particular part links four of the Oise's most attractive and historic towns and cities; Beauvais, Clermont de l'Oise, Pont-Sainte-Maxence and Senlis via a succession of attractive small stone villages. Clermont has a lovely ancient centre and Pont-Sainte-Maxence a charming waterside setting but it's Senlis that has retained the most reminders of a rich past; as you wander around its cobbled streets and the graceful outline of its cathedral it's not hard to see why it was chosen as the backdrop to several celebrated French films.

Route Info

Distance 67 kilometres / 42 miles

Terrain & Route Surface Largely easygoing gradients with plenty of excellent traffic-free tarmac along the course of the Trans-Oise greenway, which the Avenue Verte uses here. The only real climbing comes, briefly, after Clermont and Pont-Sainte-Maxence. A wonderful traffic-free cycleway through the forest is used to approach the grandeur of Senlis.

Off-road 34% traffic-free, mainly on tarmac surfaces

Profile

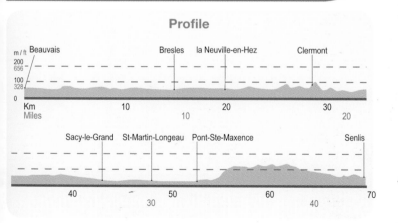

What to See & Do

• Pretty villages with pretty churches such as Bresles and Agnetz herald your arrival in lovely **Clermont-de-l'Oise**. In a pretty hill top setting (Clermont actually means clear mountain) you'll find the ruins of a twelfth-century tower, the Nointel gateway, the church of Saint-Samson and the chapel of Lardières.

• After passing through the Sacy marshlands comes your first sight of the river Oise at **Pont-Sainte-Maxence**. There's a relaxing marina and a flamboyantly styled church overlooking an attractive town centre. Nearby and en-route is Moncel Abbey, with sprawling grounds. More detail at www.abbayedumoncel.fr

© Wikimedia Creative Commons

One of the ancient gateways to the city in Clermont-de-l'Oise

© Wikimedia Creative Commons

The historic
Henri IV square
in Senlis

• The royal city of **Senlis** is a
wonderfully picturesque end to
the day's riding and a former
haunt of French kings. Its timeless
atmosphere is largely thanks to its
ancient, encircling walls and the
central and very graceful Notre-
Dame cathedral combined with a
patchwork of squares and alleys,
peppered with monuments and
mansions. With this rich architectural
backdrop it's not surprising French
films *Peau d'Âne* and *La Reine
Margot* were shot here.
The town claims an unusual
collection of museums too; art and
archaeology, history and architecture
(Hôtel de Vermandois), North African
military history (Spahi museum) and
the art of hunting.

105

Directions

For Beauvais detail see page 101.

1 In the city centre,continue ahead on Rue des Jacobins. At the busy boulevard cross the road and turn right onto the cycle track. Follow the signed route round the train station and retail park. At the busy boulevard bear right towards the railway station, then left past the station. The route joins rue du Wage, through a commercial area. Where this road bears left and joins another road, turn right into the narrow rue Matheas. Follow the bend to the left, then turn right and cross another road into rue des Aulnaies. This street leads to an attractive woodland path, which emerges into a residential area. Turn sharp left then at the main road turn right. Continue straight ahead through an industrial area to the edge of the city.

2 Cross over the A16 into open countryside, follow the road left then right to Therdonne. Continue through the village and turn left at a roundabout to join a cycle track, part of the ambitious Trans'Oise network. The purpose built cycle track continues by the D931 to Bresles' outskirts, a small town with an impressive church and castle.

3 Turn left after the town centre then right onto a superb new traffic-free railway path. Just before the end turn right onto a minor road, then left onto the D931. On leaving the second village, rejoin the impressive cycle track beside the main road. The route passes through a forest, which is marred by passing traffic on the road.

4 After leaving the forest, turn right into the attractive old village of Agnetz and follow gentle, undulating quiet roads into Clermont. You may catch sight of the impressive church spire on top of the hill that Clermont occupies.
Follow the one-way system through the town – at a T-junction turn left, then right and right again into rue de la Croix Picard, which climbs steadily to the attractive town centre. Turn sharp left into rue de la République, with the historic main street and church straight ahead up the hill. Turn right into rue du Chatelier below the church, then right and downhill into rue Marcel Duchemin.

5 Turn right again into rue du Mont de Crème and leave the town behind, crossing under a main road and over a railway at a level crossing. Turn right to Breuil-le-Vert, where you turn left at a cross-roads. Cross the river La Brèche with its marshy woodland and continue to the village of Breuil-le-Sec. From Brueil-le-Sec continue on quiet roads through delightful Nointel and Catenoy.

6 After leaving Catenoy turn right onto the D10, a fairly busy and uninspiring road through agricultural land.

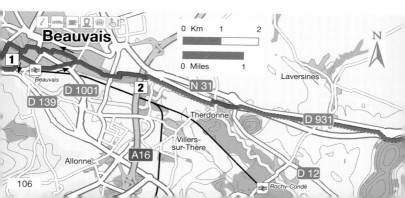

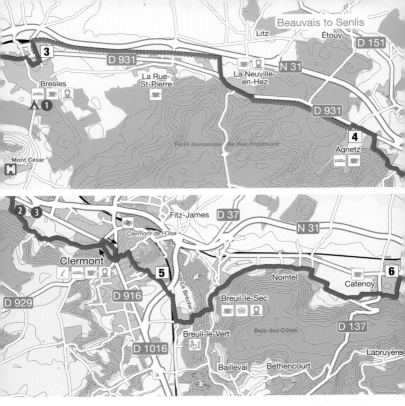

Accommodation

▲ ① CAMPING DE LA TRYE
rue de Trye 60510 Bresles
03 44 07 80 95
www.camping-de-la-trye.com

② HÔTEL AKENA
rue des Buttes 60600 Agnetz
03 44 50 69 59 www.hotels-akena.com

③ LE CLERMOTEL
60 rue des Buttes, Zone Hôtelière
60600 Agnetz
03 44 50 09 90 www.clermotel.fr

There are Paris Nord,
bike carrying train links to
Clermont (45 mins) and Pont-Sainte-
Maxence (40 mins)

Catenoy

Avenue Verte

137

Grandfres

Sacy-le-Petit

Labruyère

Sacy-le-Grand

D 1017

7

D 10

St-Martin-
Longueau

D 13

Bazicourt

Houda

Verderonne

D 20

L'Oise

Cinqueux

D 200

Les Ageux

Pont-Sainte-Maxence

i

Pont-Ste-Maxence

N

D 29

Brenouille

L'Oise

Pontpo

Rieux D 200

8

Abbaye Royale
du Moncel

4

D 120

D 120

i Clermont 19 place de l'Hôtel de Ville
03.44.50.40.25
Pont-Sainte-Maxence 18 Rue Louis Boilet
03.44.72.35.90
www.pontsaintemaxence-tourisme.fr
Senlis place du Parvis Notre Dame 03.44.53.06.40
www.senlis-tourisme.fr

Mont
Pagnotte

Mont-la-Ville

Fleurines

Villers-
St-Frambourg

❹ LES GAUDINS
60700 Pontpoint
03 44 70 03 98
http://www.chambre-pontpoint.fr
B&B 12 km (7.5 miles) from Senlis,
rural and cosy.

D 1017

D 932a

9

D 1330

Chamant

A

7 Pass through Sacy-le-Grand onto a straight run into St-Martin-Longeau, where the route turns right into the D1017. Join the slightly rough cycle track beside the road, downhill to Les Ageux and the river Oise. Cross the river over the bridge with its distinctive curved arch structure to the town of Pont-Ste-Maxence.

8 Turn left onto the D123 for Pontpoint, passing close by Moncel Abbey. Turn right and climb steeply into the extensive and beautiful Fôret d'Halatte. Turn right again at the top and follow tarmac roads for several kilometres through the forest. The second half is closed to motor traffic and is wonderfully quiet and isolated.

9 After emerging from the forest, turn left into the village of Chamant and right onto the busy D932A, where an alternative route is planned. Cross over the D1330 dual carriageway and continue straight ahead where the main road bears left at traffic lights.

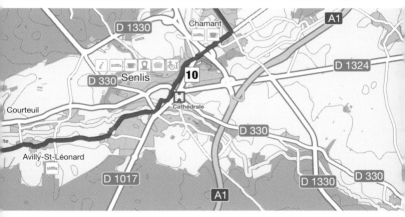

Senlis' intimate centre

10 At the bridge over the river bear left into rue Carnot into the heart of this attractive medieval town with narrow streets and old stone buildings (see map overleaf). Continue into rue St Pierre, rue St Hilaire and place de la Halle to the old town with attractive streets and numerous shops and restaurants.

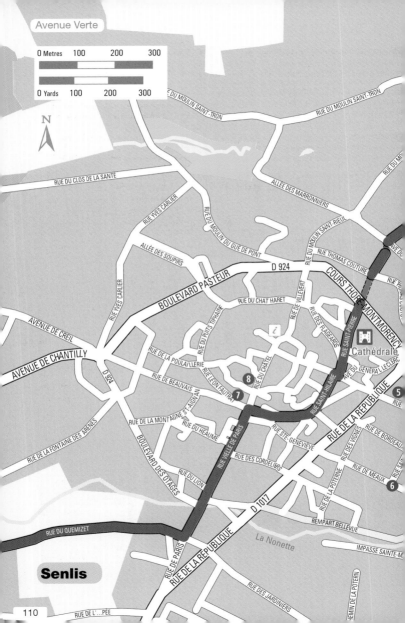

5 HOSTELLERIE DE LA PORTE BELLON
1 rue Bellon 60300 Senlis
03 44 53 03 05 http://www.portebellon.fr

6 LE RELAIS DES REMPARTS
3 rue Des Meaux 60300 Senlis
03 44 60 83 42 http://www.relaisdesremparts.fr
Small apartments from 90 Euro a night

7 LE CATEL ECOSSAIS
rue de Beauvais 60300 Senlis
06 63 90 78 09 isa.bataille@wanadoo.fr

8 CHEZ SYLVAINE REERINK
3 rue de la Chancellerie 60300 Senlis
03 44 53 06 16 03 44 53 94 82
http://perso.orange.fr/bbsenlis

There is a good stock of chain hotels on avenue
Général de Gaulle (to the north-east of the centre
off rue Maréchal de Foch) about
1.5 km (1 mile) from the town centre. Try Ibis
Budget Senlis 08 92 68 08 24, Ibis Senlis 03 44 53
70 50 or Hôtel Campanile Senlis 03 44 60 05 07.

Senlis' graceful cathedral

*An idyllic traffic-free approach to
Chantilly on the Avenue Verte*

Senlis ~ L'Isle Adam

Heading back towards the river Oise from Senlis you get a glimpse of France's aristocratic history. Tracks lead through old hunting forests and the splendours of horse-racing Chantilly can't fail to impress, whether it's the moat-encircled château, the sumptuous horse stables or the surrounding lawned expanses that capture the imagination. An equally impressive reminder of the past is found in the beautiful cloisters and gardens of Royaumont Abbey. After skirting the charming town of Asnières-sur-Oise the eponymous river provides a charming backdrop to the final few kilometres riding into L'Isle Adam.

L'Isle Adam has plenty of services but is also a charming destination, with its own riverside beach and even a Chinese pavillion all waiting to be explored.

Route Info

Distance 37 kilometres / 23 miles

Terrain & Route Surface Easy gradients along intimate valleys and through woods on a variety of minor roads and tracks before some fine riverside riding along the Oise (though some sections may be a little rough).

Off-road 30% traffic-free on wide, smooth tarmac and rough tracks.

Profile

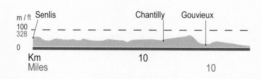

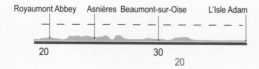

What to See & Do

• The charming Nonette valley and lovely traffic-free section of forest riding give you a chance to explore the grandeurs of **Chantilly**. Known as the Newmarket of France because of the racecourse and training stables here, it's a fascinating place to explore. Thoroughbreds can be seen exercising along the forest rides that surround the town and the two big races of the season, the Jockey Club and the Prix de Diane are incredibly popular.

The towering **17th century stables** are themselves a sight to behold but there are also acres of lawns around the town and its main draw, a fairytale-like **château** on its eastern edge, surrounded by a moat.

Art as well as architecture lovers might be tempted inside the château as it houses an incredible art collection. The library here also houses one of the most celebrated ever Books of Hours (a kind of 'primer' for devoted Christians of the time, with chosen prayers to be said at allotted times), this one being one of the most lavishly and painstakingly illustrated of all.

The Musée Vivant du Cheval is, as the name suggests, a museum with real live horses as the centrepiece and is housed in the huge stable blocks. There is a collection of worldwide breeds housed around a central ring where demonstrations of horsemanship are held.

Chantilly Château

Royaumont Abbey

© Joël-Damase

• **Gouvieux** is a pleasant town most notable for its troglodyte dwellings that were largely occupied up until the 19th century then progressively abandoned (today a few are occupied, others used for wine storage)

• **Royaumont** is the largest Cistercian abbey in the Île-de-France (the area including Paris and its surroundings) and it is also a beautiful building in a lovely wetland and forest environment, its music season attracting worldwide attention. Access to the grounds and parts of the abbey 365 days a year with tearooms open weekends and public holidays. www.royaumont.com

• **L'Isle Adam** is a small-scale holiday resort on the river Oise, with two attractive wooded islands, one with a beach, 'constructed' around 1910 (currently open April-June weekends then daily until September) and originally conceived with slides, diving boards and waterfalls. Other things to see include a very reasonably priced local museum of art and history (Louis Senlecq), a wonderful and very old indoor market, and a Chinese Pavilion. There's also a lovely walk on the east side of the river Oise, across two small wooden bridges.

Accommodation

Chantilly, some 13 km (8 miles) on from Senlis, is a fascinating place with a good stock of hotels. They include reasonably-priced options such as Hotel l'Avenue in the heart of the town and the usual chain offerings from Campanile and Kyriad as well as a host of luxury establishments, befitting the grand royal buildings here.

Bike carrying services from Paris Nord to Chantilly-Gouvieux (SNCF), Nointel-Mours (RER) and L'Isle Adam-Parmain (RER). www.voyages-sncf.com www.ratp.com

Directions

1 In the town centre turn left into Rue de Paris, down hill and across the river. Turn right into Rue du Quemizet past gardens and orchards. Whe the road bears left, join a track beside allotments. Rejoin the road and turn right into a pastoral landscape in the Nonette valley, a tributary of the Oise.

2 In the village of Avilly (not Avilly-St-Léonard), turn left into the attractive main street rue du Calvaire. At the next junction bear right and at the next six-way junction go straight ahead into route de l'Entonnoir. Bear left onto a woodland track, which follows the fenced boundary of the Chantilly estate.

3 The track emerges into a car park outside the magnificent Chantilly château. Turn left at the chateau entrance up a cobbled road and at the roundabout turn right into woodland again. At the next roundabout the road bears left and a woodland path continues straight ahead. This path emerges beside the Hippodrome de Chantilly, the world famous racecourse. Continue beside the racecourse and rejoin the road through woodland.

4 At the roundabout bear right and pass in front of Chantilly station. At the main road D909 turn left and pass under the railway bridge. There are two route options into Gouvieux, either use the cycle route beside the D909 or turn left after the bridge, then right onto the quieter chemin des Aigles.

5 Continue on the D909 through Gouvieux and where the main road bears right, continue ahead onto avenue de la République. This becomes a rough track through woodland, which emerges at a roundabout onto a private estate with limited signing. Bear left onto 9ème avenue. Continue through the wooded estate and join a gated road through open countryside, which leads to the village of Baillon.

6 At the far end of the village turn right, then right again to pass through an attractive parkland landscape with lakes and the Abbey of Royaumont. Cross the D909 onto a short stretch of old road, then cross the D922 into Asnières.

7 The route on grand rue skirts round Asnières' attractive old centre (worth a visit). Continue on the road towards Noisy-sur-Oise and on the outskirts turn right then immediately left onto the farm track, which leads to a bend on the river Oise and an attractive picnic area.

The magnificent racecourse at Chantilly

8 After Noisy-sur-Oise the route rejoins the main road then bears right to pass under the D922, joining a rough track towards Beaumont-sur-Oise. Cross the busy D929 and enter the town. Pass the bridge over to the industrial area of Persan and leave the town on rue Saint Roch.

9 At a large roundabout, bear left onto rue de la Cimenterie and through the small town of Mours. Once back into open countryside, the route leaves the road to the right and joins a rough track. Cyclists with narrow tyres may prefer to follow the D922 into L'Isle Adam. At the time of writing (2013) this section was rough, stony and muddy in places, although improvements are planned. The track passes under the D922 through a subway and drops back down to the river Oise.

10 Passing under two wide road bridges that cross the river, the route joins a woodland path set back from the river. This path can be muddy and slow going, but it soon emerges onto a road for a short distance. The route rejoins the delightful riverside path, passing fields and woodland. Passing a lock, the path continues alongside an access road and emerges onto the road adjacent to the attractive stone bridge, where the route turns right. A visit to the interesting old town of L'Isle Adam is well worthwhile, not least for the numerous shops and restaurants.

© Titou Lannes Creative Commons

L'Isle Adam

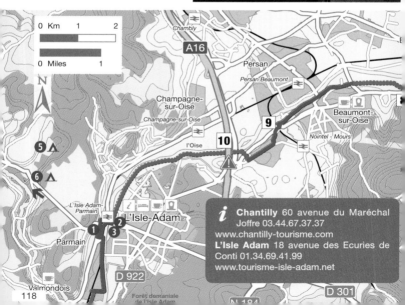

i **Chantilly** 60 avenue du Maréchal Joffre 03.44.67.37.37
www.chantilly-tourisme.com
L'Isle Adam 18 avenue des Ecuries de Conti 01.34.69.41.99
www.tourisme-isle-adam.net

1 MAISON DELALAU

131 rue du Maréchal Foch 95620 Parmain
01 34 73 02 92
chambresdhotes.parmain@wanadoo.fr
Bike-friendly b&b in Parmain, just across the
bridge from L'Isle Adam

2 AU BONHEUR DE L'ISLE

6 place du Pâtis 95290 L'Isle Adam
01 34 69 03 08
Budget option next to several restaurants

3 LE CABOUILLET

5 quai de l'Oise 95290 L'Isle-Adam, France
01 34 69 00 90 logishotels.com
Luxury option on an island in the river

There are several camping options a little distance from L'Isle Adam:

▲ 4 CAMPING LES PRINCES

route des Princes
95270 Asnières-sur-Oise 01 30 35 40 92
www.lesprinces.fr
Camping and mobile home rental
(see map on page 116)

▲ 5 CAMPING PARC DE SÉJOUR DE L'ÉTANG

10 chemin des Belles Vues
Nesles-a-Vallée 95690 01 34 70 62 89

▲ 6 CAMPING DU VAL DE NESLES

chemin de Chambly Nesles-a-Vallée 95690
01 34 70 63 24 levaldenesles@gmail.com

The Chinese Pavillion
in L'Isle Adam

© Titou Lannes Creative Commons

The historic port town of
Conflans-Sainte-Honorine

L'Isle Adam ~ St-Germain

From L'Isle Adam to St-Germain the Avenue Verte continues alongside the river Oise through an area that has inspired many famous French artists. After a fine riverside stretch the route takes to the main street of Auvers-sur-Oise, Vincent van Gogh's resting place, and not surprisingly something of a visitor magnet because of this. Another highpoint of this section is the town of Pontoise; like Senlis before it, it is full of picturesque old buildings and a favourite of film directors such as Roman Polanski. The route runs alongside the last stretch of the Oise before it reaches the Seine, having come more than 300 km (175 miles) from its source in Belgium. For the route from Neuville-sur-Oise to St-Germain see pages 92-93

Route Info

Distance 41 kilometres / 25 miles

Terrain & Route Surface Riverside riding in the main, first alongside the Oise, then the Seine on a real mixture of roads and tracks, some traffic-free tarmac and some unsealed surfaces.

Off-road 36% traffic-free on a wide variety of surfaces.

Profile

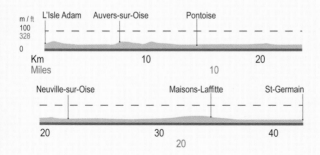

What to See & Do

• **Auvers-sur-Oise** was once home to Vincent Van Gogh and he and brother Theo are buried here. The 'Way of the Impressionists' walk follows the river and famous artists have signature paintings displayed at the spots they depict. Van Gogh only spent around seventy days here but painted more than seventy pictures. You can visit his room upstairs at Auberge Ravoux which is still a working restaurant.

Other artists also figure prominently in the town's history including Cézanne, Daubigny, Pissarro and Rousseau.
Daubigny's house is now both the town museum and home to a permanent collection of his paintings. Other buildings with strong links to the impressionist painters include the church and the house of Dr Gachet, Van Gogh's physician (open to the public).

Auvers

© Auvers Tourism

122

© Auvers Tourism

The church at Auvers

• **Pontoise's** old town is built on a limestone peak above the Oise valley. Ancient squares and cobbled streets lead to the 12th century cathedral of Saint-Maclou and what remains of the Carmel monastery nearby. The town's ancient ambience combined with an astonishing network of cellars have attracted filmmakers from Roman Polanski to Olivier Dahan; it claims to be the third most filmed town in France.

• For details of **Ham, L'Axe Majeur, Maisons-Laffitte** and **St-Germain** see page 87.

© Auvers Tourism

Directions

1 The bridge crosses two channels of the river Oise into the town of Parmain. After crossing the railway line, there is a one-way system through the town. Heading south, continue past the station then turn left onto the D64 and D4. Turn left into rue de l'Abreuvoir, cross another road then drop steeply down to the river and pass under a railway bridge. Continue on the beautiful riverside avenue to the edge of the town and turn right away from the river.

Van Gogh's lodgings, Auvers

2 Just before reaching the railway, turn left onto a footpath that leads through to Valmondois station. Join a cycle track beside the road, pass under the railway bridge and follow another one-way system. Turn right into rue des Rayons, which runs close to the river but is separated from the water by private properties.

3 Turn right away from the river once more, cross the railway and the main road D4 and climb to join rue du Montcel. We are now in Auvers-sur-Oise, associated with Vincent van Gogh. The elevated street runs parallel to the D4 and passes several old buildings, with extensive views of the river. Continue on the old street past the church, Château d'Auvers and the Musée de l'Absinthe. Cross the D928 and rejoin the quiet road on the edge of the built-up area, with wooded slopes above.

4 The route eventually rejoins the D4, a busy but attractive road beside the river, with significant commercial traffic on the water. Pass the Pont de l'Oise, which gives the town of Pontoise its name, and pass under the railway bridge.

5 The route joins a gravel path through an attractive park beside the river. The path passes under the A15 autoroute and becomes rough and stony in places, before passing under another road and entering a pleasant agricultural landscape. The road follows the bend of the river with vegetables presumably destined for the plates of Paris on the left hand side.

Accommodation

❶ GITE D'AUVERS SUR OISE
5 bis rue de Borgogne
95430 Auvers-sur-Oise
01 30 36 81 44 http://www.giteauvers.com
Reasonably priced rooms in Auvers-sur-Oise

❷ LA PETITE FUGUE
30 rue François Coppe 95430 Auvers-sur-Oise
06 82 99 03 88 http://lapetitefugue.canalblog.com

▲❸ CAMPING MUNICIPAL BELLERIVE
chemin de Bellerive 95430 Auvers-sur-Oise
01 34 48 05 22
Open from May to October

Parmain Mairie,
place Georges Clémenceau
01.34.69.67.05 www.ot-otos.fr
Mériel place Jean Gabin
01.34.21.50.77 www.ville-de-meriel.fr
Auvers-sur-Oise rue de la Sansonne
01.30.36.10.06 www.auvers-sur-oise.com
Pontoise 6 place de Petit Martroy
01.34.41.70.60 www.ot-cergypontoise.fr
Maisons-Laffitte 41 avenue de Longueil
01.39.62.63.64
www.tourisme-maisonslaffitte.fr
Saint-Germain-en-Laye 38 rue au Pain
01.30.87.20.63
www.ot-saintgermainenlaye.fr

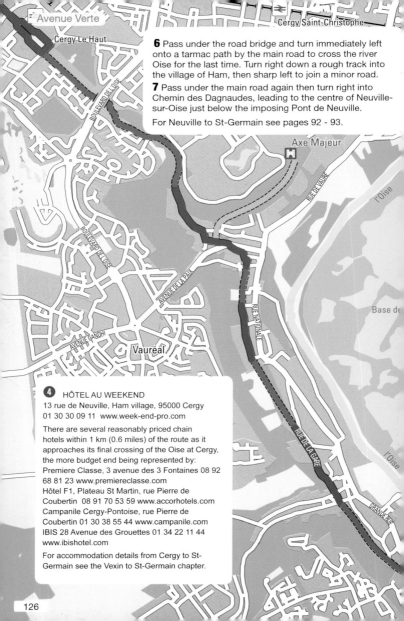

6 Pass under the road bridge and turn immediately left onto a tarmac path by the main road to cross the river Oise for the last time. Turn right down a rough track into the village of Ham, then sharp left to join a minor road.

7 Pass under the main road again then turn right into Chemin des Dagnaudes, leading to the centre of Neuville-sur-Oise just below the imposing Pont de Neuville.

For Neuville to St-Germain see pages 92 - 93.

❹ HÔTEL AU WEEKEND
13 rue de Neuville, Ham village, 95000 Cergy
01 30 30 09 11 www.week-end-pro.com

There are several reasonably priced chain hotels within 1 km (0.6 miles) of the route as it approaches its final crossing of the Oise at Cergy, the more budget end being represented by:
Premiere Classe, 3 avenue des 3 Fontaines 08 92 68 81 23 www.premiereclasse.com
Hôtel F1, Plateau St Martin, rue Pierre de Coubertin 08 91 70 53 59 www.accorhotels.com
Campanile Cergy-Pontoise, rue Pierre de Coubertin 01 30 38 55 44 www.campanile.com
IBIS 28 Avenue des Grouettes 01 34 22 11 44 www.ibishotel.com

For accommodation details from Cergy to St-Germain see the Vexin to St-Germain chapter.

Kilometres   0.5

Miles   0.5

N

Cergy

6

BOULEVARD DE L'HAUTIL

CHEMIN DES VOIES

4

RUE DE JOUVILLE

7

D203

l'Oise

CHEMIN DES DAGNAUDES

Neuville-
sur-Oise

Neuville
Université

BOULEVARD CONDORCET

AVENUE DES SAULES BRULES

BOULEVARD SALVADOR ALLENDE

l'Oise

A mixture of local Parisian trains
(Transilien) and RER services
(express trains) travel from the following
stations to central Paris: Valmondois,
Auvers-sur-Oise, Pontoise, Cergy-
Préfecture, Neuville-Université, Conflans
Fin d'Oise, Maisons-Laffitte, Sartrouville
and St-Germain.

Avenue Verte

A Vélib hire bike heads along the
Canal St-Martin in Paris

St-Germain ~ Paris

Like London's own Thames, the river Seine is the heart and soul of Paris. Between the cultured attractions of St-Germain and Rueil-Malmaison the Avenue Verte passes through the idyllic landscapes captured by Impressionist painters such as Renoir and Monet. The scenery becomes even greener, virtually a countryside ride, along the Seineside *Promenade Bleu* between Rueil-Malmaison and Colombes. Waterside riding of a different kind, along the canals St-Denis and St-Martin, herald your arrival in Paris proper and journey's end at Notre Dame cathedral. Here on the Île de la Cité it crowns one of the most famous and beautiful views in the world at the very centre of one of the world's most beautiful cities.

Route Info

Distance 23 miles / 37 kilometres

Terrain & Route Surface Largely following the river Seine, cycling into Paris along numerous easy, flat sections, is a pleasure. With many newly constructed cycle paths (though some of the route may still be under construction) you have what must be one of the most laid-back cycling approaches to one of the world's major cities.

Off-road 61% traffic-free on a mixture of tarmac and unsealed tracks, generally of a high quality

Profile

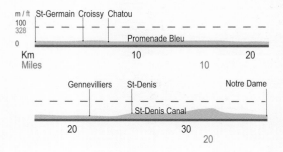

129

What to See & Do

• **Rueil-Malmaison** is an elegant suburb of Paris. It lies just to the south-east of the route, immediately after it crosses the Seine at the Pont de Chatou. The park of Bois Préau houses a grand château and there are fine walks and cycle rides along the east bank of the Seine and past the Île des Impressionnistes.

The town is strongly associated with Napoléon Bonaparte and his famous Empress Joséphine. The town walk in their honour links various buildings, such as the château bought by Joséphine with the money she expected him to bring back from his Egyptian campaign.

• **St-Denis** is a little way off the route after it has again crossed the Seine, this time over the Pont d'Île St-Denis, and is best known for its huge cathedral whose necropolis holds most of the tombs of French kings. The town was once a stronghold of the French communist party which drew its strength from the area of heavy industry that surrounded it. The area around the Stade-de-France (France's equivalent of Wembley) is currently being redeveloped and already houses 'Cinema City', a massive film production facility aiming to attract film making back to France.

The wonderful Sunday market at St-Denis

Family cycling and markets; a Sunday Parisian scene

• **Paris's canals** may not be what the city is best known for but are a joy and a delight. Whilst the canal St-Denis is more functional transport artery than recreational facility, the canal Saint-Martin provides a glorious series of elegant locks, is lined with cycle lanes and on sunny weekends becomes a centre for those simply wanting to sit and enjoy their surroundings.

• The Avenue Verte's official end is at the world famous facade of **Notre Dame cathedral,** whilst at the other end of the Île-de-la-Cité are **Sainte-Chappelle,** remains of a splendid palace built by early Frankish kings, and the **Conciergerie,** where

Marie Antoinette and other leading opponents of the French Revolution were held before meeting their grisly end.

Once in the heart of Paris you can experience some of the world's most glamorous locations and some of its greatest museums easily on two wheels on the city's expanding cycle network. Whilst the **Louvre** and the **Eiffel Tower** top the list in the fame rankings there are a myriad of other delights here, especially around the River Seine and the canals, lined by ranks of stylish apartments and idyllic picnic spots such as the **parc de la Villette** and the **Tuileries gardens.**

131

Seineside riding near St-Germain

Directions

1 On leaving the urban area, the riverside path again reverts to a gravel surface up to the first of many large riverside properties in Croissy. One of the first properties is the British School of Paris. The riverside road here is very quiet, mainly serving residential properties. A notable feature of the route between Sartrouville and Chatou is that there are no commercial properties on the river, no shops or cafes – so make sure you are well supplied The centre of Croissy is some distance from the river.

2 The riverside path / access road comes to an end at the railway bridge in Chatou, where you will find several shops. Pass under the bridge and join a cycle track beside the road for a short distance. The route crosses the Seine at Chatou and you need to turn left just before the bridge, up the slope and follow round to the right to join the cycle track on the south side of the bridge. Cross the river and take the zigzag ramp back down to the riverside. After a short distance on an access road, the path runs for several kilometres to Pont de Bezons with a good compacted stone surface. There is one water crossing, a substantial footbridge over the port access channel. There is a wheeling ramp beside the steps, but if you are heavily loaded you may prefer to use the lift.

3 Between Pont de Bezons and Pont de Colombes the riverside path is well surfaced through a popular public park, but please note that the park closes at night.

Rueil-Malmaison is a fine Parisian suburb

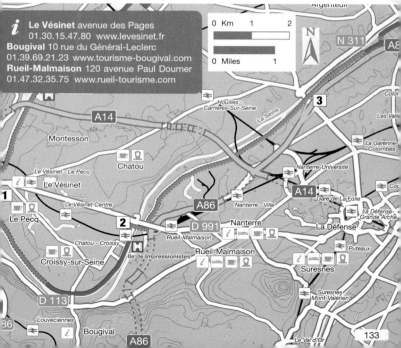

i **Le Vésinet** avenue des Pages
01.30.15.47.80 www.levesinet.fr
Bougival 10 rue du Général-Leclerc
01.39.69.21.23 www.tourisme-bougival.com
Rueil-Malmaison 120 avenue Paul Doumer
01.47.32.35.75 www.rueil-tourisme.com

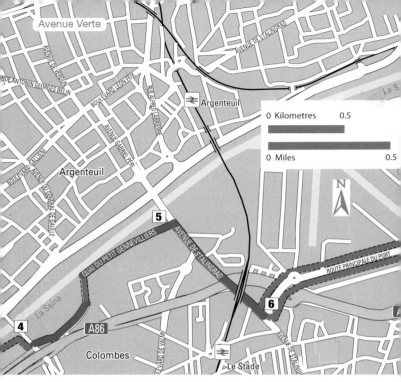

4 At the time of writing, the area around the Pont de Colombes was under construction, so if this is still the case look out for diversion signs. Stay on the river side of the motorway flyover and use pedestrian crossings to access the footway beside an impressive brick building. At the end of this building leave the marked cycle track and turn left into an industrial access road. Just when you think you have taken a wrong turn, you will see a wide rough track between concrete walls. This looks uninviting, but it leads back to the riverside and a quiet road.

5 Cross the busy main road and turn right onto the shared footway. At the next traffic lights cross the road again and join cycle lanes on the road. Pass over the motorway and under the railway before turning left into the port access road.

6 This can be a busy junction and you may prefer to use the pedestrian crossing to access the cycle track in the middle of the road. The cycle track continues through the port area and you can get glimpses of the wharves on your left. The road bends gently round to the right and the cycle track comes to an end, turning into cycle lanes on the road.

7 Follow the road round to the right, crossing over the motorway. Turn left at the large roundabout, where we recommend the use of the pedestrian/cycle crossings to join a two-way cycle track alongside the newly built tramway.

The Avenue Verte follows excellent cycle paths near Gennevilliers

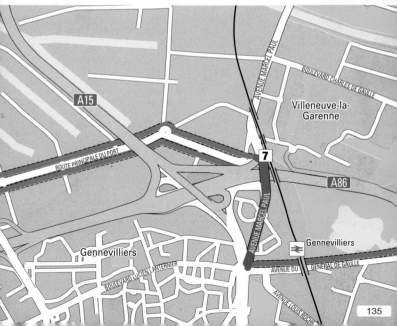

i **Saint-Denis** 1 rue de la République
01.55.87.08.70 www.saint-denis-tourisme.com

0 Kilometres 0.5

0 Miles 0.5

8 Follow the tramway all the way down to St-Denis, crossing two branches of the river Seine. The area around St-Denis railway station is a construction site, so look out for diversion signs.

9 The aim is to cross railway and canal, then turn right to follow the east bank of the Canal St-Denis. The towpath is very good where renovated, with a wide smooth concrete surface. At the locks cobbles have been retained, with a narrow concrete strip for bikes. Elsewhere, the surface is bumpy with the original cobbled wharves and railway tracks. This is a great way to enter the city, sailing under busy roads and railways along the way.

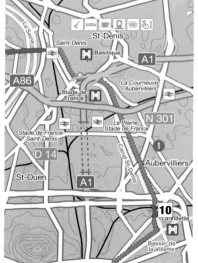

10 At Porte de la Villette you cross the road and the canal. Cross diagonally to join a two-way cycle track on the west side of the canal. At the canal junction, continue round to the right up to a metal lifting bridge. Turn right then immediately left to join another cycle track running parallel to the canal.

11 At the end of this track turn left and go round the circular building. Keep right and cross over the busy road and under the elevated railway. Get into the cycle lane in the middle of the road opposite and fork left at the lights for the cycle route beside the canal. Continue alongside the canal which bends round to the left.

12 Turn right into rue de Lucien Sampaix, which has a contraflow cycle lane (easy to miss).

13 Cross the busy boulevard de Magenta and turn right at rue René Boulanger.

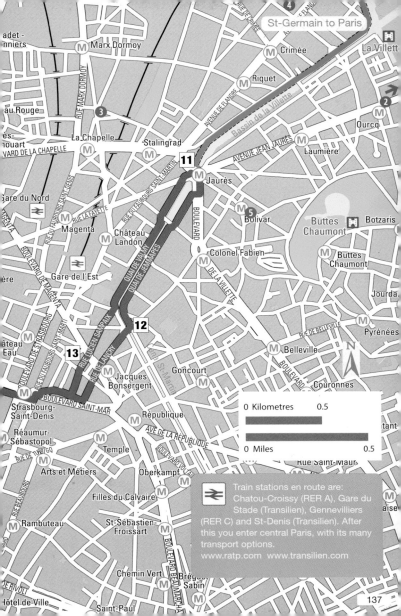

St-Germain to Paris

adet-
nniers

M Marx Dormoy

au.Rouge

ès-
ouart
VARD DE LA CHAPELLE

La Chapelle

Stalingrad

M

Crimée

Riquet

Bassin de la Villette

M Ourcq

M Crimée

La Villett

2

Gare du Nord

Magenta

M

Château
Landon

M

Gare de l'Est

Jaurès

M

BOULEVARD

M Bolivar

5

Colonel Fabien

M

DE LA VILLETTE

AVENUE JEAN JAURÈS

M Laumière

Buttes
Chaumont

M Buttes
Chaumont

Botzaris

Jourda

âteau
Eau

République

Strasbourg-
Saint-Denis

BOULEVARD SAINT-MAR

Réaumur-
Sébastopol

ère

Jacques
Bonsergent

M

Goncourt

M

RUE DE BELLEVILLE

M Belleville

Pyrénées

M

Couronnes

M

N

Temple

M

Arts et Métiers

Oberkampf

M

Rue Saint-Maur

Filles du Calvaire

M

Rambuteau

St-Sébastien-
Froissart

M

Chemin Vert

M

DE RIVOLI

ôtel de Ville

Saint-Paul

M

Brégu
Sabin

0 Kilometres   0.5

0 Miles   0.5

Train stations en route are:
Chatou-Croissy (RER A), Gare du
Stade (Transilien), Gennevilliers
(RER C) and St-Denis (Transilien). After
this you enter central Paris, with its many
transport options.
www.ratp.com www.transilien.com

137

14 Great care is required at the impressive Porte St-Martin where you cross the main road and follow the cycle route markings into rue Ste Apolline. Cross another main road and turn left into rue St-Denis and continue into the heart of the city.

15 This lower half of the street is pedestrianised and can get busy, but cycling is permitted at all times despite the crowds (see overleaf for larger scale map of end of route).

16 At the bottom end of rue Saint-Denis look for signs off to the right leading you to a signal crossing of the rue de Rivoli. Continue to the bank of the Seine.

17 Here turn left then right to cross the river on Pont au Change. Continue straight ahead but don't cross the river again. Instead turn left for your final destination – Notre Dame de Paris.

Accommodation

1 ETHIC ÉTAPES EUGÈNE HÉNAFF
1 rue de la Commune de Paris
93300 Aubervilliers
1 43 52 29 69 01 43 52 78 15
ttp://www.alj93.fr/
Hostel style accommodation with restaurant and
ike store. See map page 136

2 AUBERGE CITÉ DES SCIENCES
, rue Jean-Baptiste Clément
93310 Le Pré-Saint-Gervais, Paris
01 48 43 24 11 http://www.hifrance.org/
Secure bike store. See map page 137.

3 AUBERGE PAJOL
20 rue Pajol 75018 Paris
01 44 89 87 27 www.hifrance.org
A brand new hostel with a superb central location
and secure bike storage. See map page 137.

A PARIS CAMPSITES
There is one campsite within reach of central Paris,
some 10 km (6 miles) from Notre Dame. Camping
Paris Bois de Boulogne is west of the Bois de
Boulogne (01 45 24 30 00) www.campingparis.fr

4 HÔTEL CAMPANILE LA VILLETTE
147 avenue de Flandre 75019 Paris
01 44 72 46 46
www.campanile-paris-19-la-villette.fr
Pricey (online discounts available). Secure car
park. Two minutes ride from the route at Porte de
la Villette. See map page 137.

5 RELAIS BERGSON
124 avenue Simon Bolivar 75019 Paris
01 42 08 31 17
www.hotel-relais-bergson-paris.federal-hotel.com
See map page 137.

6 HÔTEL PICARD
26 rue de Picardie 75003 Paris
01.48.87.53.82 www.picardparis.com
Unpretentious, reasonably priced and with
overnight bike storage.
Shared facility rooms are good value for central
Paris.

Journey's end,
Notre Dame

© Olivier Bruchez Creative Commons

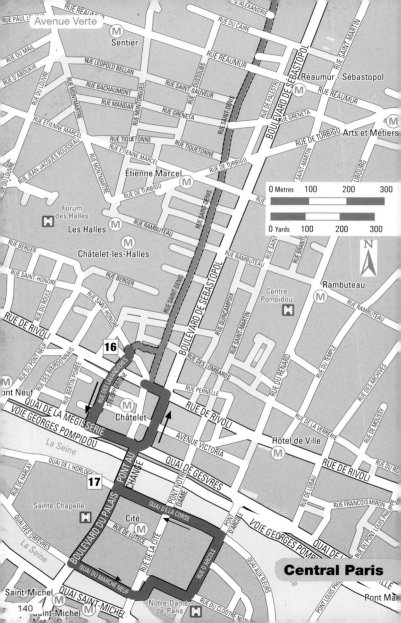

Central Paris

The Île St-Louis is right next to your end point, Île de la Cité, and is a quiet contrast

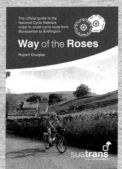